Deep Dive into Power Automate

Learn by Example

Goloknath Mishra

Apress®

Deep Dive into Power Automate: Learn by Example

Goloknath Mishra
Singapore, Singapore

ISBN-13 (pbk): 978-1-4842-9731-5   ISBN-13 (electronic): 978-1-4842-9732-2
https://doi.org/10.1007/978-1-4842-9732-2

Managing Director, Apress Media LLC: Welmoed Spahr
Acquisitions Editor: Smriti Srivastava
Development Editor: Laura Berendson
Coordinating Editor: Shaul Elson
Copy Editor: Kezia Endsley

Cover designed by eStudioCalamar

Cover image by Sven Dressler on Pixabay (www.pixabay.com)

Distributed to the book trade worldwide by Apress Media, LLC, 1 New York Plaza, New York, NY 10004, U.S.A. Phone 1-800-SPRINGER, fax (201) 348-4505, e-mail orders-ny@springer-sbm.com, or visit www.springeronline.com. Apress Media, LLC is a California LLC and the sole member (owner) is Springer Science + Business Media Finance Inc (SSBM Finance Inc). SSBM Finance Inc is a **Delaware** corporation.

For information on translations, please e-mail booktranslations@springernature.com; for reprint, paperback, or audio rights, please e-mail bookpermissions@springernature.com.

Apress titles may be purchased in bulk for academic, corporate, or promotional use. eBook versions and licenses are also available for most titles. For more information, reference our Print and eBook Bulk Sales web page at http://www.apress.com/bulk-sales.

Any source code or other supplementary material referenced by the author in this book is available to readers on GitHub (https://github.com/Apress). For more detailed information, please visit https://www.apress.com/gp/services/source-code.

Paper in this product is recyclable

Table of Contents

About the Author

 **Goloknath Mishra** is a Microsoft Most Valuable Professional (MVP), Microsoft Certified Trainer (MCT), and Power Platform Solution Architect Expert with over 14 years of experience in digital transformation using Microsoft Tech stack as an enabler. He has worked with various organizations in different domains and is currently associated with NCS Group, Singapore as a senior IT architect.

During his tenure, he has been involved in enterprise solution architecture and design, delivery management (scaled agile, agile, and waterfall), pre-sales, project management, client consulting, and business analysis.

He is active in the tech community and participates in different Microsoft Programs. He is an Udemy instructor, speaker, blogger, and YouTuber. He runs the Microsoft User Group in Singapore and Odisha, focusing on Microsoft Dynamics 365 and the Power Platform. He is also one of the founding members of #PowerPlatformClassmates.

About the Technical Reviewer

Aroh Shukla's enthusiasm lies in acquiring fresh skills, with a specific concentration on Microsoft technologies. He possesses a deep understanding of the Microsoft Cloud platform and remains dedicated to keeping up with the latest advancements. Through remarkable communication skills, he can effectively explain complex technical concepts clearly and concisely. He readily extends his assistance to individuals, be they students or professionals, as they begin their exploration of Microsoft technologies. As a leader in the community, he exhibits strong interpersonal talents, attentive listening, and a genuine commitment to driving the community forward.

Introduction

This book is intended for those who are interested in improving processes using Power Automate, a leading RPA tool. The target audience ranges from business executives, to citizen developers, to IT professionals and computer scientists who want to automate monotonous work efficiently.

Deep Dive into Power Automate is a practical guide for learning the basics of flows and the implementation guidelines for different real-life scenarios, including RPA capabilities. The book covers how flows evolved to be a full-fledged RPA called Power Automate.

This book covers the basic building blocks of Cloud Flows, Desktop Flows (RPA), and Business Process Flows. It covers their types, triggers, and actions. You learn to schedule, manage, share, and transfer flows to different environments. It also includes best practices, troubleshooting steps, practical use cases, and tips and tricks.

This book is intended for those who want to understand flows, learn how to write them, and see where to use them. You also learn what RPAs are and how to identify a candidate for RPA implementation. You learn how to improve processes using RPAs.

This book also covers AI Builder as an Intelligent Process Automation (IPA). You learn how to build, train, manage, publish, and share models, as well as use models in different scenarios. After completing this book, you will be comfortable with Power Automate and will be able to implement it in real-life scenarios.

Happy learning!

CHAPTER 1

Introduction

This chapter discusses process automation, including how it led to RPA (Robotic Process Automation) and its history. Microsoft entered the RPA market with its Cloud Flows and subsequently transformed it into a full-fledge RPA with the introduction of Desktop Flows. They named the RPA product *Power Automate*. You will also see a comparison view of Power Automate and the leading RPA in the market.

Human demands are never-ending—they crave comfort, luxury, and lavishness. Nothing is more important to humans than their comfort and convenience. It is human nature to seek physical and mental comfort. Everybody wants an easy and comfortable life. This desire triggered scientific innovation and automation. Narrowing this down to the business realm, humans need automation to simplify processes, increase productivity, increase reliability, and control costs.

A business process is a group of activities that must be completed to achieve an organizational goal. It can be simple or complex. Simple methods require fewer steps to execute, whereas complex processes involve many steps, so they demand governance.

Business process automation (BPA), also known as *business automation* or *digital transformation,* is the technology-enabled automation of complex business processes.

What Is Process Automation?

Process automation replaces humans with machines when executing a sequence of activities.[1]

Process automation improves a system by removing human input, which includes the following benefits:

- Decreases errors
- Increases the speed of delivery
- Boosts quality

© Goloknath Mishra 2023
G. Mishra, *Deep Dive into Power Automate*, https://doi.org/10.1007/978-1-4842-9732-2_1

- Minimizes costs

- Simplifies the operation

- Incorporates software tools, people, and processes to create a completely automated workflow

What Is RPA?

Process automation uses technology to automate human tasks that are manual, rule-based, or repetitive. This is called Robotic Process Automation (RPA).

(*Robotic* refers to the capability to mimic human actions, *process* refers to a sequence of steps, and *automation* refers to tasks performed without human interaction.)

Blue Prism says, "*Robotic Process Automation or RPA is a term for a piece of software, or a 'robot,' which carries out tasks and activities within systems, or applications, in the same way a human would. The software is perceived as a 'robot' because it works robotically, completing tasks automatically in the same way a human would.*" [2]

Automation Anywhere states, "*With RPA, software users create software robots, or "bots," that can learn, mimic, and execute rules-based business processes. RPA automation enables users to create bots by observing human digital actions. Show your bots what to do, then let them do the work.*" [3]

UiPath states, "*RPA is a software that makes it seamless to build, deploy, and manage software robots that imitate human's actions interacting with digital systems and software.*" [4]

Microsoft states, "*Robotic process automation (RPA) uses software bots to emulate human interaction within a graphical user interface (GUI) to automate repetitive and manual tasks, saving businesses time, effort, and headaches.*" [5]

Before 1990, businesses tended to automate single tasks, so that was the era of macros, because businesses heavily relied on management information systems. Subsequently, companies marched toward automation to optimize business processes. Blue Prism first released an RPA in 2003, based on the Microsoft .Net Platform, to automate processes. Then, Automation Anywhere released its first RPA around 2009. In 2012, UiPath came to the market with its RPA product, due to massive demand in the RPA market.

RPA helps automate structured data. AI subsequently came into the picture to automate unstructured data, also called *intelligent process automation* or *hyper-automation.*

Figure 1-1 shows the evolution of RPA.

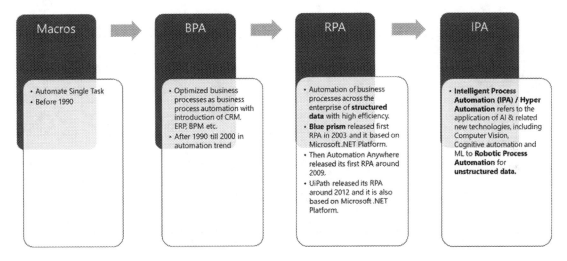

Figure 1-1. Evolution of RPA

RPA developed automated applications, called software robots or *bots,* that mimic and execute rule-based business processes. RPA can be classified into two broad categories (see Figure 1-2):

- *Attended*

  - If bots developed in RPA require human intervention while executing, the process is called attended RPA

  - Manually triggered

  - Sign-in is not required because the automation system assumes that the system is already signed in

- *Unattended*

  - If bots developed in RPA do not require human intervention while executing, the process is called unattended RPA

  - Automatically triggered

  - Windows sign-in is automated with predefined user credentials

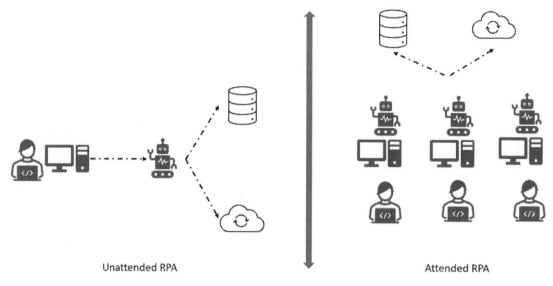

Figure 1-2. *Attended vs unattended RPA*

Figure 1-3 shows a diagram to identify where to start RPA.

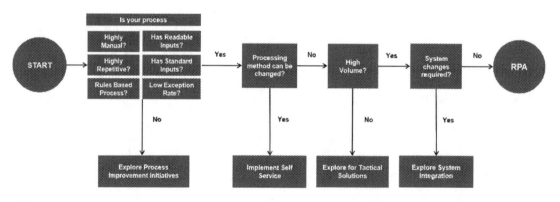

Figure 1-3. *Where to start RPA*

After you know what to do with automation, the next issue to consider are the benefits of RPA. Here are a few advantages of RPA:

- *Saves time*: Repetitive administrative tasks are done daily in many business processes. RPA allows businesses to automate and perform repetitive tasks quickly. The business and its employees benefit from RPA, as they spend more time on productive work.

- *Increases ROI*: RPA tools are more efficient at managing redundant tasks than humans, and they help businesses improve productivity. That is why one of the most significant benefits of RPA is its +ve impact on return-on-investment. By incorporating robotic process automation, a business can improve several processes, which helps manage costs more efficiently.

- *Eliminates human error*: Realistically, human error and fatigue are always factors, no matter how skilled a person is in their role. Robots never get tired, so tasks are performed accurately each time.

- *Elevate security*: Cybersecurity is essential to a business, and RPA solutions protect against security breaches. RPA improves security by reducing human interactions with sensitive information, which helps prevent data leaks and non-compliance. RPA helps keep businesses secure.

- *Increases compliance*: Compliance is essential for the sustainability of a business, and RPA solutions adhere to guidelines with great accuracy. Additionally, RPA can be audited centrally rather than performing multiple application audits, reducing compliance risks. RPA can be applied to contract workflows and submissions, form updates, compliance-related notifications, and related alerts.

- *Scales business process automation*: As a company applies an RPA tool to business activities, the automation of processes and tasks expands throughout the organization. RPA also allows businesses to scale to meet seasonal increases in demand and projected targets with greater confidence, whether processing orders or invoices, managing inventory, or dealing with other forms of production and service.

- *Increases employee satisfaction*: When tedious processes are automated, employees are freed up to focus on more critical business needs. As RPA reduces repetitive tasks typically performed by humans, employee satisfaction increases. Employees can then apply their skills to jobs that require strategic thinking, like business planning, public relations, and brainstorming.

Figure 1-4 shows the who, what, and why of RPA.

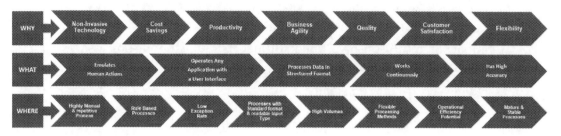

Figure 1-4. *Summary of RPA*

RPA can be used in different industry verticals, including the following.

Banking:

- Mortgage lending

- Compliance reporting

- Customer service

- Client onboarding (KYC/CDD)

- Compliance and risk management

- Equity research

Logistics:

- Order scheduling and tracking

- Invoicing and credit collection

- Researching loads

Manufacturing:

- Supply chain automation

- Inventory tracking and processing

- Pricing and procurement

Healthcare:

- Patient eligibility

- Customer service

- Scheduling

- Physician credentialing

- Customer service

Insurance:

- Claims processing

- Compliance reporting

- Customer service

Retail and travel:

- Competitive intelligence and price monitoring

- Brand monitoring and fraud protection

RPA can be used in different departments within an organization, including the following.

Finance:

- Process to pay

- Order to cash

- Record to report

Supply chain:

- Inventory management

- Demand and supply

- Planning

IT:

- Server and app monitoring

- Routine maintenance and monitoring

HR:

- Payroll

- Onboarding and offboarding

- Benefits administration

Customer service:

- Address change

- Password reset

- Payments

Microsoft Flow and Its Evolution to Power Automate

Figure 1-5 shows the evolution of Power Automate.

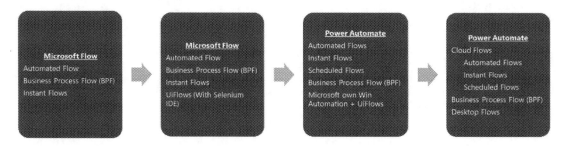

Figure 1-5. *Evolution of Power Automate*

Microsoft Flow was initially a cloud-based SaaS service introduced in 2016 and was mainly used in the Microsoft ecosystem. It allowed users to automate workflows across multiple applications and services without requiring coding skills. It enabled the creation of automated workflows or "flows" that integrated different software services and automated repetitive tasks, such as data collection, synchronization, notification, and management.

In July 2019, Microsoft rebranded Microsoft Flow as Power Automate to reflect the product's growing capabilities and evolution. The core functionality and features of Power Automate are the same as Microsoft Flow. The name change represents the broader vision of the platform as an automation tool that enables users to drive business productivity and efficiency.

Microsoft added RPA capabilities by introducing Uiflows (with Selenium IDE). In May 2020, Microsoft acquired Softomotive and incorporated the desktop automation functionality by Win Automation, one of the market's leading RPAs. They merged its Uiflows to introduce Desktop Flow.

Microsoft then renamed Desktop Flow Power Automate Desktop (PAD). Power Automate has the following features:

- Cloud Flows: Cloud-based digital process automation (DPA)

- Power Automate Desktop (aka Desktop Flow): Desktop-based Robotic Process Automation (RPA)

- AI Builder: Intelligent Process Automation (IPA)

Power Automate integrates with over 500 services, including Microsoft applications such as Excel, SharePoint, and Teams, as well as other popular services like Dropbox, Google Drive, Twitter, and Slack. Users can create flows using prebuilt templates or customize them based on their specific needs. Users can also monitor and manage their flows from a central dashboard. Power Automate is designed to improve productivity, reduce errors, and simplify business processes. It does the following:

- *Automates repetitive tasks*: Power Automate allows users to automate repetitive tasks that would otherwise require manual effort, saving time and reducing errors.

- *Connects different applications and services*: Power Automate integrates with over 500 services, enabling users to connect various applications and services and automate complex workflows and tasks.

- *Enhances productivity*: By automating workflows, Power Automate frees up time for employees to focus on more valuable tasks, which can help improve productivity and efficiency.

- *Improves accuracy*: Automating tasks reduces the risk of human error, which can improve the accuracy and quality of work.

- *Enables collaboration*: Power Automate can automate and streamline collaboration processes between teams, which can help enhance communication and cooperation.

- *Reduces costs*: By automating processes and workflows, organizations can reduce costs associated with manual labor and streamline their operations.

Overall, Power Automate can help organizations be more efficient, effective, and competitive in their respective industries. As per Microsoft, you can automate your business processes with Power Automate. The basic steps are as follows (see Figure 1-6):

- **Plan:** Identity the who, what, when, and why.

- **Design:** Design your new automated process "on paper" and consider various automation methods.

- **Make:** Create the Power Automate flows.

- **Test:** Try the automation you created.

- **Deploy and refine:** Start using the automation in production, identify processes that can be refined, and decide what to change or add.

Figure 1-6. *Business process automation steps*

Comparing Power Automate and the Leading RPAs in the Market

As of February 2023, the five-year trend analysis per Google Trend (`https://trends.google.com/trends/`—see Figure 1-7) shows how Microsoft Power Automate compares to leading RPAs in the market:

- UiPath (`www.uipath.com/`)

- Automation Anywhere (`www.automationanywhere.com/`)

- Blue Prism (`www.blueprism.com/`)

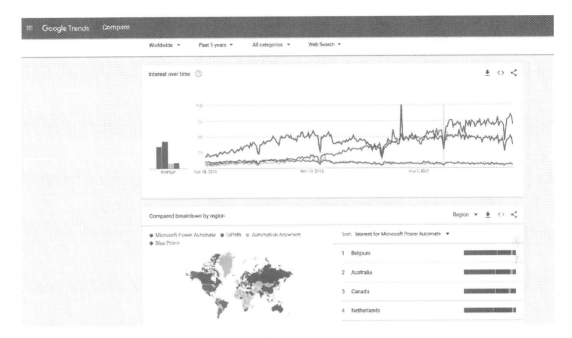

Figure 1-7. *Google Trend view of the leading RPAs*

As per Gartner Magic Quadrant[6], Power Automate is in the leader segment, along with the leading RPA tools.

Comparing UiPath and Power Automate

There are many RPAs in the market, but UiPath is the leader, so it's smart to compare it to Power Automate.

Similarities:

- Both support cloud-based and on-premises environment setup.

- Both provide unattended and attended automated orchestration and AI solutions for businesses.

- Power Automate has AI Builder, whereas UiPath has AI Center, which provides the same drag-and-drop usability for bringing machine learning models into automated workflows.

- Both need a Windows environment to run the Desktop Flows.

Differences:

- The Power Automate licensing and implementation costs are comparatively cheaper.

- UiPath has a very active developer community with new flows being rolled out every day, while Power Automate's society is still growing.

- UiPath bots are comparatively more scalable than Power Automate flows.

- Power Automate is available on desktop, mobile, web, and Microsoft Teams; the user interface is more straightforward than UiPath.

- In Power Automate, it's simpler to integrate with other Microsoft platforms, which have a vast library of connectors in comparison to UiPath.

- UiPath is easier to maintain and debug, whereas Power Automate still needs improvement.

- Power Automate has templates to quickly create flows, whereas UiPath allows saving templates for reuse.

Power Automate can be targeted to smaller businesses, whereas UiPath targets customers from SMBs to enterprises when cost is not a concern.

If cost is a concern, Power Automate is a better option. It has massive potential if Microsoft keeps investing in it and it can compete with other RPA competitors. Also, if the customer IT ecosystem heavily relies on Microsoft technologies, Power Automate is a better option than UiPath.

Intelligent Process Automation (IPA) vs. Robotic Process Automation (RPA)

As per UiPath, *"Intelligent Process Automation (IPA) refers to the application of AI and related new technologies, including computer vision, cognitive automation, and machine learning to Robotic Process Automation."*[7]

As per Automation Anywhere, *"Intelligent Automation (IA) is a fusion of Robotic Process Automation (RPA) and artificial intelligence (AI) technologies, which together help end-to-end business process automation and accelerate digital transformation."*[8]

What Is Intelligent Process Automation (IPA)?

IPA is the fusion of RPA, Business Process Management (BPM), and AI to automate complete, end-to-end business processes.

It is the evolution of basic, rules-based task automation of structured data into managing and automating entire business processes of unstructured data using AI technologies. See Figure 1-8.

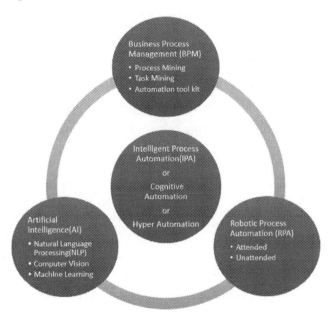

Figure 1-8. *Type of process automation at a glance*

Components of IPA are classified into three categories:

- **Robotic Process Automation (RPA)**: This is the automation of repetitive, rules-based business tasks using attended or unattended bots/programs.

  - *Attended*: During execution, requires human intervention.

  - *Unattended*: During execution, no human intervention is required.

- **Artificial Intelligence (AI)**: Technology that mimics human intelligence by analyzing data faster than humans and makes decisions based on past learnings.

  - *Natural Language Processing (NLP)*: Software that can understand, interpret, and manipulate language, spoken or written.

  - *Machine Learning (ML)*: A process that uses algorithms to find patterns in structured, historical data and uses those patterns to make precise predictions on outcomes.

  - *Computer Vision*: Technology that enables computers to parse and interpret images. It includes tools such as OCR (Optical Character Recognition) that scan and transform documents into text.

- **Business Process Management (BPM)**: Businesses want to know the scope and candidates for automation, including the cost-benefit analysis, including maintenance.

  - *Process mining*: Helps take the event data from your system of records and visualize the processes happening in your organization. Process mining provides novel insights that can help you identify automation opportunities and address performance and compliance opportunities.

  - *Task mining*: Helps to quickly capture detailed steps for each process in your organization to help you better understand places to streamline workflows.

Review Questions

1. What is the difference between RPA and IPA?

2. What is the difference between attended and unattended RPA?

3. What is hyper-automation?

4. What are the benefits of RPA?

5. What is computer vision (CV)?

6. Name three leading RPA applications.

Summary

This chapter started with process automation and moved to intelligent process automation. It also covered identifying RPA as necessary for the specific organization and its benefits. It explained how flow transformed to Power Automate, a full-fledged RPA. It also ran a comparative analysis of Power Automate with leading the RPA, UiPath.

The next chapter dives deep into power automation environments and covers the different types of offerings in Power Automate.

References

1. https://www.outsystems.com/glossary/what-is-process-automation/

2. https://www.blueprism.com/resources/white-papers/what-is-rpa-what-is-intelligent-automation-heres-a-glossary-of-automation-terminology/

3. https://www.automationanywhere.com/rpa/robotic-process-automation

4. https://www.uipath.com/rpa/robotic-process-automation

5. https://powerautomate.microsoft.com/en-us/rpa-tool/

6. https://www.gartner.com/en/documents/4016876

7. https://www.uipath.com/rpa/intelligent-process-automation#:~:text=Intelligent%20Process%20Automation%20(IPA)%20refers,Learning%20to%20Robotic%20Process%20Automation

8. https://www.automationanywhere.com/rpa/intelligent-automation

9. https://learn.microsoft.com/en-us/power-platform/admin/

Keywords

RPA

Artificial intelligence (AI)

Attended RPA

Business process automation (BPA)

Computer vision

Intelligent process automation (IPA)

Machine learning (ML)

Natural language processing (NLP)

Robotic process automation (RPA)

Unattended RPA

CHAPTER 2

How to Kickstart Using Power Automate

In the first chapter, you learned about the basics of automation and RPA, including where to use it and its benefits. You also learned about intelligent process automation and about the journey of Power Automate. That chapter also compared Power Automate to the leading RPA in the market.

This chapter dives deep into Power Automate. You learn how to access it, what its components are, and what flows are. The chapter also explains what Power Automate offers to citizen developers (without having to code), as well as what it offers to professional code developers.

Before starting Power Automate, you should understand its ecosystem, the Microsoft Power Platform (see Figure 2-1). It's a low-code platform for quickly building customized end-to-end business solutions. It is comprised of the following tools and services:

- **Power Apps:** Provides a low-code development environment for building custom business applications. It has services, connectors, data services, and an app platform called Microsoft Dataverse that allow integration and interaction with existing data. Power Apps enables the creation of web and mobile applications that run on all devices.

- **Power Automate:** Allows users to create automated workflows between different applications. It helps automate repetitive business processes such as communications, data collection, and decision approvals. It is used to automate processes and orchestrate activities across different services that use integrated/custom connectors. Using Power Automate, users can create web-based Cloud Flows or Desktop Flows.

© Goloknath Mishra 2023
G. Mishra, *Deep Dive into Power Automate*, https://doi.org/10.1007/978-1-4842-9732-2_2

- **Power BI:** A business analytics service or BI tool from Microsoft that gives insights into data analysis. It can share insights through data visualizations, which create reports and dashboards for easy decision-making. Power BI scales across an organization, and it has built-in security and governance, allowing businesses to focus on using data over managing it.

- **Power Virtual Agents:** It helps create powerful chatbots using a no-code graphical interface, without the need for data scientists or developers.

- **Power Pages:** An enterprise-grade, low-code software as a service (SaaS) environment for creating, hosting, and administering external-facing websites. Makers can easily design, configure, and publish websites seamlessly, supporting cross-browsers and devices. Developers can extend these capabilities by writing code to address advanced business requirements.

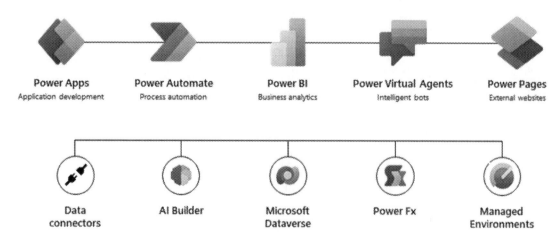

Figure 2-1. *The Power Platform ecosystem*

As you can see in Figure 2-1, the Power Platform consists of those five products and includes cross-cutting features that enable it to be leveraged to its full potential. Some of these include:

- **AI Builder**: Allows users and developers to add AI capabilities to workflows and Power Apps that they create and use. AI Builder allows users to seamlessly add intelligence to apps and predict outcomes to help improve business performance without writing code.

- **Microsoft Dataverse**: A scalable data service and app platform that allows users to securely store and manage data from multiple sources and integrate that data into business applications using a standard data model. This ensures ease and consistency for users. Microsoft Dataverse is the common currency that enables the components of Microsoft Power Platform to work together. It is the foundation that enables data consolidation, display, and manipulation.

- **Data Connectors**: Enable a connection of apps, data, and devices in the cloud. Consider connectors the bridge across which information and commands travel. There are over 600 connectors for the Microsoft Power Platform, enabling all user data and actions to connect cohesively. Popular connectors include Salesforce, Office 365, Twitter, Dropbox, Google services, and more.

- **Power Fx**: The low-code language used across the Microsoft Power Platform. It is a general-purpose, strongly-typed, declarative, and functional programming language.

- **Managed Environments**: Allow admins to manage Power Platform at scale in a controlled manner with less effort and more insights. Admins can use Managed Environments with any environment except the developer environments. You need admin privilege to enable or disable a Managed Environment. You should also have these roles:

  - Global Admin

  - Power Platform Service Admin

  - Dynamics 365 Admin

You can enable Managed Environments in the Power Platform Admin Center (`https://aka.ms/ppac`) by navigating to Environments. Select the check mark to the left of the environment. On the command bar, you'll see the following options:

- Enable Managed Environment (if not enabled)

- Edit Managed Environment (if already enabled)

The following table lists a few of the settings under Managed Environments:

Setting	Description
Limit sharing	Helps reduce risk by limiting how widely the Canvas app can be shared
Don't set limits	Select to not limit sharing of canvas app
Exclude sharing with security groups	Select if makers aren't allowed to share canvas apps with any security groups. Admins may share with a limit
Limit total individuals who can be shared to	If Exclude Sharing with Security Groups is selected, select to limit the number of people that makers can share canvas apps with
Usage insights	Select to include insights for this environment in the weekly scheduled email
Data policies	Help safeguard your organizational data by restricting available connectors
See active data policies for this environment	View the policies that define the consumer connectors that specific data can be shared with

People often need clarification about Dataverse as a database, but it is not because Dataverse has more built-in capabilities than a database, which is explained next and in Figure 2-2, from the Microsoft documentation.

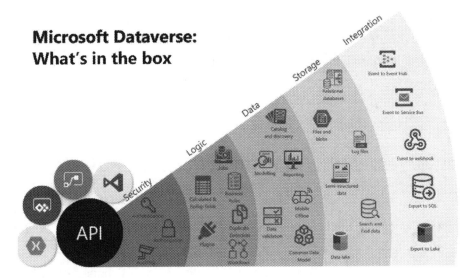

Figure 2-2. *Microsoft Dataverse in a box*

Microsoft Dataverse offers a series of functionalities, as follows:

- **Security**: Dataverse handles authentication with Azure AD for conditional access and multi-factor authentication (MFA). It supports authorization up to the row and column level and provides auditing features.

- **Logic**: Dataverse allows you to apply business logic easily, regardless of how a user interacts with the data. These rules can be duplicate detection, business rules, and workflows.

- **Data**: Dataverse offers the control to shape data, allowing it to discover, model, validate, and report on it. This control ensures that data looks the way a user wants.

- **Storage**: Dataverse stores data in the Azure cloud. This cloud-based storage architecture removes the burden of worrying about where data resides or how it scales. These concerns are handled by a user.

- **Integration**: Dataverse integrates with different ways to support business needs. APIs, webhooks, events, and data exports allow data to get in and out.

In summary, Power Automate is a part of the Power Platform. It also uses Dataverse as its storage on the cloud, which allows easy integration with different products, either within the Power Platform or outside it, along with other associated features. The next section explains how to create the Power Automate environment, so you can see all these components in action.

Creating a Power Automate Environment

This section walks you through the process of setting up a Power Automate environment, step by step:

1. First, navigate to the website `https://powerautomate.microsoft.com/`. Then click Sign In if you have a valid license, or click Start Free, as shown in Figure 2-3.

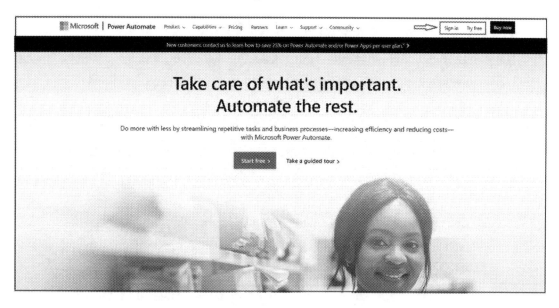

Figure 2-3. *The Power Automate website*

2. Then enter a valid email address and click Start Free, as shown in Figure 2-4. Note that if you use a work or school email, you can avail the Premium Connectors feature, whereas personal emails restrict the premium features.

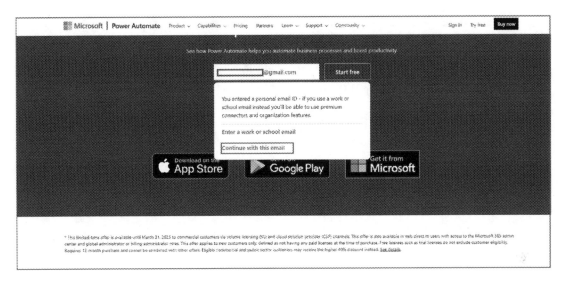

Figure 2-4. *Enter a valid email address*

3. The first time, you have to select your region and click Get Started, as shown in the Figure 2-5.

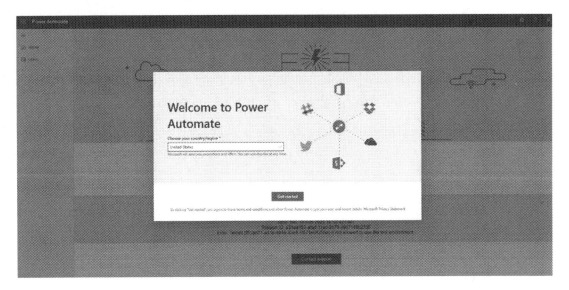

Figure 2-5. *Choose your region*

4. Once the home page is loaded, you can see the environment at
    the top right, as shown in Figure 2-6, along with the navigation
    pane on the left side, which is collapsible. In contrast, the central
    panel displays standard templates to kickstart the flow, training
    materials, and news.

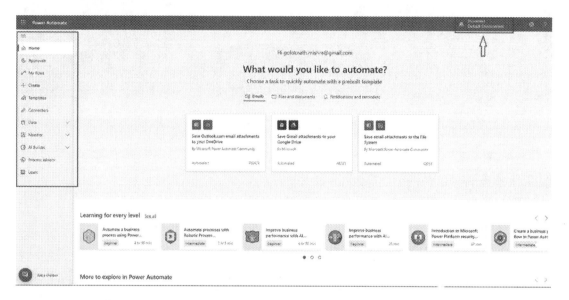

Figure 2-6. *The Power Automate environment*

5. The left navigation pane displays the following options:

    • Home: The default landing page.

    • Approvals: Displays the flow using Microsoft Teams approvals
      and requires a premium account.

    • My Flows: Displays any flows that you are working on; not visible
      to other users.

    • Create: This is where you can create different types of flows.

    • Templates: This holds different types of templates available to use
      to build the flow.

    • Connectors: This holds different types of connectors used in
      the flows.

- Data: This includes Tables, Connections, Custom Connectors, and Gateways. You need a premium account to use Custom Connectors and Gateways.

- Monitor: This includes the Cloud Flow Activity, Desktop Flow Activity, Desktop Flow Runs, and Machines options.

- AI Builder: This includes the Explore, Models, and Document Automation options and requires a premium account.

- Process Advisor: This includes a Process Advisor and requires a premium account.

- Learn: This will redirect you to Microsoft Learn for learning.

Navigating the Power Automate Portal

Once you have created the environment, the landing page will display the home page, as shown in Figure 2-7. The Power Automate portal can be broadly classified into three sections:

- Top navigation pane

- Left navigation pane

- Central workspace

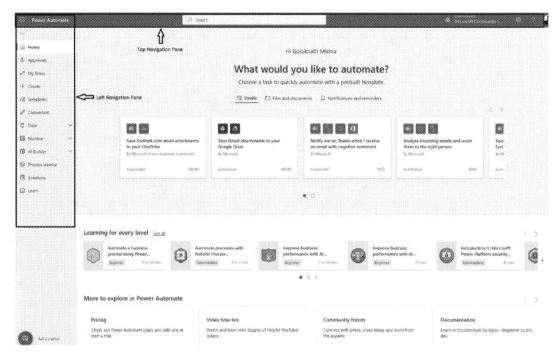

Figure 2-7. *The Power Automate portal*

On the top-left corner of the top navigation pane, the dotted icon navigates to other Microsoft 365 apps. In the middle of the top navigation pane is a search box, where you can search the website. The top-right corner of the page contains Help, Settings, and Environments tabs. Figure 2-8 includes a Settings dialog with features like Admin center, Power Automate Settings, View Licenses, and Password Change.

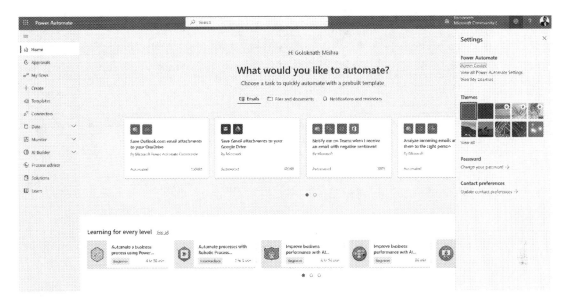

Figure 2-8. *Power Automate Settings window*

The left navigation bar displays Home, Approvals, My Flows, Create, Templates, Connectors, Data, Monitor, AI Builder, Process Advisor, Solutions, and Learn. You can expand and collapse the left panel, as shown in Figure 2-9, and Home is selected by default.

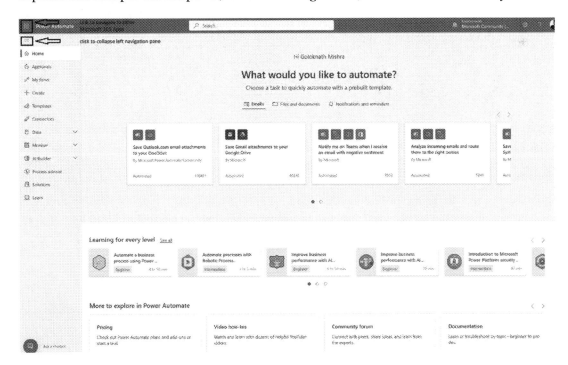

Figure 2-9. *The left navigation bar*

When you click Approvals, you'll see the Microsoft team's approval communications, categorized as Received for the received approvals, Sent for sent approvals, and History for all communication history (see Figure 2-10). Teams' approvals are covered in Chapter 3.

Figure 2-10. *The Approvals panel*

When you click My Flows, you'll see the flows specific to your account; you can also see options for flow creation along with different sample Cloud Flows, as shown in Figure 2-11.

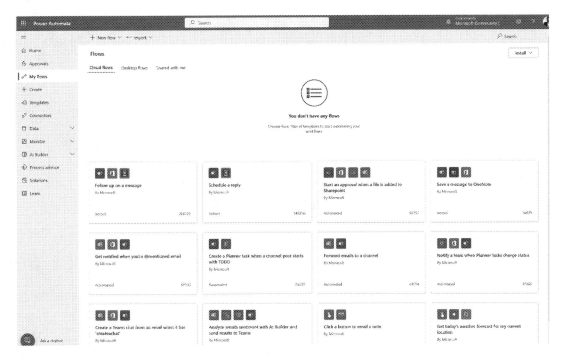

Figure 2-11. *Sample cloud Flows*

When you click Desktop Flow under My Flows, you'll see any Desktop Flows specific to your account and you'll have the option to launch a Desktop Flow directly from the page. See Figure 2-12.

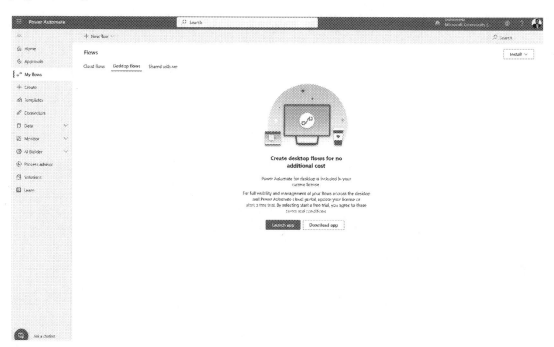

Figure 2-12. *Desktop Flows pane*

When you click the Shared with Me option, it displays a list of flows shared with you, which can be used as templates for building or enhancing your flows (see Figure 2-13).

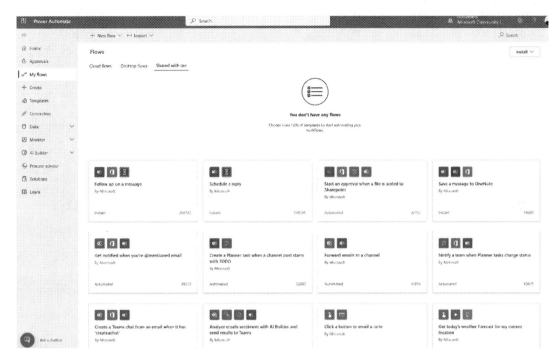

Figure 2-13. *The Shared with Me option*

When you click the Install button, it will show a Power Automate for Desktop link and an On-Premises Data Gateway Installer, which can be clicked to install the respective Windows application. See Figure 2-14.

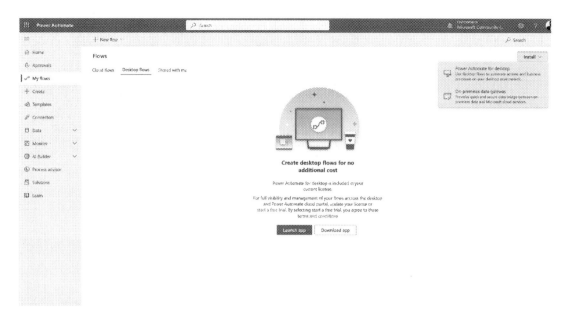

Figure 2-14. *Install Power Automate from here*

When you click the +New Flow button, Power Automate will display options to create different types of flows, as shown in Figure 2-15. I discuss creating different types of flows in upcoming chapters.

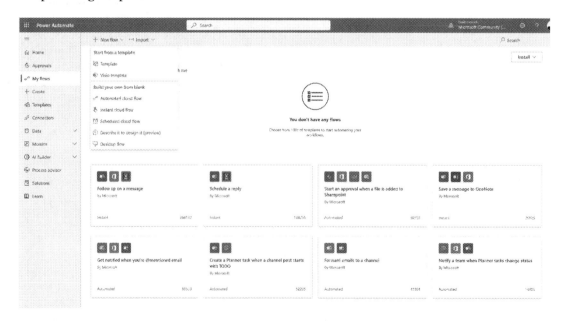

Figure 2-15. *Creating different types of flows*

When you click +Create button, Power Automate will display different options for flow creation, as shown in Figure 2-16.

- Start from Blank

- Start from a Template

I discuss these options in detail in upcoming chapters.

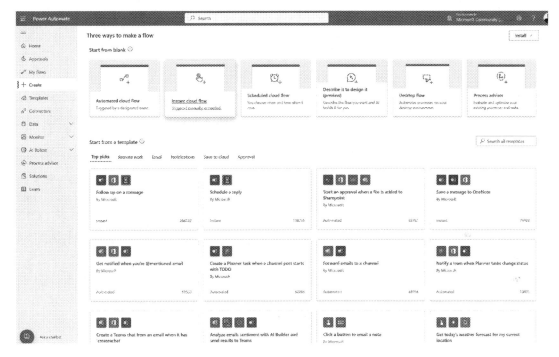

Figure 2-16. *Different options for creating flows*

When you click Templates, you'll see the different types of available templates, which are categorized and sorted for easy navigation and searching, as shown in Figure 2-17.

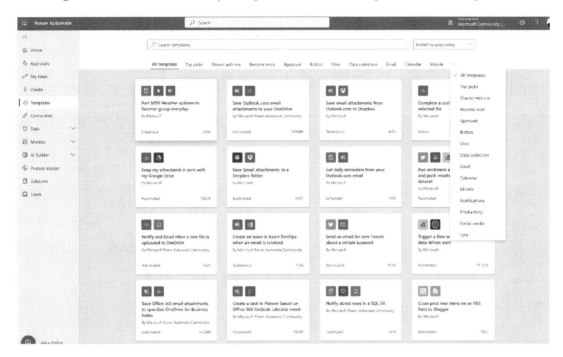

Figure 2-17. *Templates available in Power Automate*

When you click Connectors, you'll see the different available connectors, which are broadly classified as follows:

- Standard connectors: Available upon purchase of Power Automate

- Premium connectors: Come with additional licensing

There is also a search option you can use to find a connector based on your requirements. See Figure 2-18.

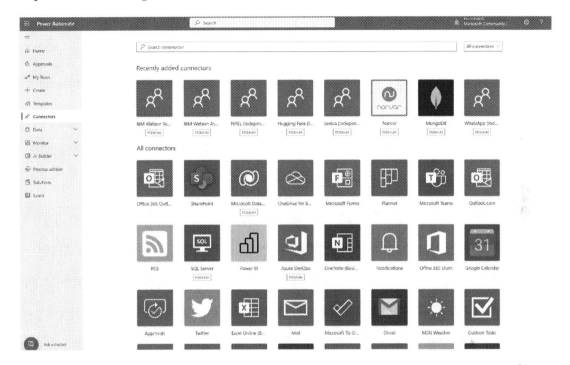

Figure 2-18. *Various connectors found in Power Automate*

When you click Data, you'll see these options:

- Tables: This is the link to power apps that will display available tables in Dataverse.

- Connections: This displays your existing connections along with the option to create a new connection. See Figure 2-19.

- Custom Connectors: This displays a list of custom connectors developed or used on top of preexisting connectors, based on the business requirements.

- Gateways: This area displays existing on-premise data gateways, which connect applications to Dataverse over the cloud.

Figure 2-19. *Connectors in the Microsoft community*

Custom Connectors can be created using different sources, as shown in Figure 2-20.

Figure 2-20. *Custom Connectors*

You can create a new gateway by clicking the +New Gateway option, as shown in Figure 2-21.

Figure 2-21. *The Gateways option*

When you click Monitor, you'll see options for monitoring different flows. When you click the Cloud Flow activity, you'll see the status of the Cloud Flows, as shown in Figure 2-22.

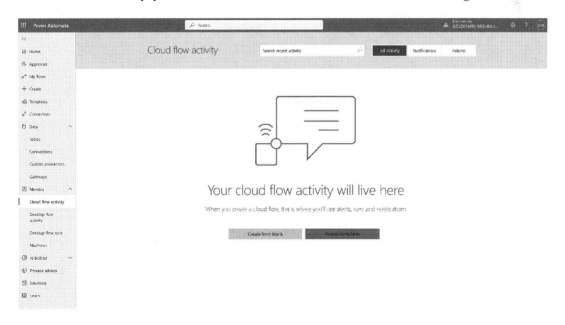

Figure 2-22. *Status of any Cloud Flows*

When you click the Desktop Flow activity, you'll see the status of the Desktop Flows, as shown in Figure 2-23.

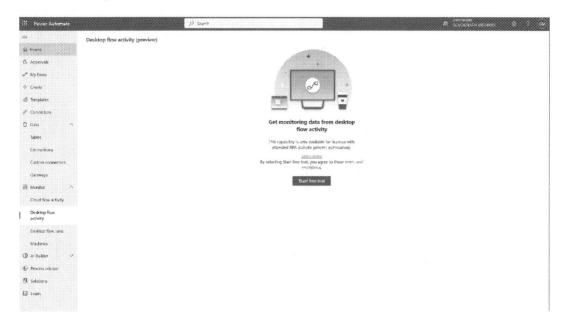

Figure 2-23. *Status of Desktop Flows*

When you click the Desktop Flow runs, you'll see the status of any running desktop Flows, as shown in Figure 2-24.

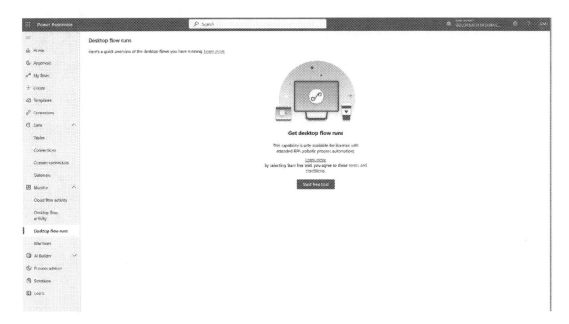

Figure 2-24. *The status of any running Desktop Flows*

When you click Machines, you'll see the following:

- Machines (see Figure 2-25)

- Machine groups (see Figure 2-26)

- VM images (see Figure 2-27)

- Gateways

I discuss machines in Chapter 4.

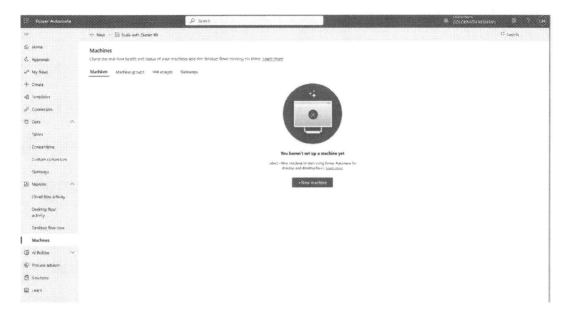

Figure 2-25. *Power Automate machines*

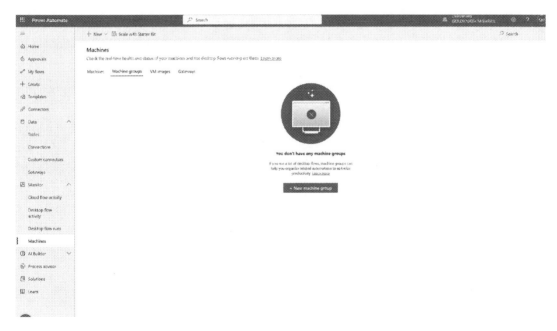

Figure 2-26. *Power Automate machine groups*

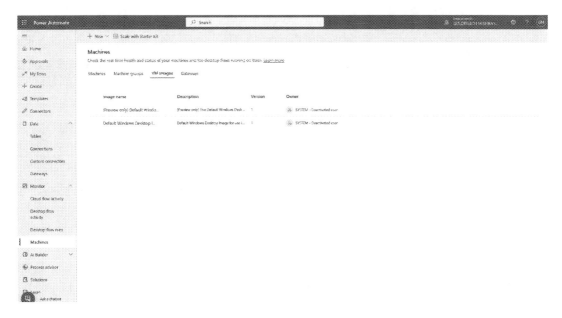

Figure 2-27. *Power Automate VM images*

When you click AI Builder, you'll see three options (see Figure 2-28). Explore shows the different AI models available under AI Builder, categorized as follows:

- Document-based models

- Text-based models

- Structured data models

- Image-based models

I discuss more this in Chapter 7.

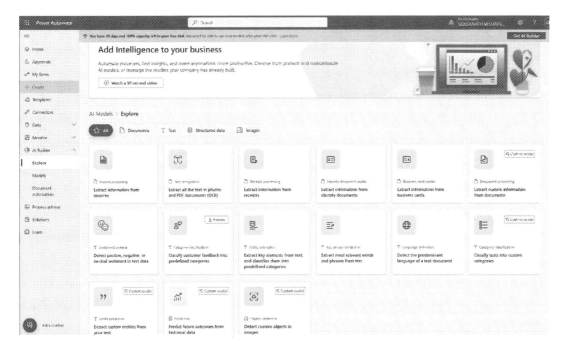

Figure 2-28. *AI Builder models*

When you build a custom model, you can see it by choosing Models, as shown in Figure 2-29.

Figure 2-29. *The Models pane shows models you have built*

When you click Document Automation, you can see how Document Automation works, how it helps in automating documents, and how to use it. See Figure 2-30.

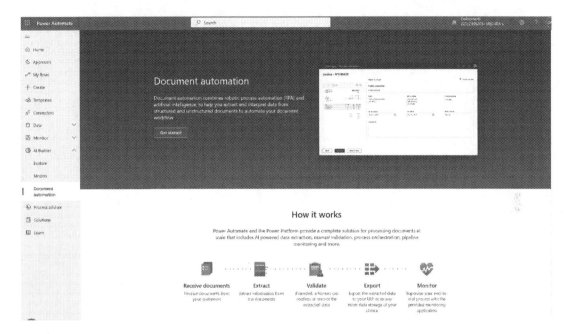

Figure 2-30. *Document Automation*

Document Automation also enables you to determine your ROI; see Figure 2-31.

Figure 2-31. *Document Automation enables you to determine your ROI*

For example, say that the average number of documents processed monthly by your company is 50,000, and they take two minutes to process. Based on the ROI calculation, your business can save 75,000+ minutes a month, which is equivalent to 1,250+ hours. Working eight hours a day saves nearly 156 person-days of effort, equivalent to 5.5 months of effort for one person.

In summary, the employee can spend those 5.5 months doing more productive work (or maybe on holiday!) after this document automation, as Power Automate can take care of that activity. See Figure 2-32.

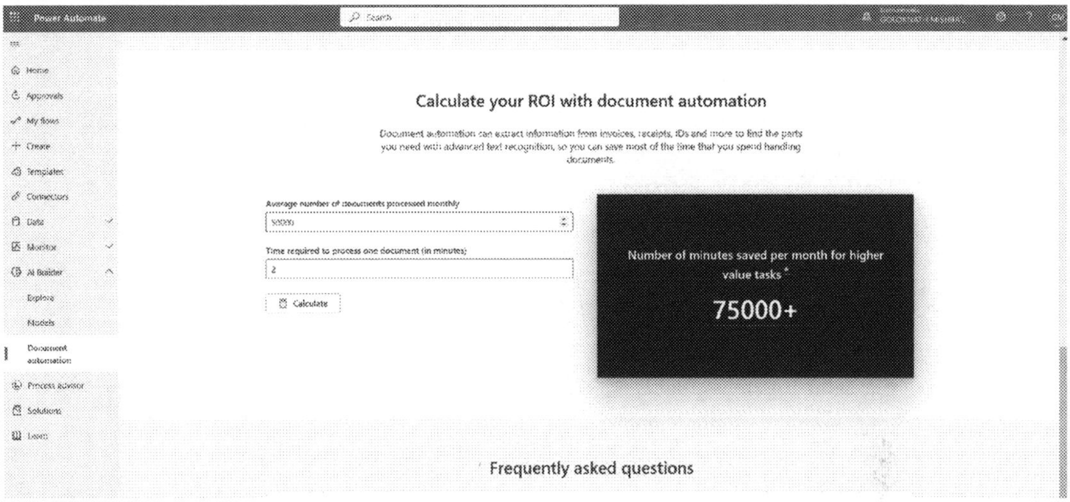

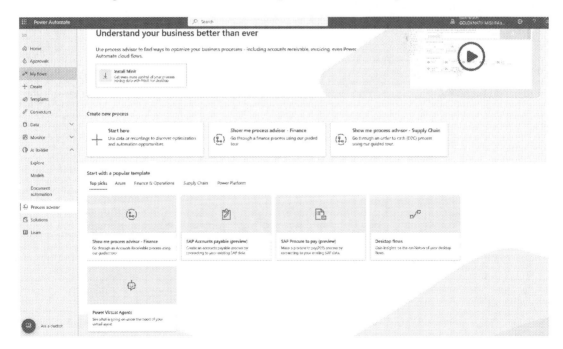

Figure 2-32. *Power Automate calculating the ROI*

When you click Process Advisor, you'll see different options for your optimizing business (see Figure 2-33). I discuss these options more in Chapter 6.

Figure 2-33. *Process Advisor helps optimize your business*

You will see different solutions for building and migrating flows when you click a specific solution. See Figure 2-34.

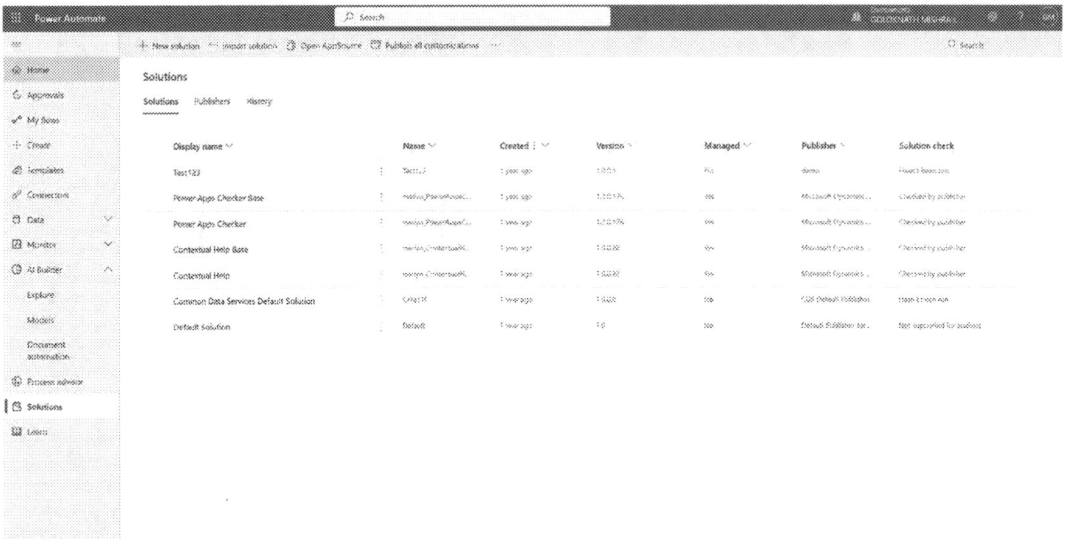

Figure 2-34. *Power Automate Solutions pane*

You can create different publishers under the solution as well, as shown in Figure 2-35.

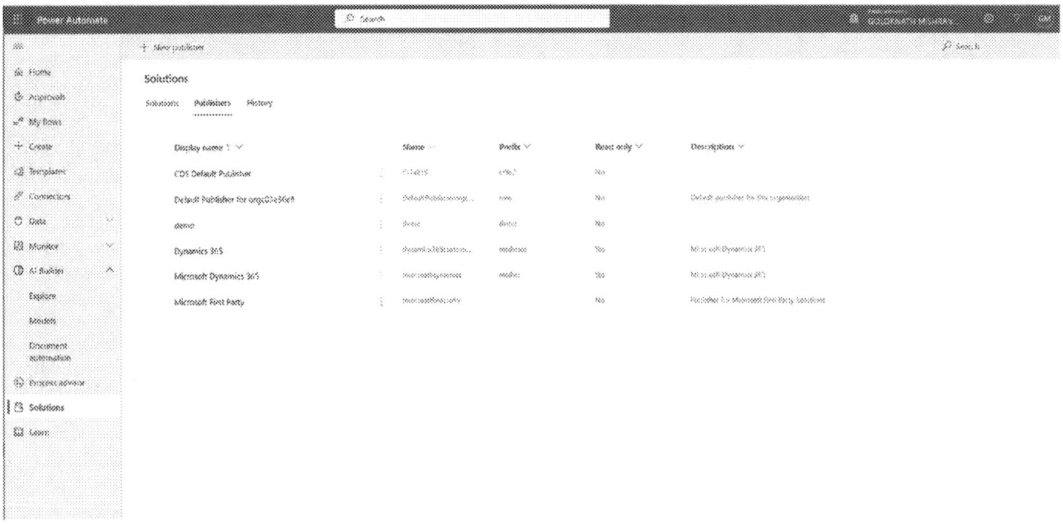

Figure 2-35. *Creating publishers in the Solutions pane*

You can also view the solution history, such as when the solution was created/ modified, what operations were performed, and their status. See Figure 2-36.

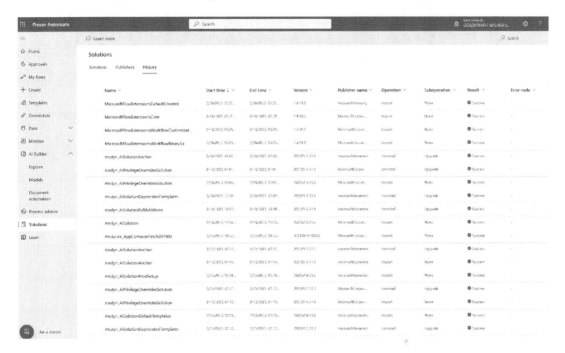

Figure 2-36. *Showing the full history of a solution*

Different Types of Flows in Power Automate

Power Automate works by creating flows, of which there are three types:

- **Cloud Flows**: Flows that you build with a trigger and one or more actions. Several triggers and actions are available, including emails from a specific person or a mention of an organization in social media. You will see these as My Flows and Team Flows in Power Automate. With a My Flow, the user is the sole owner, while Team Flows have more than one owner.

- **Business Process Flows**: These flows are built to provide the experience when using model-driven apps and Microsoft Dataverse. Use these to create a guided experience in your model-driven apps.

- **Desktop Flows**: These RPA flows allow you to record yourself performing actions on your desktop or in a web browser. You can then trigger a flow to perform that process. Users can also pass data in or get data out of the process, letting the user automate "manual" business processes.

Plug-and-Play Offerings from Power Automate

Microsoft Power Automate has the following plug-and-play offerings:

- Approval flows, which are seamless integrations of flow with the Microsoft Teams approval app.

- Preexisting connectors are available for nearly all standard applications. They can be used to integrate seamlessly (e.g., Workday, Salesforce, Google Drive, box, etc.).

- You can create a flow from a description, which uses AI functionality. (Note: This functionality is not available in all regions.)

- You can create a flow from a Visio diagram.

Summary

This chapter explained how to create the Power Automate ecosystem and explored its various components and navigation. In the next chapter, you learn more about each type of flows.

Keywords

AI Builder

Approvals

Cloud Flow

Connectors

Dataverse

Desktop Flow

Document Automation

Gateways

Machines

Model

Monitor

Power Apps

Power BI

Process Advisor

Publisher

ROI

CHAPTER 3

Cloud Flow

Earlier chapters explained what RPA and IPA are. You also learned about the history and components of Power Automate. You learned how to create a Power Automate instance and navigate Power Automate.

You learned that flows are the core of Power Automate. This chapter dives deep dive into flows. It dives deep into Power Automate Cloud Flows, so you learn how to create them, how to use their triggers, actions, controls, connectors, variables, and expressions, as well as how to share and move flows from one environment to another. You will also learn about custom connectors, which can help you integrate with third-party systems.

Cloud Flows help automate over the cloud, whether automatically, instantly, or via a schedule. There are three types:

- Instant flow
- Automated flow
- Scheduled flow

© Goloknath Mishra 2023
G. Mishra, *Deep Dive into Power Automate*, https://doi.org/10.1007/978-1-4842-9732-2_3

Instant Cloud Flows are triggered manually, as shown in Figure 3-1.

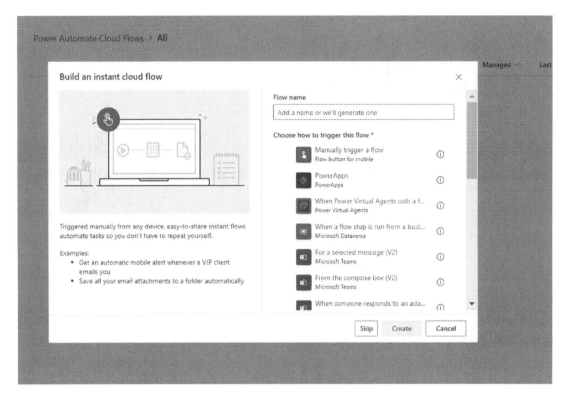

Figure 3-1. *Instant cloud flows are triggered manually*

Automated Cloud Flows are triggered as a sequence of external events, as shown in Figure 3-2.

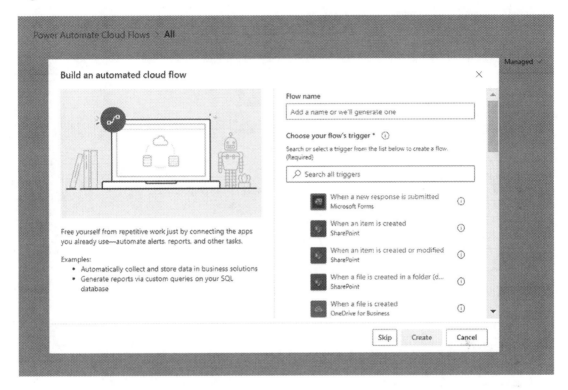

Figure 3-2. *Automated Cloud Flows are triggered as a sequence of external events*

Scheduled Cloud Flows are triggered based on the configured schedule/recurrence, as shown in Figure 3-3.

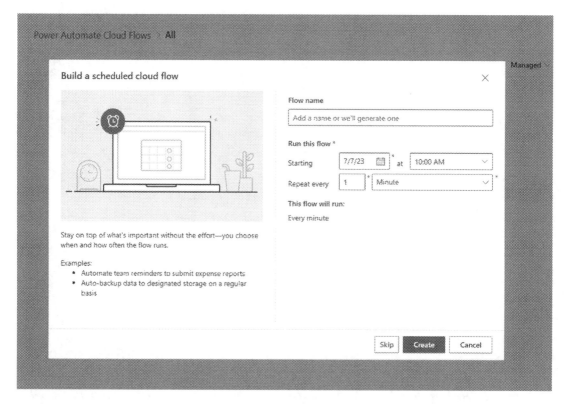

Figure 3-3. *Scheduled Cloud Flows are triggered based on a set schedule*

Creating Cloud Flows

Cloud flows can be created in three ways:

- From a template

- From a description

- From scratch or blank, which is discussed in the next chapter

Creating a Cloud Flow from a Template

To create a Cloud Flow from a template, click + Create and then choose All Templates to see list of templates under the Start From a Template section, as shown in Figure 3-4.

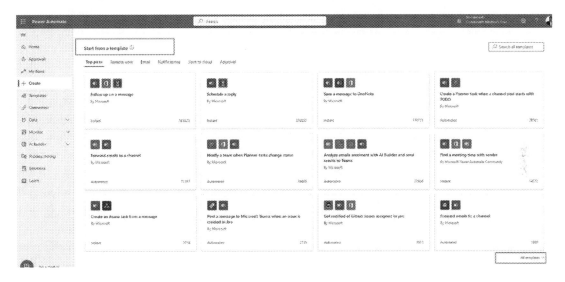

Figure 3-4. *Creating a Clow Flow from a template*

Power Automate will display all the templates and you can sort them

- By popularity

- By name

- By published time

Templates can also be segregated by different operations and features, as shown in Figure 3-5.

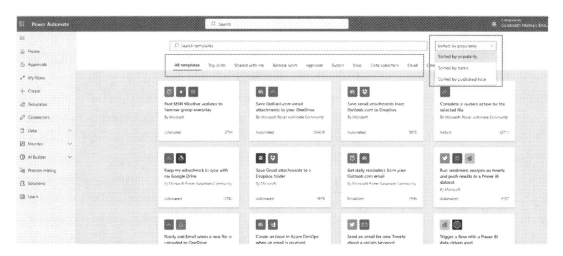

Figure 3-5. *You can sort templates by popularity, name, and when they were published*

For this example, select a template that will display the weather when it's asked in Microsoft Teams. See Figure 3-6.

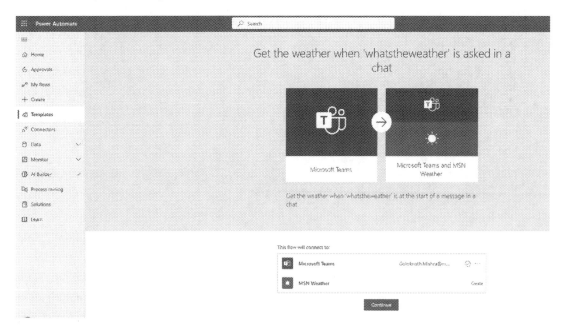

Figure 3-6. *A template that will report the weather*

Click Continue to establish connection of connectors, as shown in Figure 3-7.

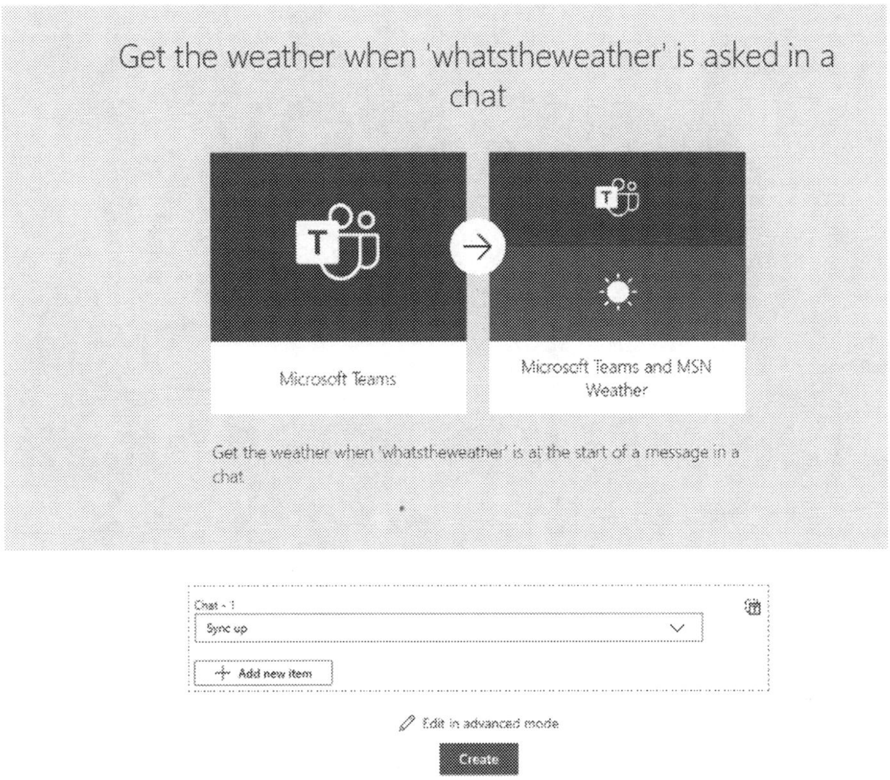

Figure 3-7. *Establishing the connection*

Then configure the Teams chat to get the weather and click Continue. See Figure 3-8.

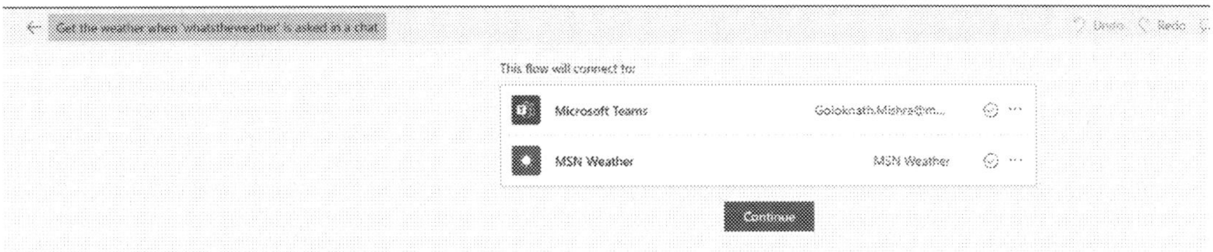

Figure 3-8. *Choose the Teams app*

After basic configuration and connection is established, the full flow will display as shown in Figure 3-9.

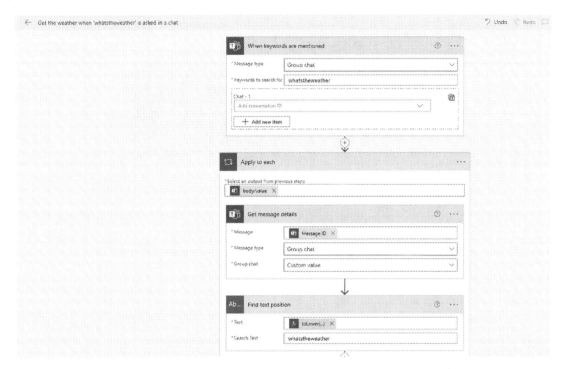

Figure 3-9. *The full flow of this weather template*

Run the flow as shown in Figure 3-10 to execute it, after entering the whatstheweather text in the Teams chat.

Figure 3-10. *The flow runs successfully*

The flow ran successfully and displayed the weather conditions.

Creating a Cloud Flow from a Description

Power Automate has an AI capability called Copilot, which creates flows from descriptions. You simply describe the flow you want to create in the box, as shown in Figure 3-11.

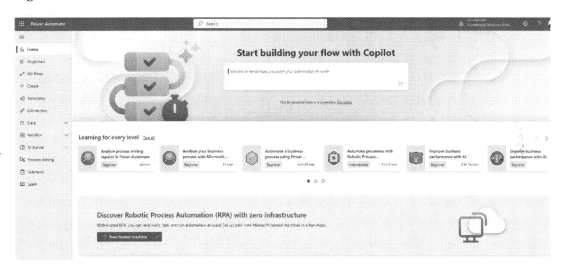

Figure 3-11. *Building a flow with Copilot*

Once you start typing a suggestion, Copilot shows some possible flows, as shown in Figure 3-12.

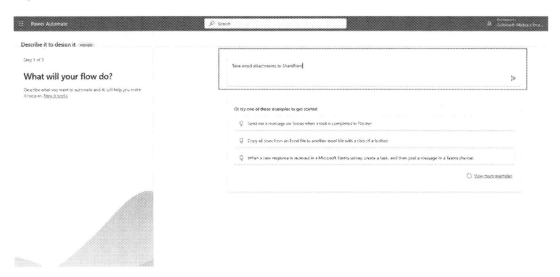

Figure 3-12. *Copilot will guess at your intentions once you begin typing*

Select the desired flow statement to start building the flow, as shown in Figure 3-13.

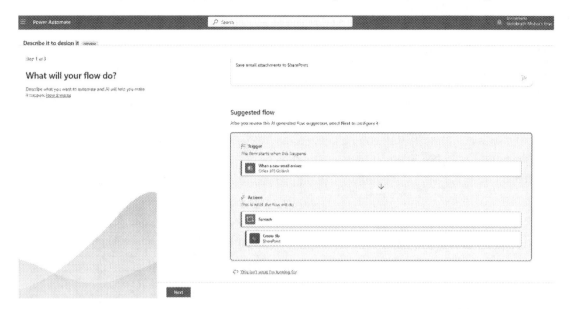

Figure 3-13. *Select the desired flow statement*

Once the flow is selected, establish the connections of the flow connectors. See Figure 3-14.

Figure 3-14. *Connect the appropriate apps to your flow*

Flows can be edited in two ways:

- With Designer

- With Copilot

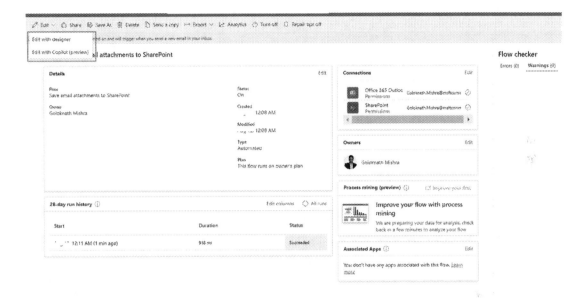

Figure 3-15. *Choose Edit in the menu bar to edit your flow*

When you choose to edit with Designer, you'll see the UI, as shown in Figure 3-16.

Figure 3-16. *Editing with Designer*

When you choose to edit with Copilot, you'll see the UI shown in Figure 3-17, which includes the Copilot bot to guide you in preparing the flow.

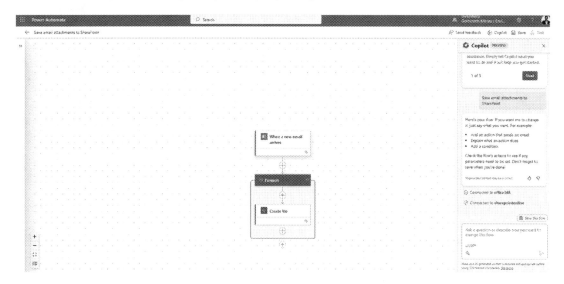

Figure 3-17. *Editing with Copilot*

Once you are finished editing your flow, run the flow. After running the flow, you can see whether the execution completes successfully, as shown in Figure 3-18.

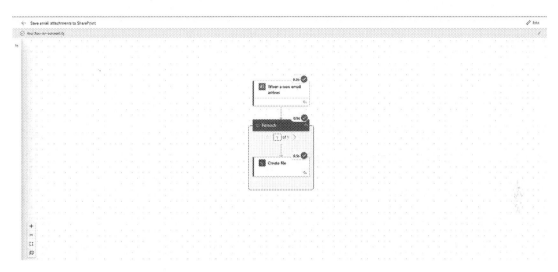

Figure 3-18. *The new flow works*

An attachment is uploaded to SharePoint because of the run, as shown in Figure 3-19.

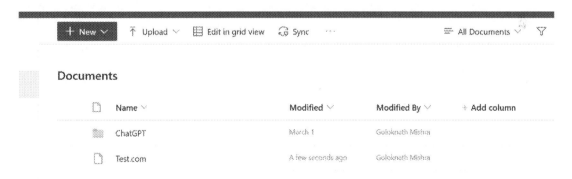

Figure 3-19. *An attachment is uploaded to SharePoint*

Building Blocks of Flows: Triggers, Actions, and Connectors

The basic building blocks of flows are categorized into three types:

- Triggers, which answer when

- Actions, which answer what

- Connectors, which answer how

A *trigger* is an event that starts the cloud flow and an *action* is the operation performed by the flow. A *connector* is the bridge between the trigger and the action.

For example, say you want to receive an email notification when someone uploads a document in OneDrive. In this case:

- The trigger is the uploading of the document.

- The action is sending the email notification.

- The connector is the intermediary that connects OneDrive and Outlook with the relevant credentials.

Always create flows for a solution that will be easy to migrate to different systems and to maintain.

Click +New Solution to create a new solution and fill in the required information. Then click Create to create the solution. See Figure 3-20.

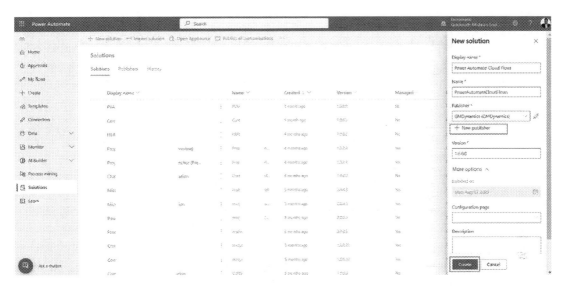

Figure 3-20. *Creating a new solution*

Once the solution has been created, it will display the solution with detailed information, as shown in Figure 3-21.

Figure 3-21. *The completed solution*

Inside the solution, you can choose +New ➤ Automation ➤ Cloud Flow to see the different flow types (automated, instant, and scheduled). See Figure 3-22.

Figure 3-22. *Viewing different flow types*

Creating an Instant Cloud Flow

Choose Instant from the cloud flow options to create an instant flow. See Figure 3-23.

Figure 3-23. *Choosing to create an instant cloud flow*

You can also click Instant Cloud Flow, as shown in Figure 3-24, to create the flow.

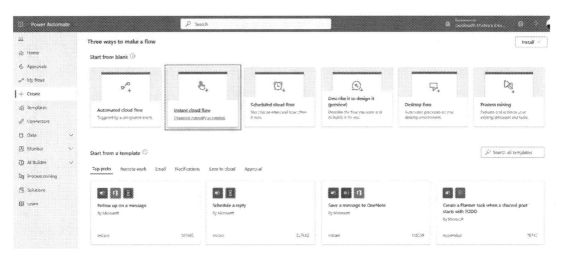

Figure 3-24. *Choosing to create an instant cloud flow*

A dialog appears, as shown in Figure 3-25. Name the flow and then click Create.

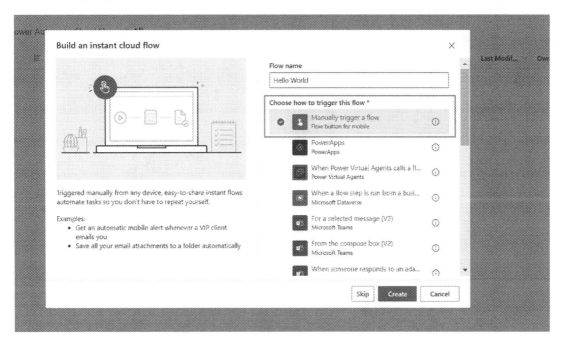

Figure 3-25. *Building an instant cloud flow*

You can create a blank flow by using the Manually Trigger a Flow option, as shown in Figure 3-26.

Figure 3-26. *Choose the Manually Trigger a Flow option*

Click +New Step to choose an operation and then type the desired operation. In this example, you want to send an email, so you would type that request. The system will display the Send an Email action, as shown in Figure 3-27.

Figure 3-27. *Sending an email as part of the flow*

When you select the Send an Email action, the system will prompt you to fill in the To, Subject, and Body fields, as shown in Figure 3-28.

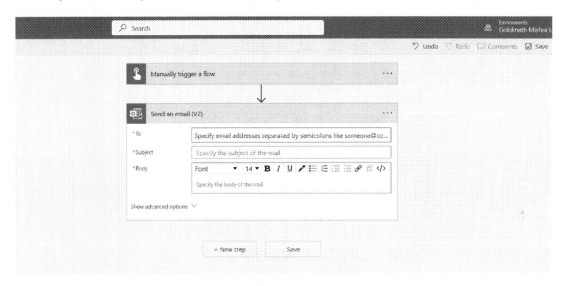

Figure 3-28. *Fill in the appropriate fields for the email*

Click the **...** icon to access the Rename option. The action can be updated by removing V2, as shown in Figure 3-29.

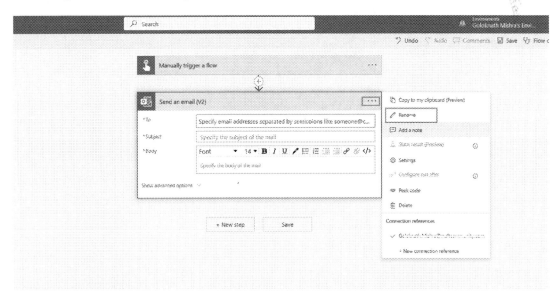

Figure 3-29. *Renaming the step*

Fill in the required information to complete the steps, as shown in Figure 3-30.

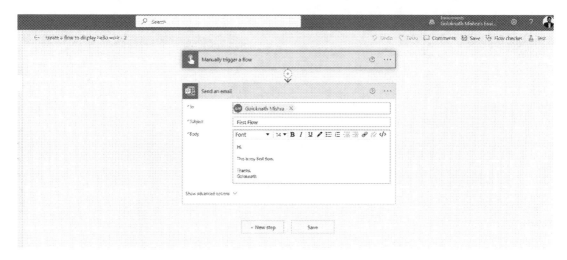

Figure 3-30. *Fill in all the required information*

When the flow runs, an email will be triggered to the mailbox, as shown in Figure 3-31.

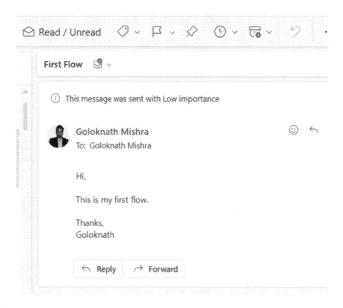

Figure 3-31. *The email has been sent*

From the ... icon, you can also choose the Peek Code option (see Figure 3-32). You can then view the code behind the flow step.

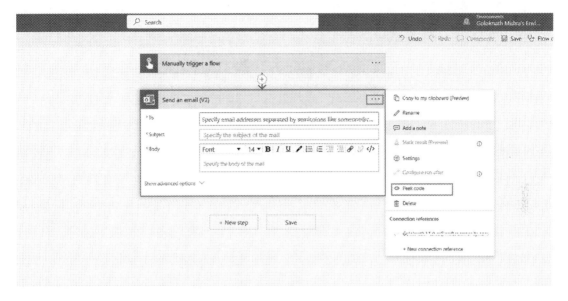

Figure 3-32. *The Peek Code option*

Figure 3-33 displays the code behind the flow step.

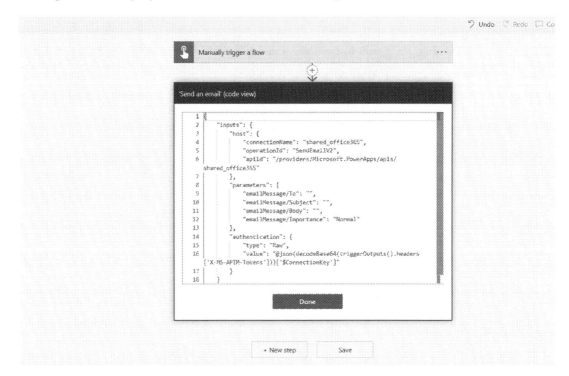

Figure 3-33. *The code you see when choosing Peek Code*

Peek Code will display the code in the Workflow Definition Language (see https://learn.microsoft.com/en-us/azure/logic-apps/logic-apps-workflow-definition-language for more information).

It is always best to add notes to the steps. You can add them using the Edit Note option, as shown in Figure 3-34.

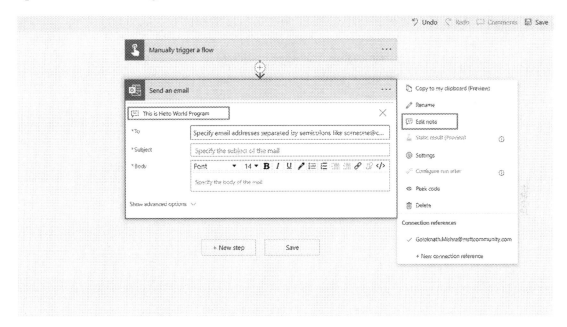

***Figure 3-34.** Adding notes*

The Settings option displays options for different settings, as shown in Figure 3-35.

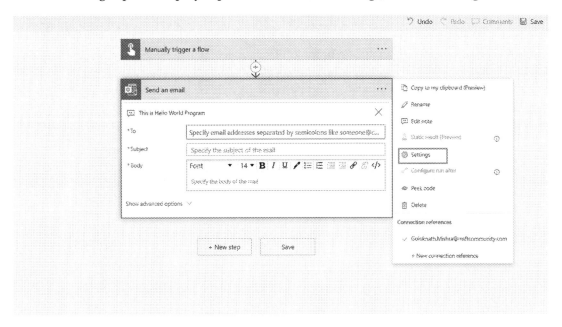

***Figure 3-35.** Choose the Settings option*

In the Settings option, you can configure Synchronous/Asynchronous, Secure Field/ Not, Timeout Period, and Retry Policy, as shown in Figure 3-36.

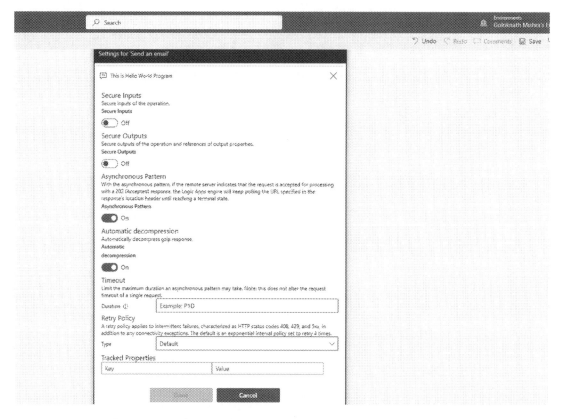

Figure 3-36.   *The settings for sending an email*

Creating a Scheduled Cloud Flow

Select Scheduled Cloud Flow from the Create + window to create a scheduled flow, as shown in Figure 3-37.

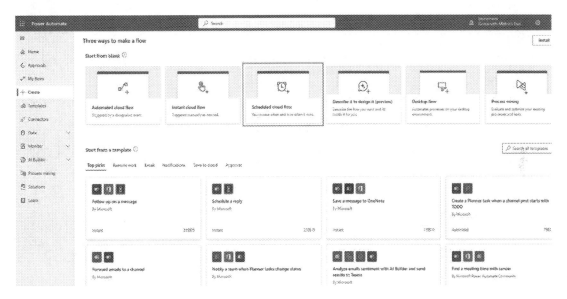

Figure 3-37. *Select Scheduled Cloud Flow*

Next, choose a name for the flow and the desired schedule, as shown in Figure 3-38.

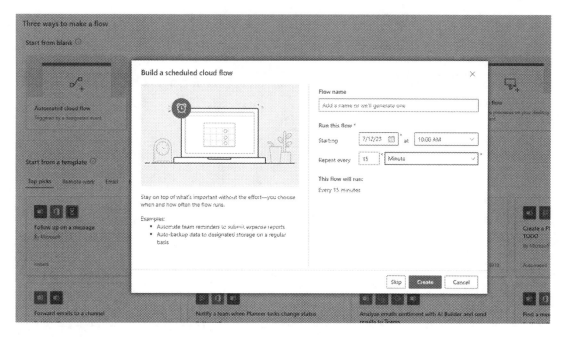

Figure 3-38. *Name your flow and set up the schedule*

Rename the flow **First Scheduled Flow** and select the necessary information, as shown in Figure 3-39.

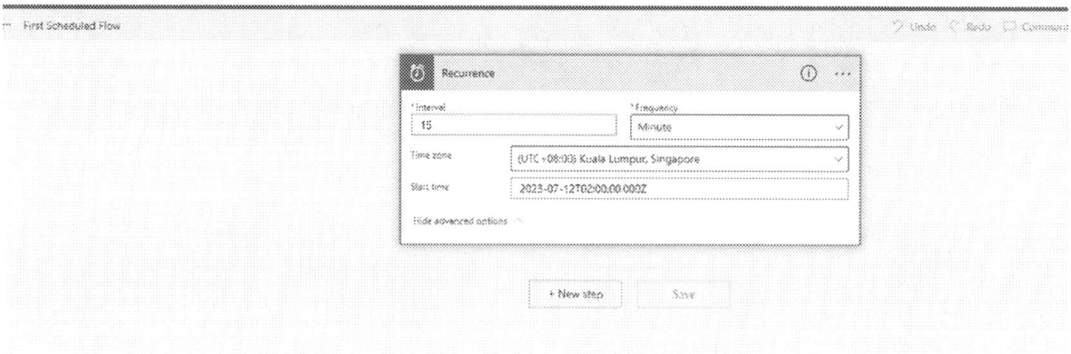

Figure 3-39. *Setting up the interval*

Add a new step and select Send an Email, as shown in Figure 3-40.

Figure 3-40. *Choose Send an Email for the operation*

Select the mandatory content, as shown in Figure 3-41.

Figure 3-41. *Add the required fields*

Click Save to save the flow. A notification will display stating that the flow has been saved, as shown in Figure 3-42. If there is an error, the flow will not be saved and the error will be displayed instead.

Figure 3-42. *The flow has been saved*

Once the flow is ready, click Flow Checker to view any errors. See Figure 3-43.

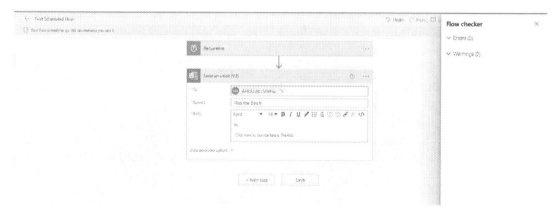

Figure 3-43. *Use Flow Checker to check for errors*

If there are no errors, click Test to test the flow. See Figure 3-44.

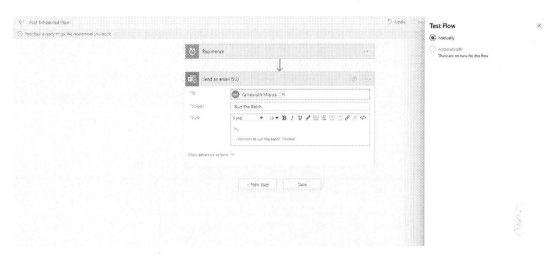

Figure 3-44. *Testing the flow*

Once the flow runs, it will display, as shown in Figure 3-45.

Figure 3-45. *The flow begins*

The flow ran successfully, as shown in Figure 3-46.

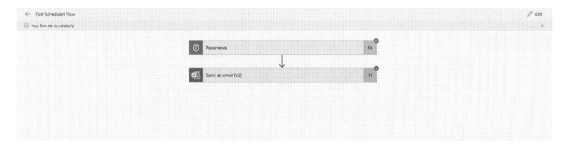

Figure 3-46. *The flow ran successfully*

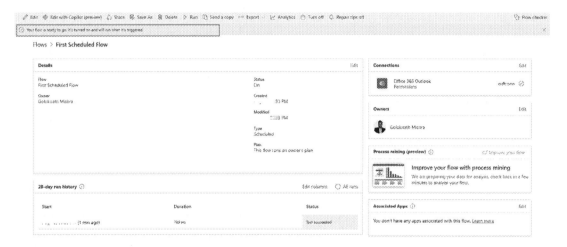

Figure 3-47. *The flow will run as programmed*

The flow is now ready to run automatically in 15 minute intervals.

The flow ran successfully, as shown in Figure 3-48.

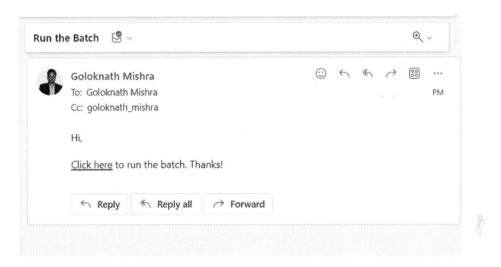

Figure 3-48. *The email was sent as expected*

Say you want to modify the email schedule. To make modifications to your flow, you click Edit on the Flow Details page, as shown in Figure 3-49.

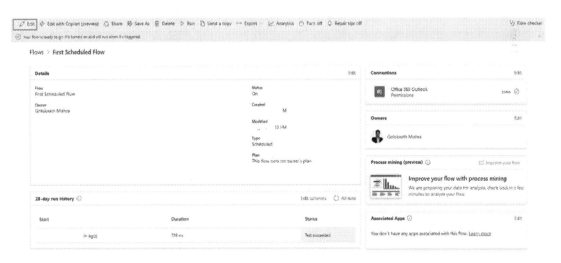

Figure 3-49. *Choose Edit on the Flow Details page*

In this example, you are modifying the recurrence, as shown in Figure 3-50.

Figure 3-50. *Changing the interval of the email*

Click All Runs to see list of flow runs. See Figure 3-51.

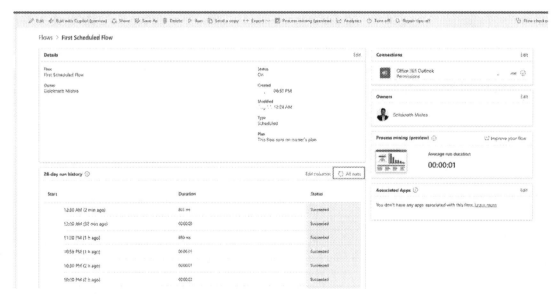

Figure 3-51. *Choose All Runs to see a list of the flow runs*

A list displays all the runs, as shown in Figure 3-52.

First Scheduled Flow › **Run history**

Start time	Duration	Add column	Status
12:30 AM (47 min ago)	803 ms		Succeeded
12:00 AM (1 h ago)	00:00:05		Succeeded
11:30 PM (1 h ago)	860 ms		Succeeded
10:59 PM (2 h ago)	00:00:01		Succeeded
10:30 PM (2 h ago)	00:00:01		Succeeded
10:00 PM (3 h ago)	00:00:02		Succeeded
09:30 PM (3 h ago)	00:00:01		Succeeded
09:00 PM (4 h ago)	585 ms		Succeeded
08:29 PM (4 h ago)	986 ms		Succeeded
08:00 PM (5 h ago)	732 ms		Succeeded
07:30 PM (5 h ago)	761 ms		Succeeded
06:59 PM (6 h ago)	735 ms		Succeeded
06:45 PM (6 h ago)	439 ms		Succeeded
06:39 PM (6 h ago)	789 ms		Test succeeded

Figure 3-52. *The run history*

Creating Automated Cloud Flows

You can create automated Cloud Flows by choosing the icon shown in Figure 3-53.

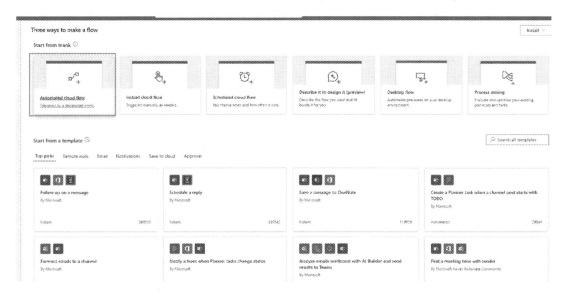

Figure 3-53. *Choose Automated Cloud Flow*

Name the flow and select the trigger criteria, as shown in Figure 3-54.

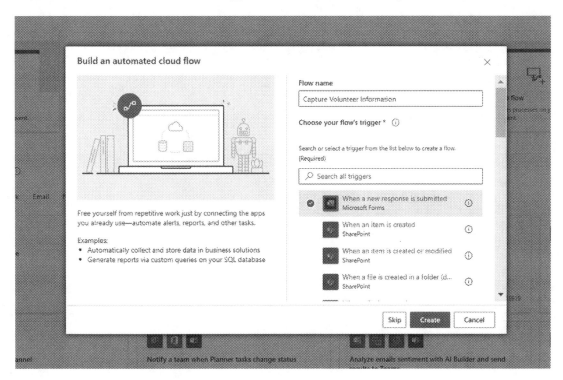

Figure 3-54. *Name your flow and select the trigger criteria*

After the trigger, add the action/operation to send an email. See Figure 3-55.

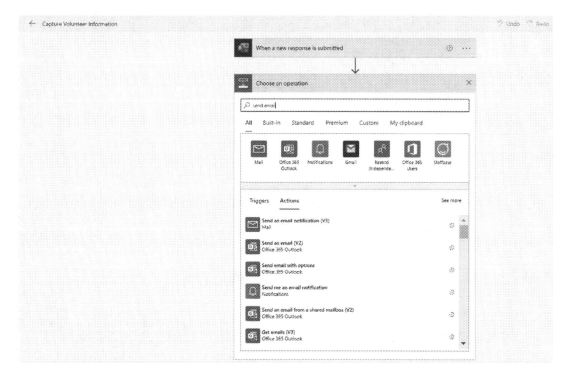

Figure 3-55. *Choose the Send an Email operation*

Fill in the required information for the trigger, as shown in Figure 3-56.

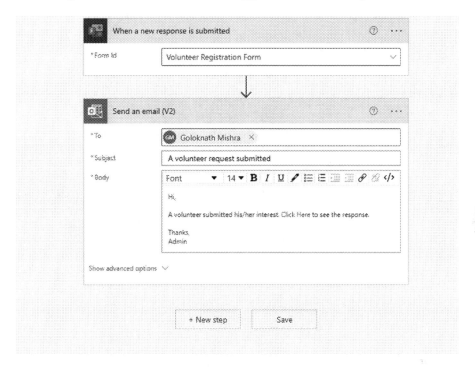

Figure 3-56. *Fill in the required fields*

The flow is now ready and waiting for a new response, which is submitted using Microsoft Forms. See Figure 3-57.

Figure 3-57. *The flow is ready*

Once a response has been submitted, the flow will execute successfully, as shown in Figures 3-58 and 3-59.

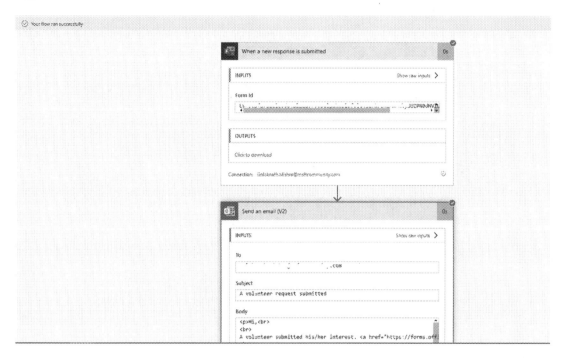

Figure 3-58. *The flow executes successfully*

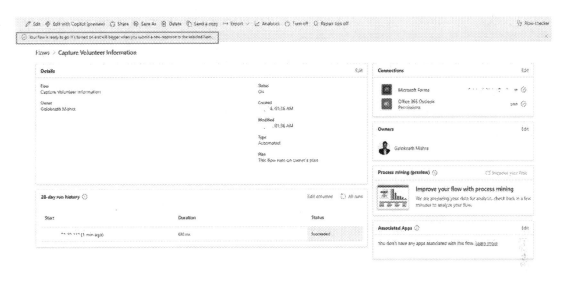

Figure 3-59. *The flow executes successfully*

Using Variables

Let's say you want to add a number to the email subject to identify the number of volunteers. To do this, you can add a variable to capture the number of volunteers.

First, you need to insert additional steps into the last flow, as shown in Figure 3-60.

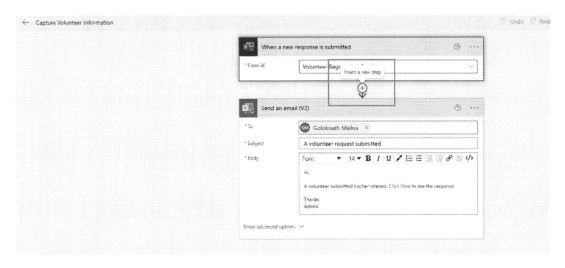

Figure 3-60. *Inserting a step into a flow*

Click Add an Action to add a new operation/action, as shown in Figure 3-61.

Figure 3-61. *Choose Add an Action*

Type **variable** to see list of variable operations, as shown in Figure 3-62.

Figure 3-62. *Typing variable shows a list of variable actions*

Select Initialize Variable, as shown in Figure 3-63.

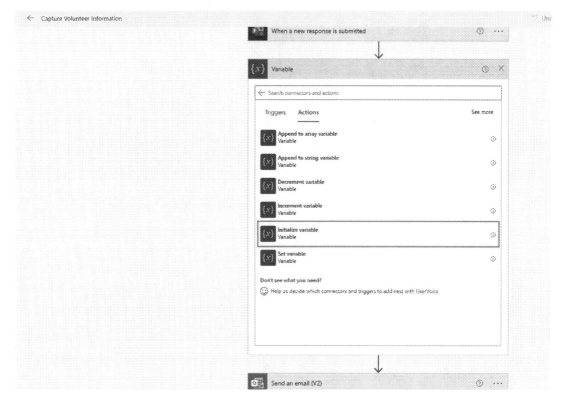

Figure 3-63. *Choose Initialize Variable*

Once Initialize Variable is selected, you need to fill in the mandatory parameters (Name and Type), as shown in Figure 3-64.

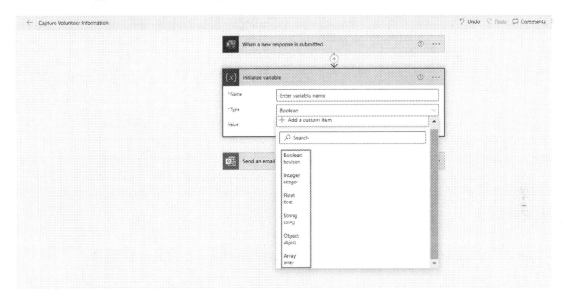

Figure 3-64. *Fill in the mandatory fields*

Supported variable types include the following:

- **Boolean**: True or False

- **Integer**: Accepts whole number numeric values (e.g., 1, 2, 3, 4, etc.)

- **Float**: Accepts decimal numbers (e.g., 1.2, 2.4, 3.45, etc.)

- **String**: Accepts text input (e.g., Hello, World, Power, Automate, etc.)

- **Object**: Contains key-value pair properties in JSON format

- **Array**: Accepts a list of objects that can be numbers or string and have the same data type

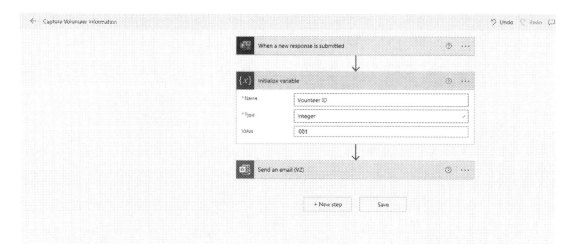

Figure 3-65. *Choose the appropriate variable type*

Add another action to increment the variable, as shown in Figure 3-66.

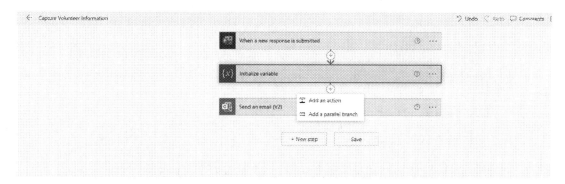

Figure 3-66. *Add another action*

As shown in Figure 3-67, the Increment Variable action has been added before sending the email.

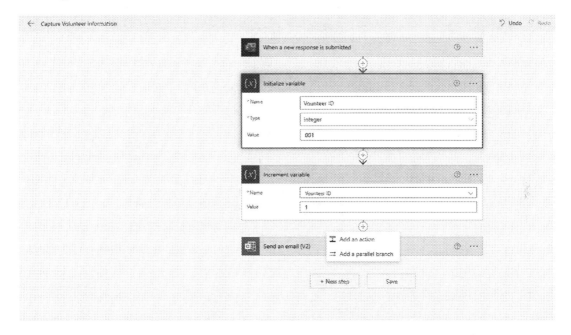

Figure 3-67. *The Increment Variable action has been added*

To perform a data operation, search for Compose in the operations.

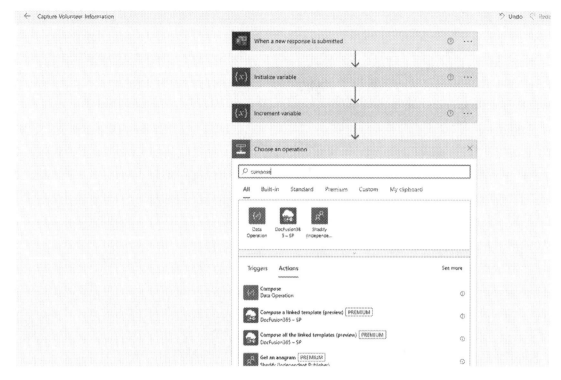

Figure 3-68. *Search for Compose*

As shown in Figure 3-69, a list of data operations is displayed. Choose the Compose operation.

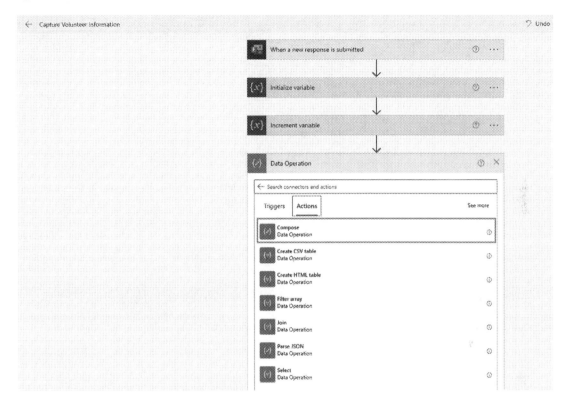

Figure 3-69. *A list of data operations is displayed*

In the Compose step, add a dynamic variable, as shown in Figure 3-70.

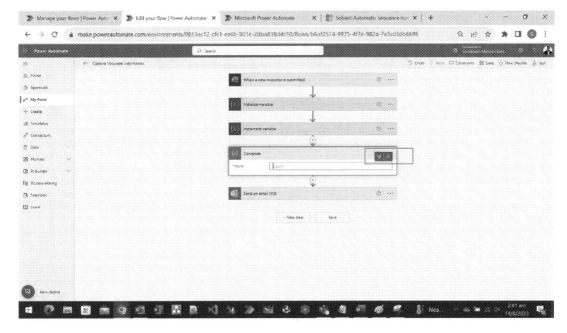

Figure 3-70. *Add a dynamic variable to the Compose step*

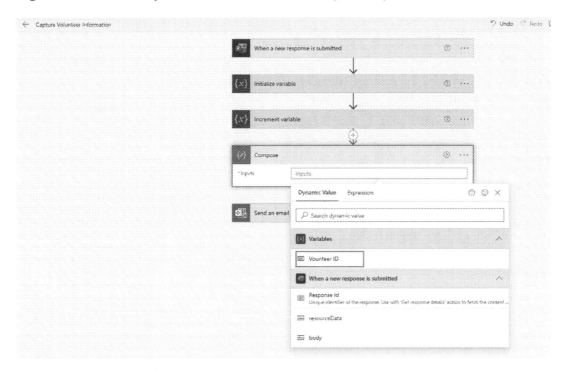

Figure 3-71. *Choose the volunteer ID*

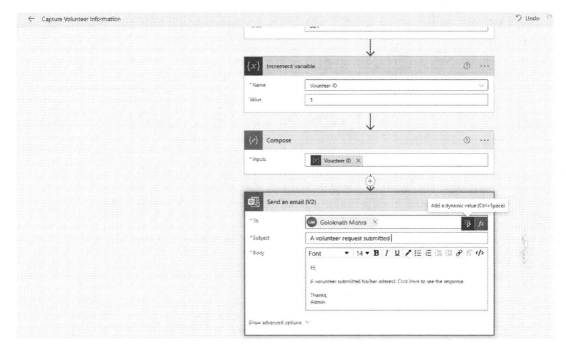

Figure 3-72. *Give the email a subject name*

Add the Compose output to the subject of the email as a dynamic value, as shown in Figure 3-73.

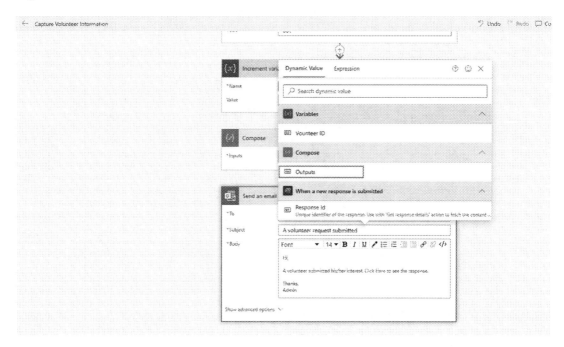

Figure 3-73. *Add the Compose output as a dynamic value*

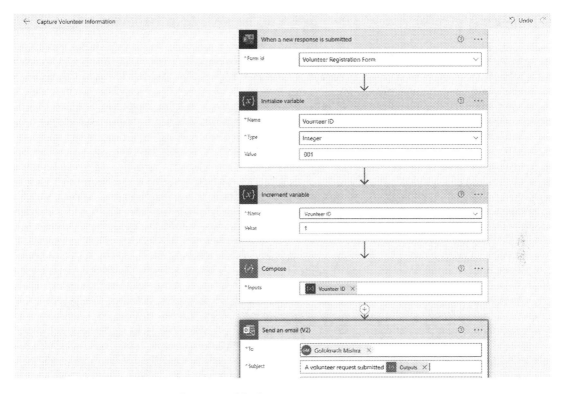

Figure 3-74. *Increment the variable by one*

This flow will display an error when it runs because it was initialized with 001, which the system considers a string. See Figure 3-75.

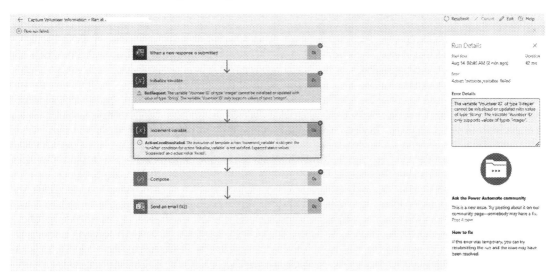

Figure 3-75. *An error is displayed*

Updated the initialize variable to 1 to execute it successfully. See Figure 3-76.

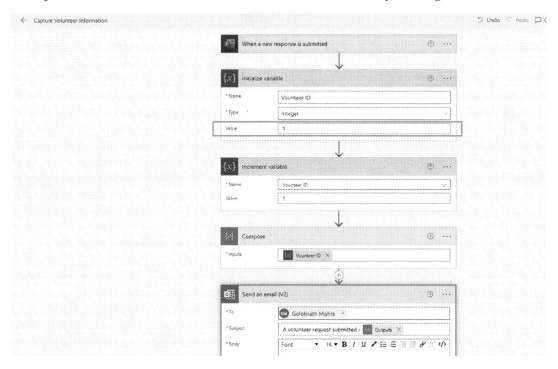

Figure 3-76. *Updated the initialize variable to 1*

The flow executes successfully after the update, as shown in Figure 3-77.

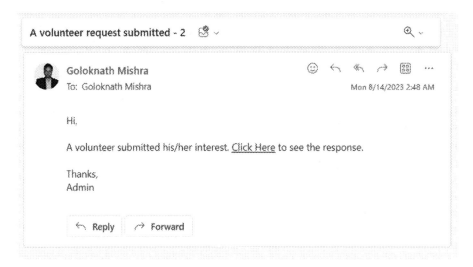

Figure 3-77. *The new flow executes successfully*

Using Expressions

In the last example, you might have noticed the two blue icons, as shown in Figure 3-78.

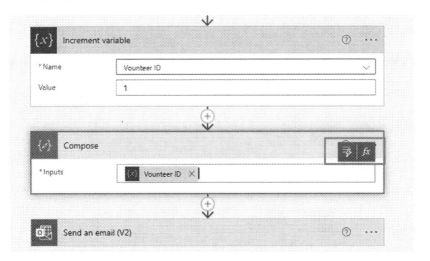

Figure 3-78. *Icons to add dynamic values and expressions*

The icon highlighted in Figure 3-79 is used to add a dynamic value. The shortcut key is Control+Space.

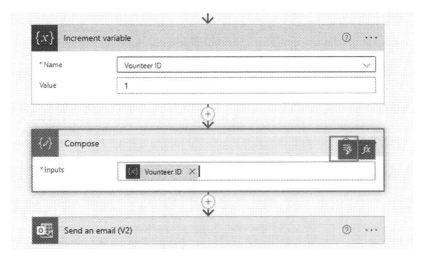

Figure 3-79. *Adding a dynamic value*

When you click this icon, it displays a dialog prompt, as shown in Figure 3-80, where you select the dynamic value you want to use.

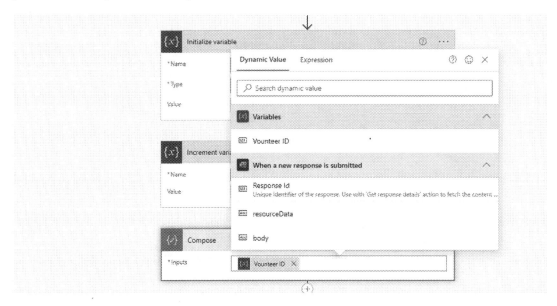

Figure 3-80. *Choose the dynamic value*

The icon highlighted in Figure 3-81 is used to add an expression. Its shortcut key is Control+Shift+Space.

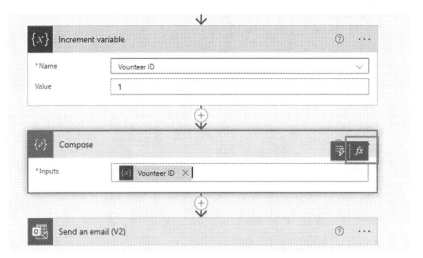

Figure 3-81. *Adding an expression*

When you click this icon, it displays the dialog prompt shown in Figure 3-82, where you create expressions with the following options:

- List of available formulas (functions)

- Dynamic values

- Canvas/area where newly created expressions will appear

- Format by example, which helps generate expressions based on patterns

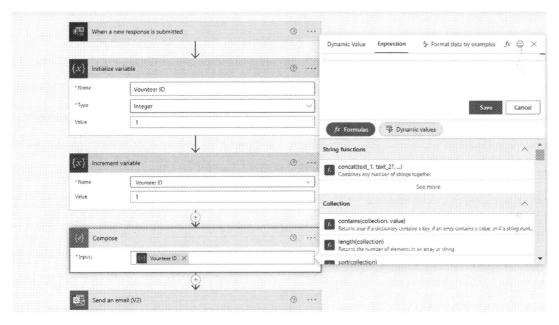

Figure 3-82. *Creating your expression*

Click Format Data by Examples. This will display the dialog shown in Figure 3-83.

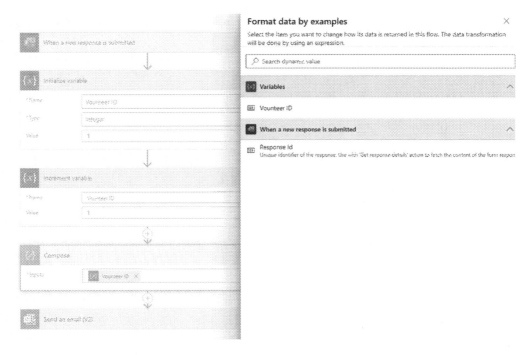

Figure 3-83. *The Format Data by Examples option*

Say you want to know which expression to use to auto-increment the Volunteer ID variable. You would follow these steps:

- Select Volunteer ID. It will display the screen shown in Figure 3-84.

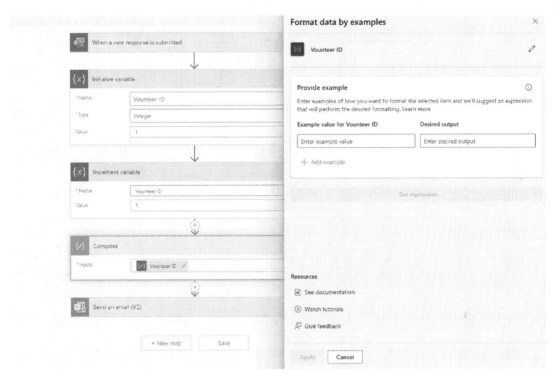

Figure 3-84. *The Volunteer ID window*

- Provide examples of the input and the desired output, as shown in Figure 3-85.

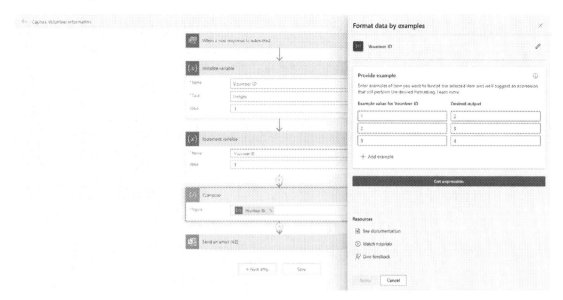

Figure 3-85. *Provide example input and output*

- Click Get Expression to display a suggested expression, as highlighted in Figure 3-86.

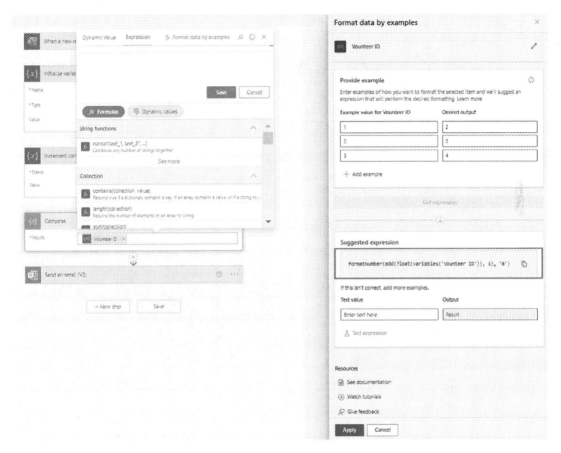

Figure 3-86. *A suggestion is displayed*

- If you want to test this expression, enter the input in the Test Value are and click Test Expression, as shown in Figure 3-87. Then click Apply to use the expression.

Figure 3-87. *Testing the expression*

It will add the expression under the Expression field, as shown in Figure 3-88.

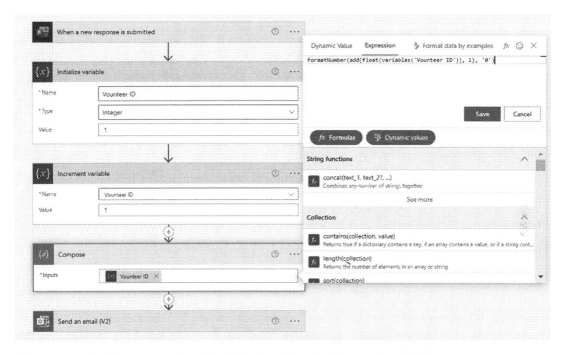

Figure 3-88. *The expression is added under the Expression field*

If you know which function you want, you can write it directly, as shown in Figure 3-89.

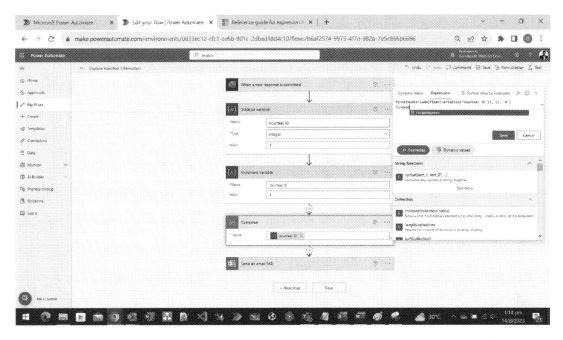

Figure 3-89. *You can write the expression directly*

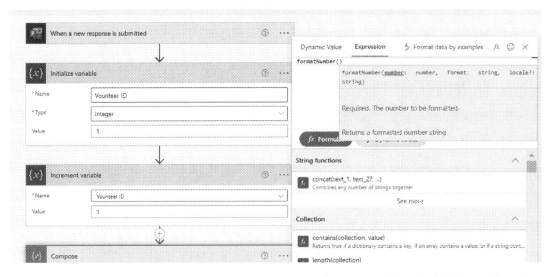

Figure 3-90. *This expression is defined with the* formatNumber(add(float(varia bles('Volunteer ID')), 1), '0') *code*

Click Save to add the expression to Compose, as shown in Figure 3-91.

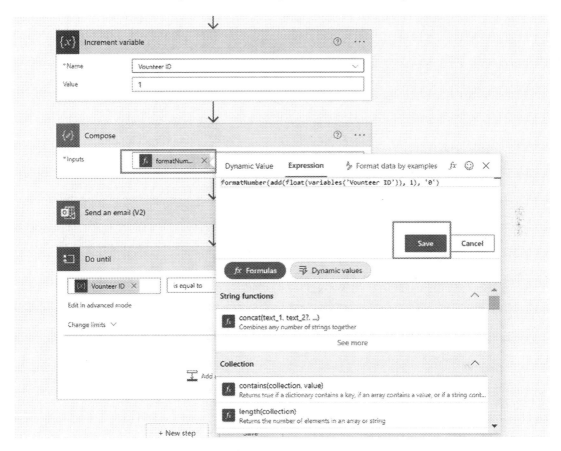

Figure 3-91. *Click Save to add the expression to Compose*

The Increment variable is not required in this case, as Compose can do the increment that was done earlier using the Increment variable.

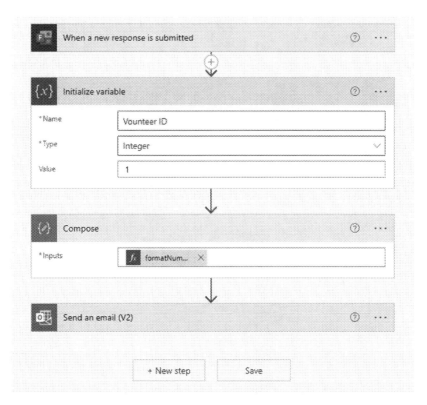

Figure 3-92. *The Increment variable is not required*

Sharing, Exporting, and Importing Your Flows

To share a flow, you can use the Share button on the menu bar (see Figure 3-93). When you click the Share button, the system will show the options in Figure 3-94. You then select the user/group to add as the co-owner of the flow.

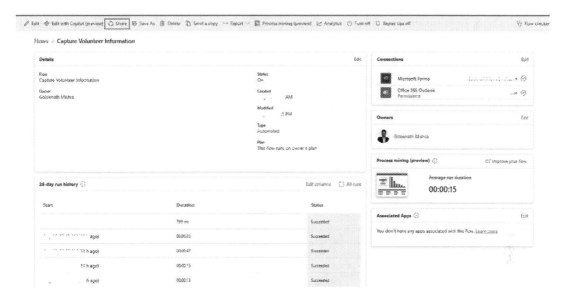

Figure 3-93. *Click the Share button to share a flow*

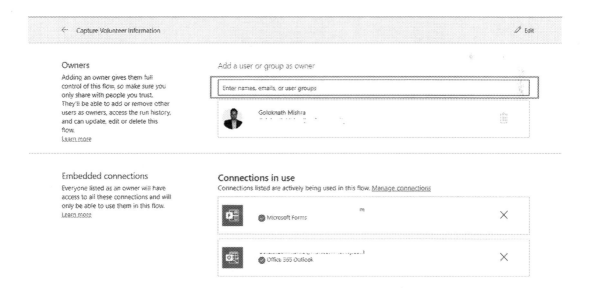

Figure 3-94. *Sharing options*

Select the correct user, as shown in Figures 3-95 and 3-96.

Figure 3-95. *Selecting the user to share the flow with*

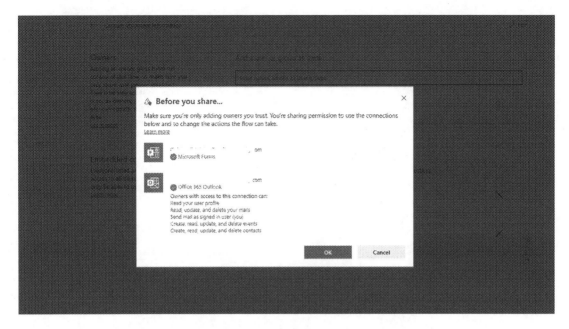

Figure 3-96. *Verify that you are sharing in a safe and secure way*

Sharing a Flow as Run Only User

This option allows you to share a flow with users, who then have run-only permissions. They won't be able to edit or manipulate the flow. See Figure 3-97.

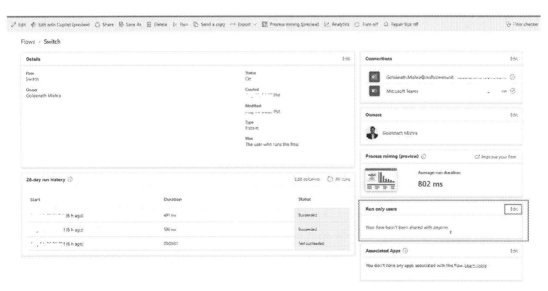

Figure 3-97. *Choose Run Only Users*

Click Edit under Run Only Users to open the dialog box shown in Figure 3-98.

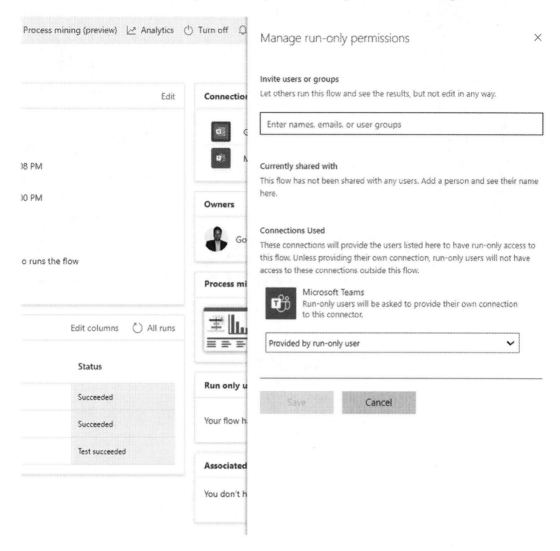

Figure 3-98. *Setting up the Run Only Users*

Enter an email address or select the person whom you want to share the privilege, as shown in Figure 3-99.

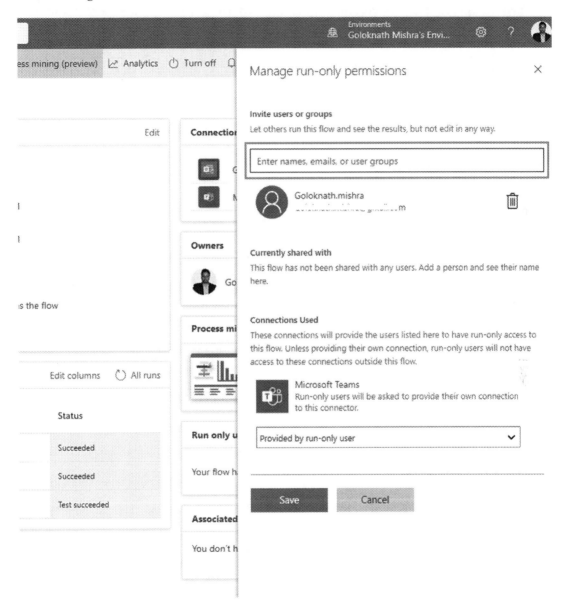

Figure 3-99. *Enter names or emails*

Setting Up Associated Apps

This feature maps a flow so a certain application can use it. To associate apps to your flow, click Edit under Associated Apps, as shown in Figure 3-100.

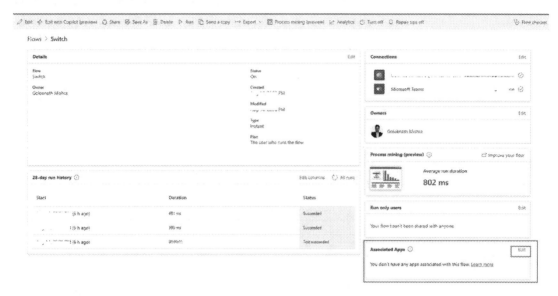

Figure 3-100. *Setting up associated apps*

A dialog box will display, as shown in Figure 3-101, with a button that says Add Association.

Figure 3-101. *Click the Add Association button here*

Click Add Association and then search for the app you want to add, as shown in Figure 3-102.

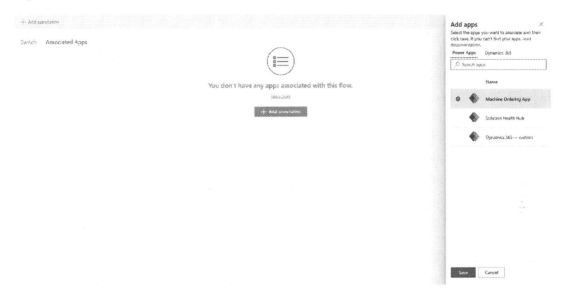

Figure 3-102. *Search for the apps you want to add*

Once the app has been added, it will appear as shown in Figure 3-103.

Figure 3-103. *The app now appears in the Associated Apps window*

Process Mining will improve the flow. Click Improve Your Flow, as shown in Figure 3-104.

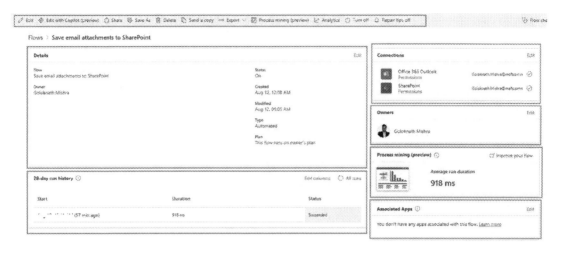

Figure 3-104. *Improving the process flow*

Process mining will generate a summary based on the total count, as shown in Figure 3-105.

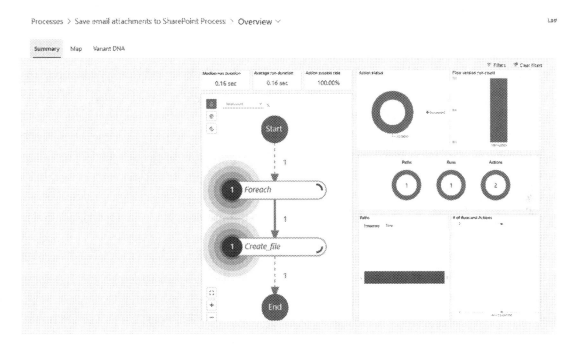

Figure 3-105. *Process mining generates a summary*

A summary based on the total duration is shown in Figure 3-106.

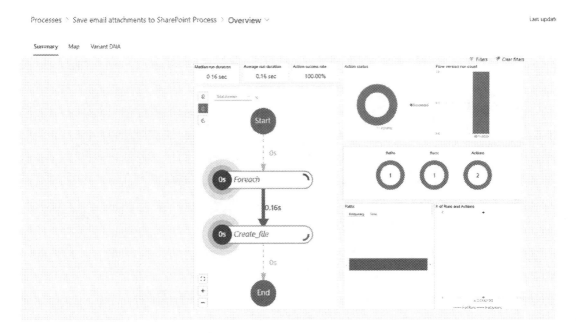

Figure 3-106. *A summary based on the total duration*

A summary based on the rework count is shown in Figure 3-107.

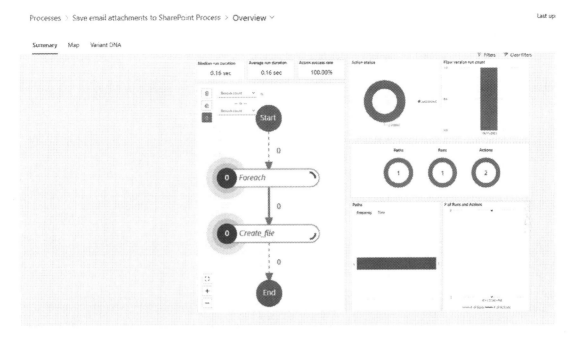

Figure 3-107. *A summary based on the rework count*

A map based on the total count is shown in Figure 3-108.

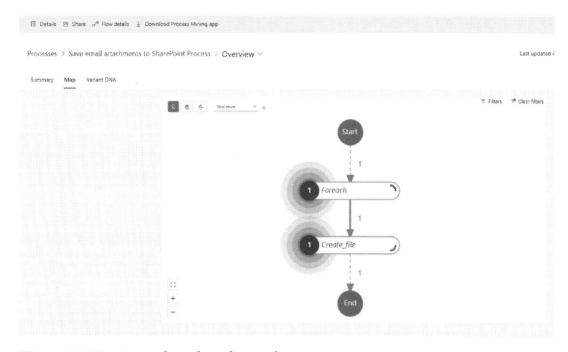

Figure 3-108. *A map based on the total count*

Variant DNA is shown in Figure 3-109.

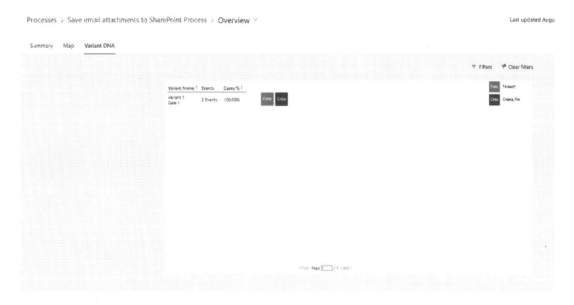

Figure 3-109. *Variant DNA*

Use can use the Save As option to create duplicates of the flow, as shown in Figure 3-110.

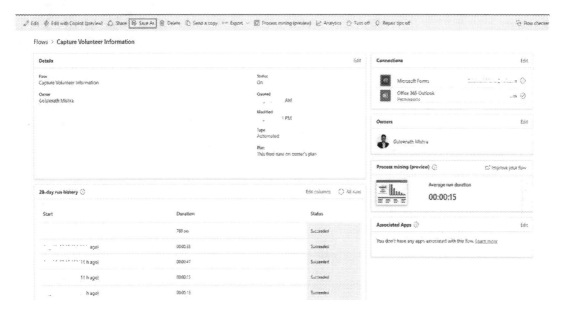

Figure 3-110.   *Creating duplicates of the flow*

Rename the flow, as shown in Figures 3-111 and 3-112.

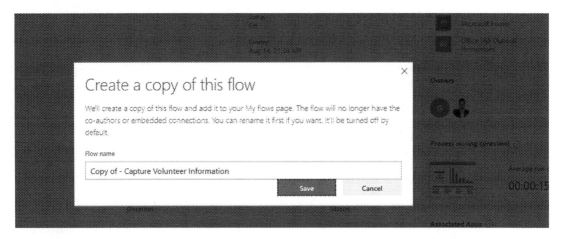

Figure 3-111.   *Name the duplicate flow*

Figure 3-112. *Rename the duplicate flow*

The Analytics button will display the flow's statistics and its use, as shown in Figure 3-113.

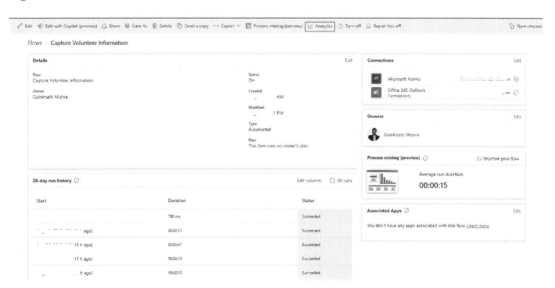

Figure 3-113. *Use the Analytics button to display the flow's statistics*

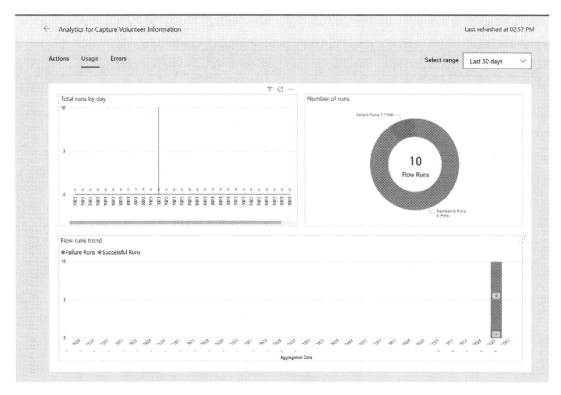

Figure 3-114. *Usage statistics for the flow*

To migrate the flow from one system to another, you can use Export option, as shown in Figure 3-115.

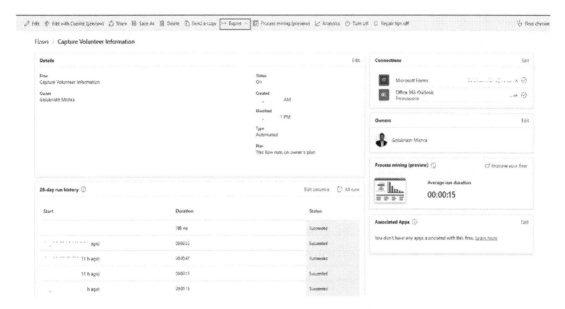

Figure 3-115. *Use Export to migrate the flow to another system*

Export has two options, as shown in Figure 3-116.

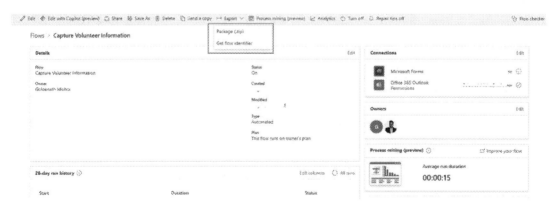

Figure 3-116. *You can export it as a package or using the flow identifier*

The Get Flow Identifier option will display the flow identifier to use, as shown in Figure 3-117.

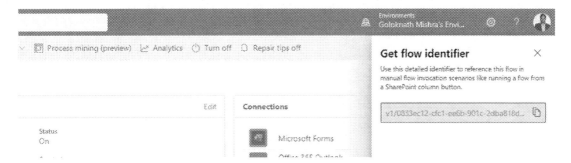

Figure 3-117. *The flow identifier is a long number that identifies your flow*

The Export package will display the options shown in Figure 3-118. You need to select the name and other information before exporting the flow as a ZIP file.

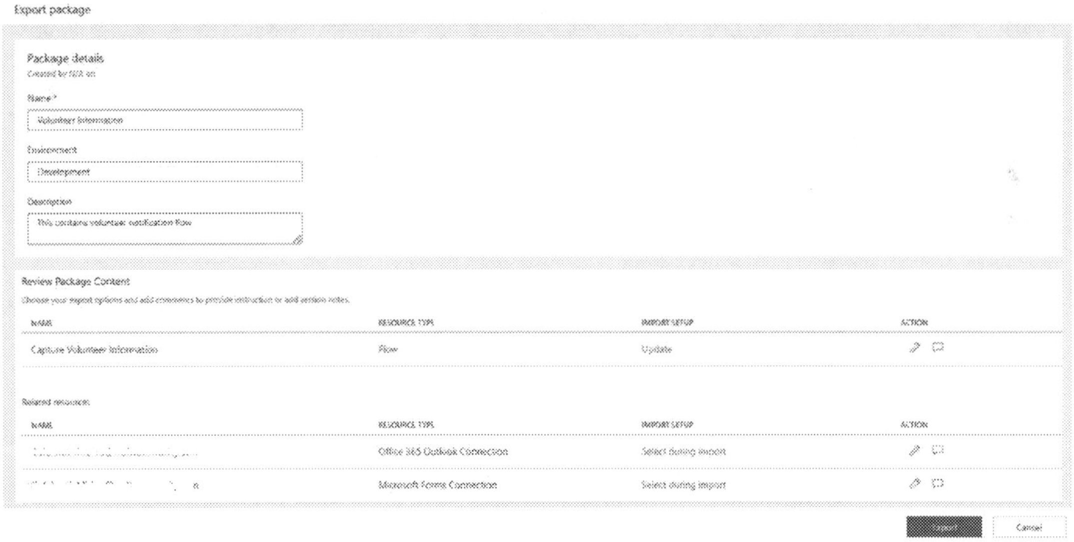

Figure 3-118. *Options for exporting as a ZIP file*

You can export a new flow or update an existing flow, so select the appropriate option, as shown in Figure 3-119.

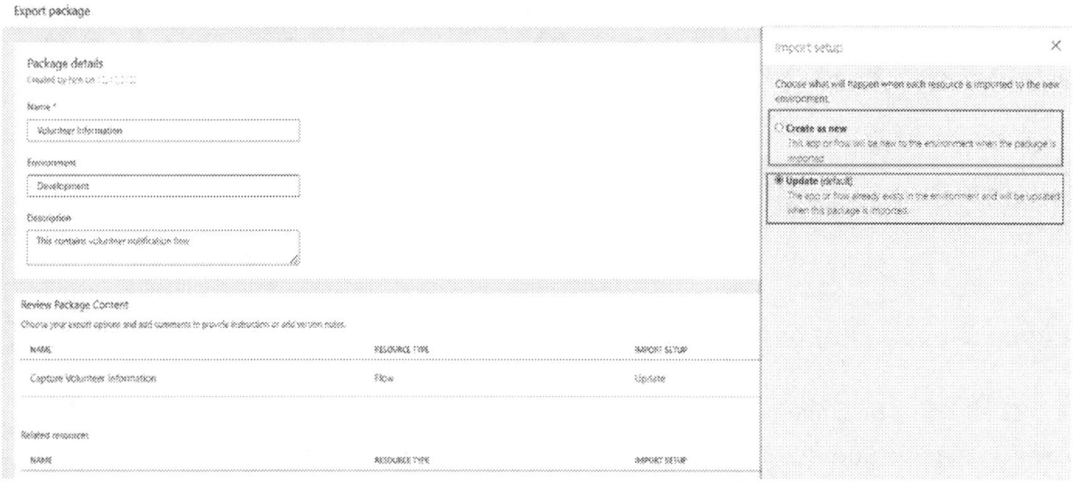

Figure 3-119. *You can export a new flow or update an existing flow*

In this example, I updated the flow and then chose Create as New, which updated the details shown in Figure 3-120.

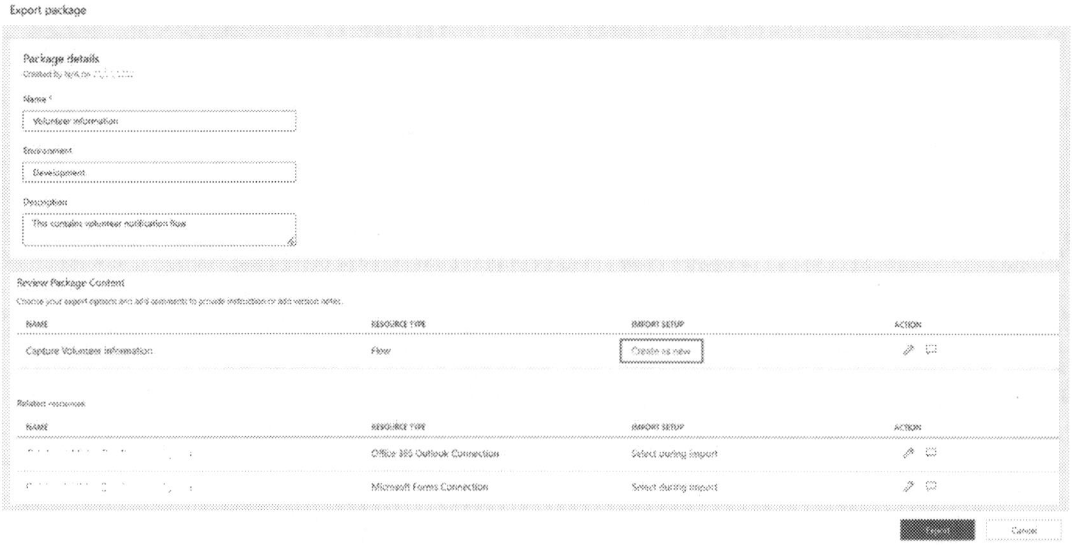

Figure 3-120. *Creating the update as a new flow*

Click Export to export the ZIP package. It will be downloaded, as shown in Figure 3-121.

Figure 3-121. *The ZIP file has been downloaded*

You can then import the package, either by importing the package or by importing the solution. See Figure 3-122.

Figure 3-122. *You can import the package or import the solution*

When you select Import Package, the dialog in Figure 3-123 will appear.

Figure 3-123. *Choose the file you want to import*

There are errors with the connectors, which need to be mapped, as shown in Figure 3-124.

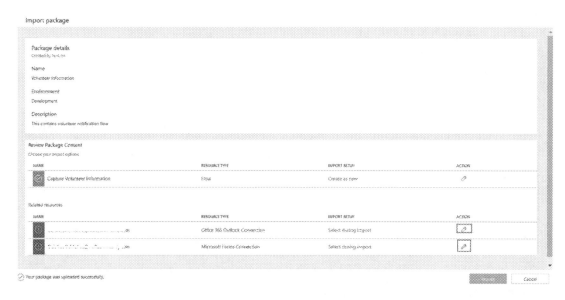

Figure 3-124. *The connectors contain errors*

Once the mapping is complete, you can import the flow, as shown in Figure 3-125.

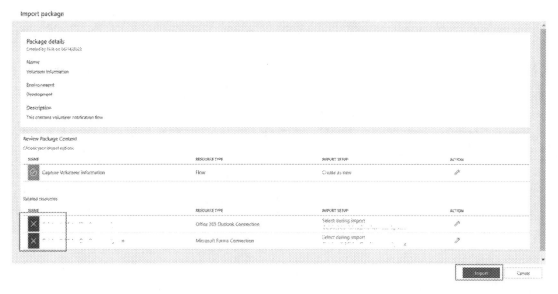

Figure 3-125. *Importing the flow*

Any solution you export can be imported for the flow migration, as shown in Figure 3-126.

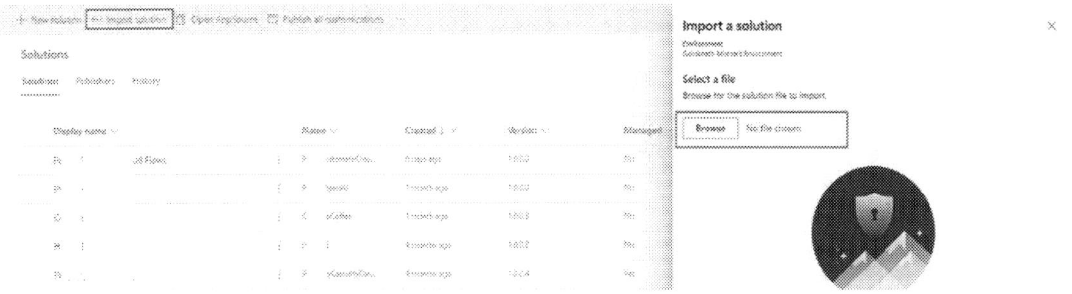

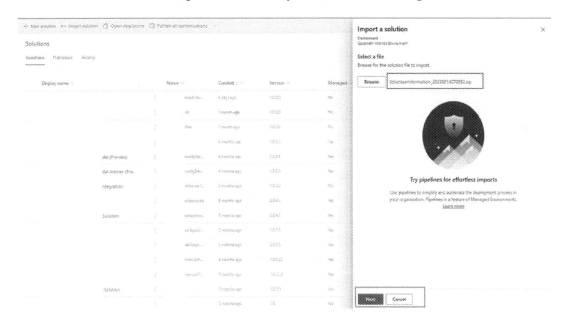

Figure 3-126. *Importing a solution*

Select the solution to import to another system, as shown in Figure 3-127.

Figure 3-127. *Select the solution to import to another system*

Flows can be deleted using the Delete button in the menu bar, as shown in
Figure 3-128.

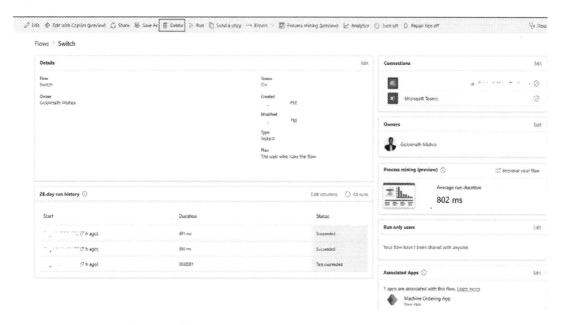

Figure 3-128. *Deleting a flow is easy*

Restoring a Deleted Flow

Deleted flows can be restored using Power Automate Management, as shown
Figure 3-129.

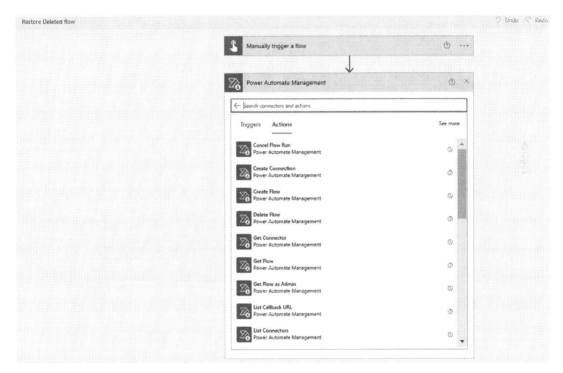

Figure 3-129. *Go to Power Automate Management*

Search Power Automate Management for List Flows as Admin. This will allow you to determine the deleted flow's ID, as shown in Figure 3-130. Set the Include Soft-Deleted Flows option to yes.

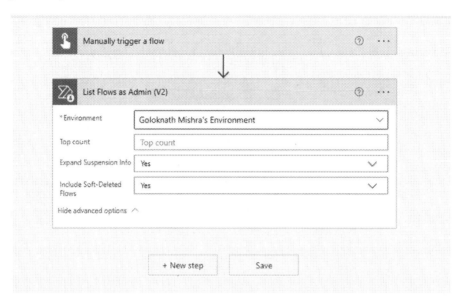

Figure 3-130. *Choose List Flows as Admin*

After running the flow, go to the flow session to get the deleted flow's ID, as shown in Figure 3-131.

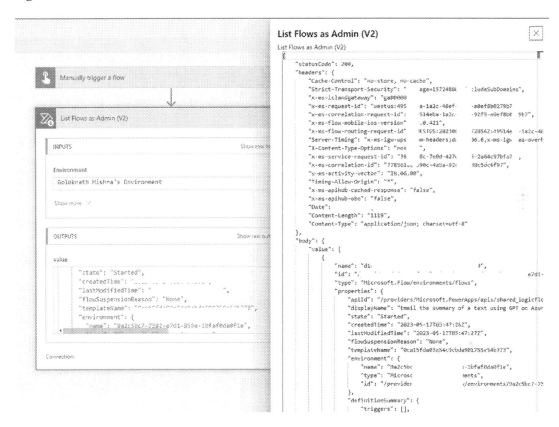

Figure 3-131. *Finding the deleted flow's ID*

Jot down the flow name. You'll pass this as a parameter to Restore Deleted Flow as Admin. See Figure 3-132.

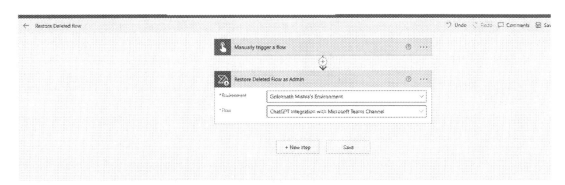

Figure 3-132. *Make sure you note the flow name*

Using the Controls in Power Automate

There are different controls available in Power Automate. This section explains a few of the commonly used ones. Figure 3-133 displays the list of available controls.

Figure 3-133. *The list of available controls in Power Automate*

As an example, you could use the Condition control, as shown in Figure 3-134, to create an exam condition for a pass or fail exam. If the score is more than 50, the person passes; otherwise, they fail.

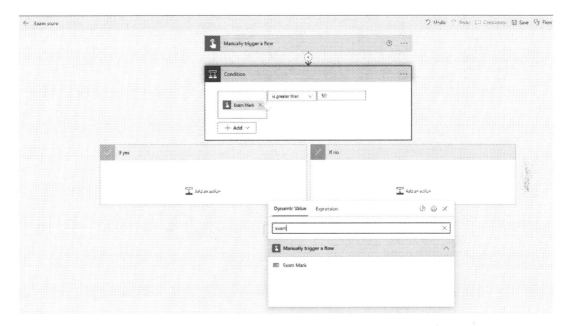

Figure 3-134. *Using the Condition control to create a pass/fail exam*

Say that, if the score is more than 50, you want to post a "pass" message in Teams. To do that, select the Post Message in Chat or Channel option, as shown in Figure 3-135.

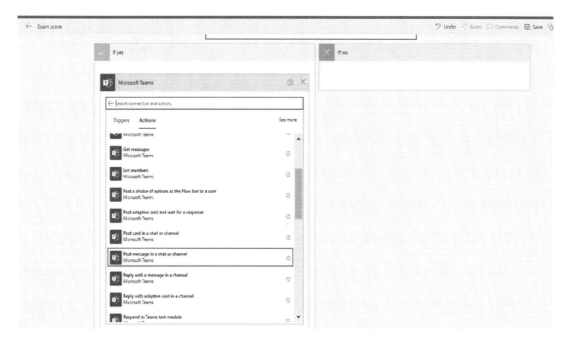

Figure 3-135. *Posting a message in a chat or channel*

Configure the Teams channel information, as shown in Figure 3-136.

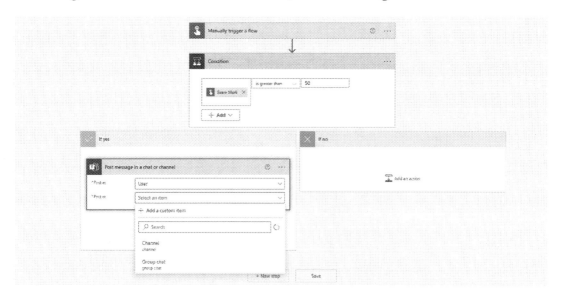

Figure 3-136. *Configuring the channel information*

The message is configured for a pass, as shown in Figure 3-137.

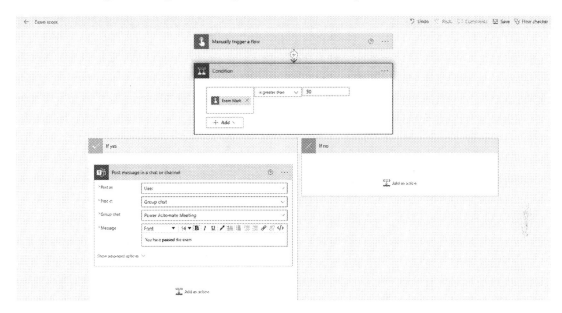

Figure 3-137. *The message will be sent if the person passed*

If the person failed, you can send an email to them notifying them of this, as shown in Figure 3-138.

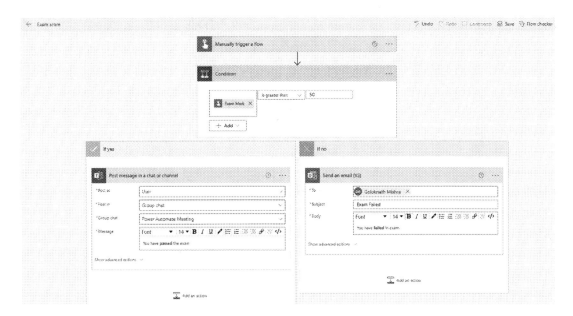

Figure 3-138. *An email will be sent if the person failed*

The flow will prompt for the score to validate the criteria, as shown in Figure 3-139.

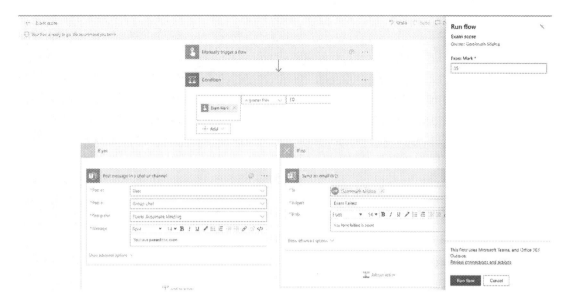

Figure 3-139. *The flow prompts for the test score*

When the score entered is 35, an email will be triggered, as shown in Figure 3-140.

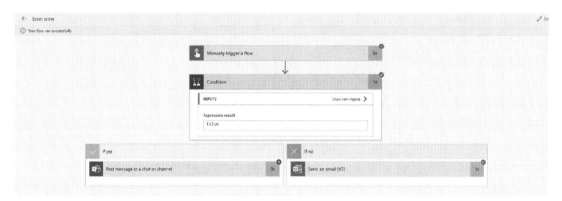

Figure 3-140. *An email will be triggered in this case*

Run the flow again, as shown in Figure 3-141.

Flows

Cloud flows   Desktop flows   Shared with me

	Name		Modified	Type
○	Exam score	▷ ◌ ⋮	3 min ago	Instant

Figure 3-141. *Run the flow again*

Enter a score of 51 to test the flow for passed scores. Then run the flow, as shown in Figure 3-142.

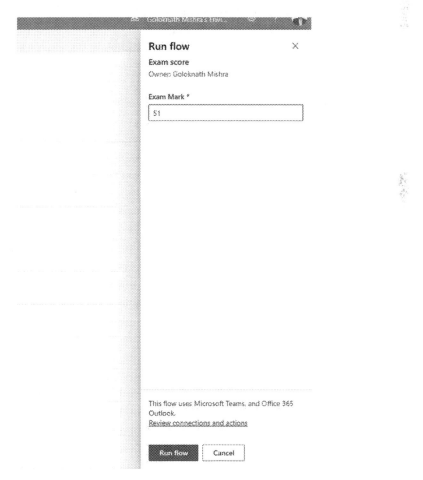

Figure 3-142. *Enter a score that indicates a passed test*

The Teams message will be triggered, as shown in Figure 3-143.

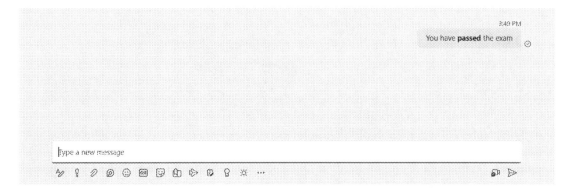

Figure 3-143. *The Teams message is sent when the person passes*

In the flow execution, you can also see that the Teams message was triggered. See Figure 3-144.

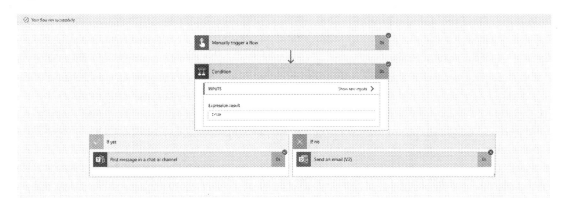

Figure 3-144. *The flow execution shows that the Teams message will be sent*

If you wanted to let people know how well they did on the test—say there are divisions of the test— you can use the Division text field and then add a drop-down list of options, as shown in Figure 3-145.

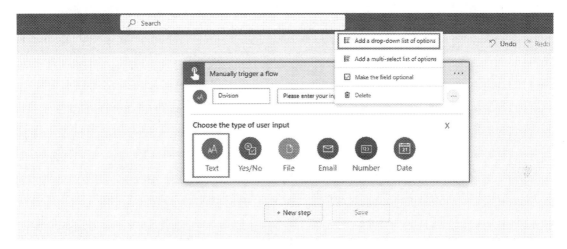

Figure 3-145. *Creating divisions of the test*

The divisions are entered, as shown in Figure 3-146.

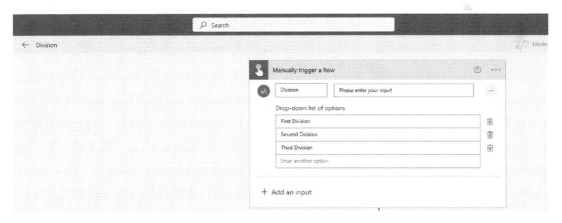

Figure 3-146. *The divisions are entered*

Add a `switch` statement to post a message in Teams for each division, as shown in Figure 3-147.

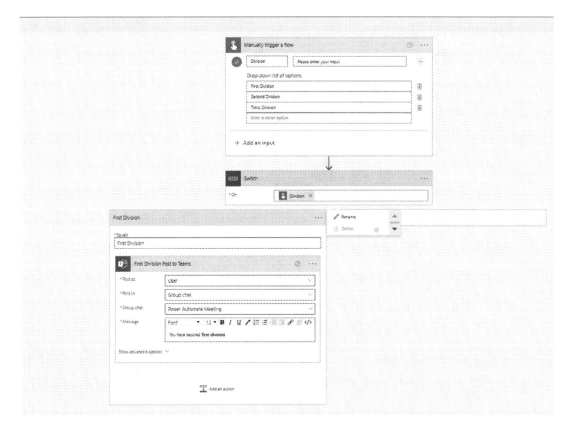

Figure 3-147. *The switch statement determines which division to post*

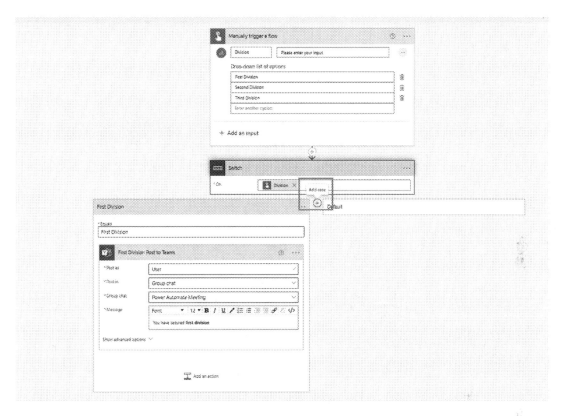

Figure 3-148. *Add the case for the first division*

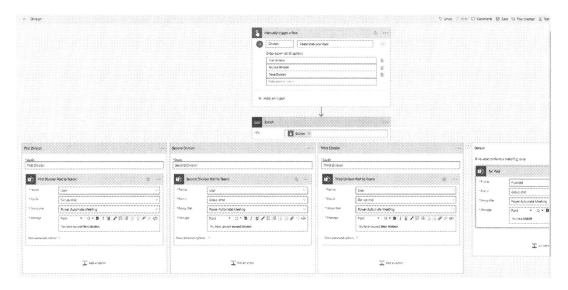

Figure 3-149. *All the divisions have been defined*

If you run the flow now, you'll see that the Teams message was triggered, as shown in Figure 3-150.

Figure 3-150. *The Teams message indicates the grade division*

Now you'll learn how to use the Apply to Each control. This use case uses an array of academic subjects, as shown in Figure 3-151. Figures 3-152 through 3-156 show the steps for setting up the Apply to Each control.

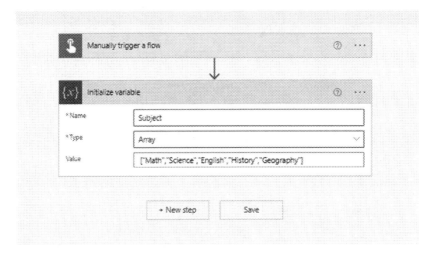

Figure 3-151. *Using an array of academic subjects to explain the Apply to Each control*

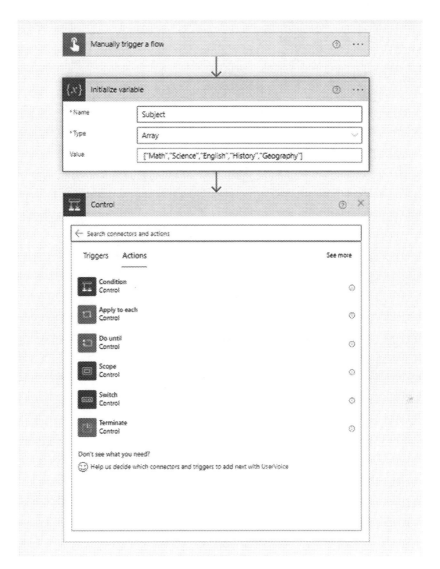

Figure 3-152. *Choose the Apply to Each action here*

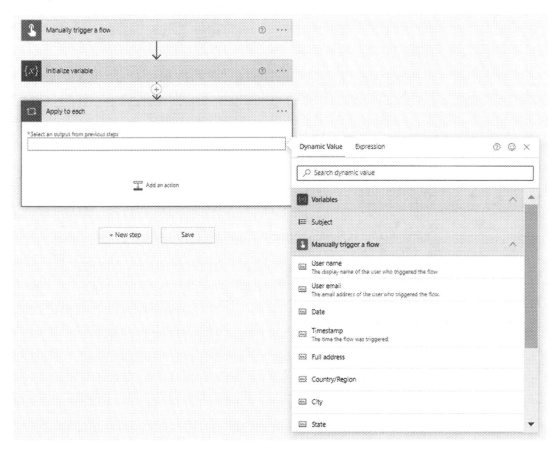

Figure 3-153. *Choose Manually Trigger a Flow here*

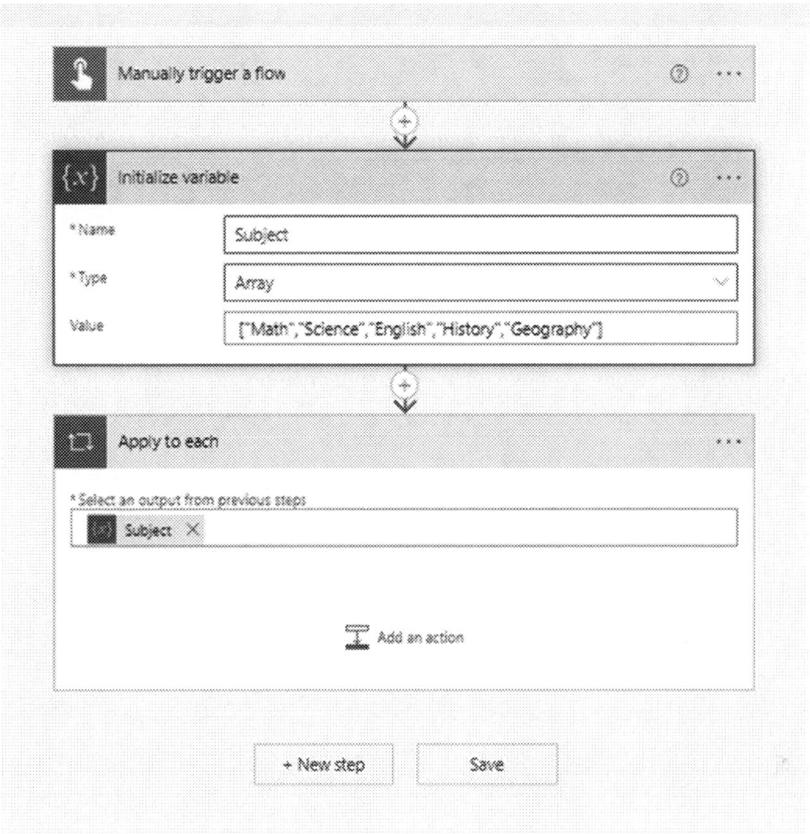

Figure 3-154. *Use the Subject output*

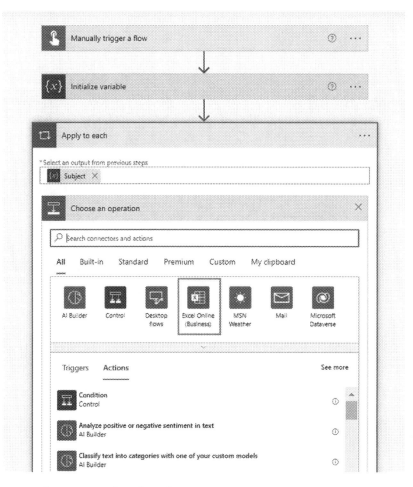

Figure 3-155. *Choose Excel Online here*

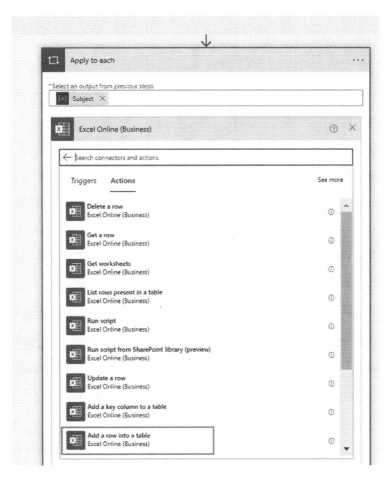

Figure 3-156. *Choose to add a row to a table*

You have now created a blank Excel Online sheet, as shown in Figure 3-157.

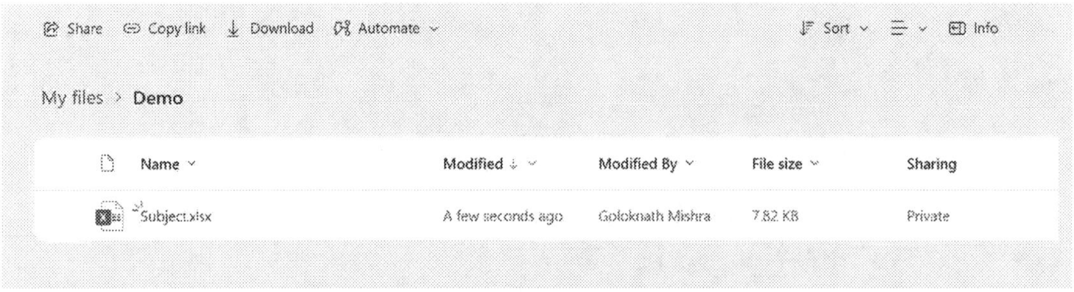

Figure 3-157. *The blank Excel Online sheet has been created*

The flow will create a tab for each subject, as shown in Figure 3-158.

Figure 3-158. *The flow creates a tab for each subject*

Figure 3-159 shows that the flow has successfully started. Figure 3-160 shows the blank sheet with the subject tabs.

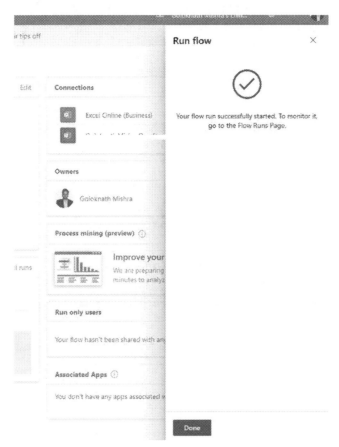

Figure 3-159. *The flow has successfully started*

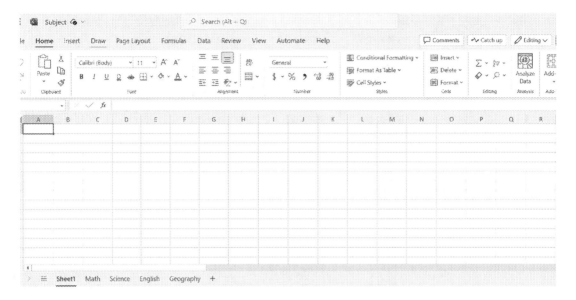

Figure 3-160. *The blank sheet contains tabs for each subject*

Different functions can be leveraged for flow building. Functions are broadly classified as follows:

- String functions

- Collection functions

- Logical comparison functions

- Conversion functions

- Implicit datatype conversion functions

- Math functions

- Date and time functions

- Workflow functions

- URI parsing functions

- Manipulation functions

For more information about functions, refer to `https://learn.microsoft.com/en-us/azure/logic-apps/workflow-definition-language-functions-reference`.

Table 3-1 lists the operators you can use in your flows.

Table 3-1. *Operators*

Operator	Description	Example
eq	Equal to	`$filter=fieldname eq 'Value'`
ne	Not equal to	`$filter=fieldname ne 'Value'`
contains	Contains	`$filter=contains(fieldname, 'Value')`
not contains	Does not contain	`$filter=not contains(fieldname, 'Value')`
gt	Greater than	`$filter=fieldname gt 'Value'`
lt	Less than	`$filter=fieldname lt 'Value'`
ge	Greater than or equal to	`$filter=fieldname ge 'Value'`
le	Less than or equal to	`$filter=fieldname le 'Value'`
and	And	`$filter=fieldname1 ge 'Value1' and fieldname2 le 'Value2'`
or	Or	`$filter=fieldname1 ge 'Value1' or fieldname2 le 'Value2'`
startswith	Start with the specified value	`startswith(fieldname, 'Value')`
endswith	End with the specified value	`not endswith(fieldname, 'Value')`

Creating Custom Connectors

To create a custom connector, navigate to the Custom Connectors section in Power Automate, as shown in Figure 3-161.

Figure 3-161. *The Custom Connectors section*

Click Create from Blank, as shown in Figure 3-162.

Figure 3-162. *Creating a connector from a blank*

Name the flow, as shown in Figure 3-163.

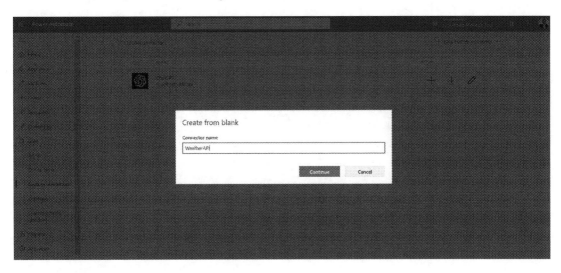

Figure 3-163. *Name the connector*

When you click Continue, it will display the window in Figure 3-164, which you need to fill in as part of the General section.

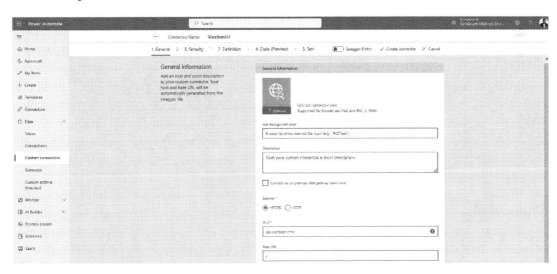

Figure 3-164. *Fill in the general information*

Change the icon, schema, and host, as shown in Figure 3-165.

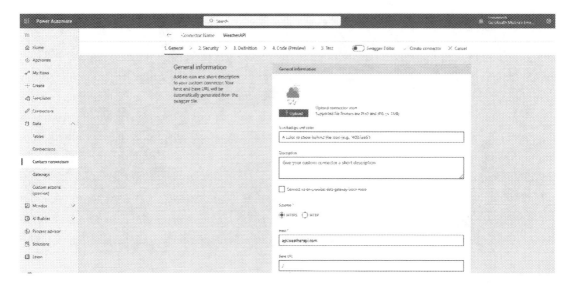

Figure 3-165. *Add the required information*

Select the type of authentication required for the connector, as shown in Figure 3-166.

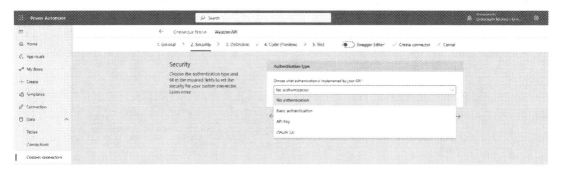

Figure 3-166. *Select the authentication type*

Select API Key to set up security, as shown in Figure 3-167.

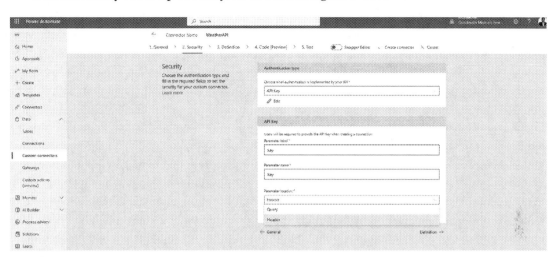

Figure 3-167. *Choose an API key for the authentication type*

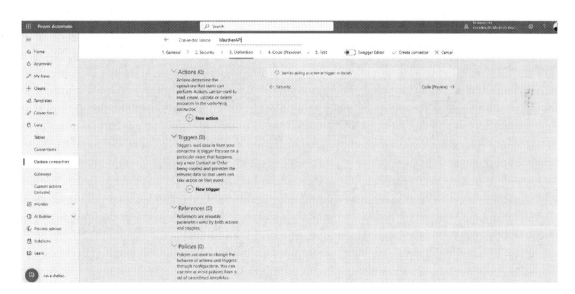

Figure 3-168. *Defining the new connector*

Enter a definition for the connector, as shown in Figure 3-169.

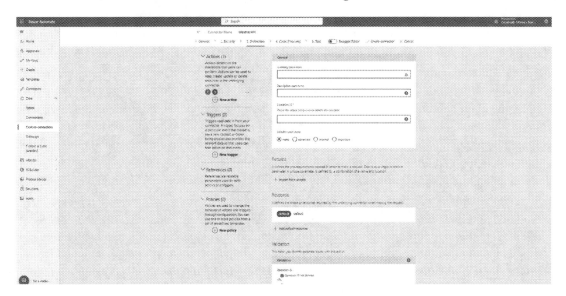

Figure 3-169. *Enter a definition*

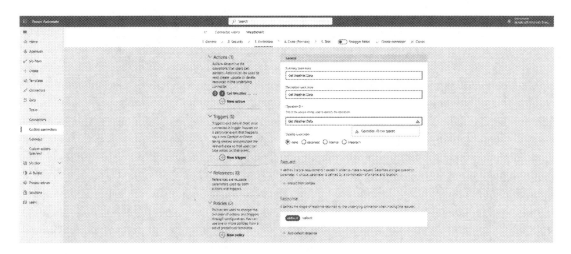

Figure 3-170. *Provide the proper information*

Update the URL, as shown in Figure 3-171.

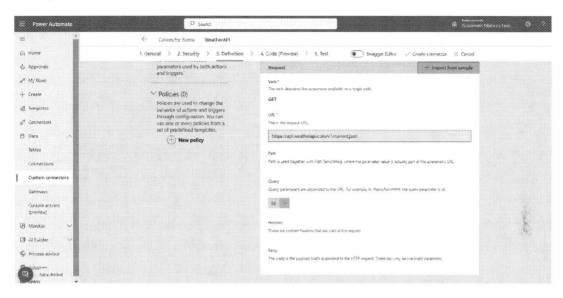

Figure 3-171. *Update the URL*

Validate the flow, as shown in Figure 3-172.

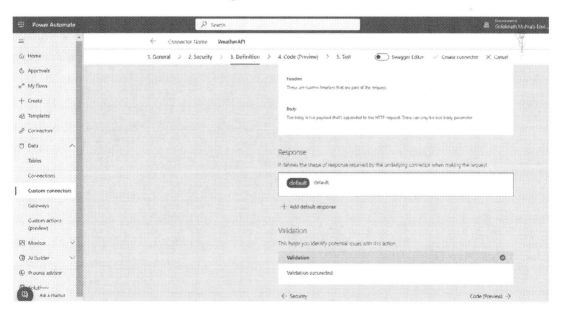

Figure 3-172. *Validating the flow*

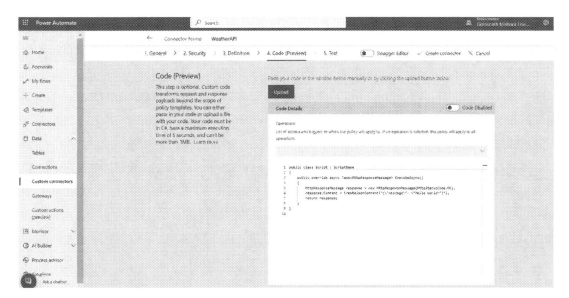

Figure 3-173. *Viewing the code*

Figure 3-174. *Testing the connector*

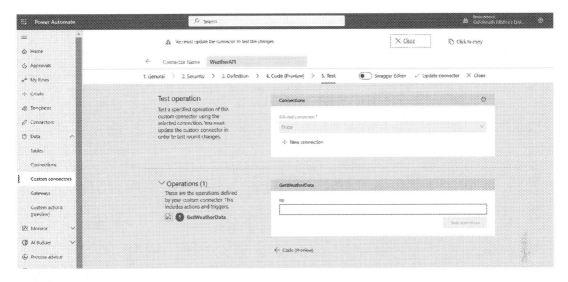

Figure 3-175. *Testing the operation*

Enter the API key, as shown in Figure 3-176.

Figure 3-176. *Enter your API key*

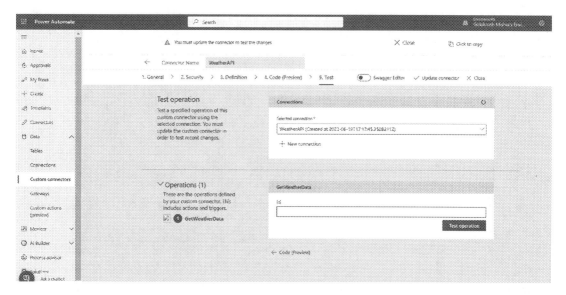

Figure 3-177. *Update the connector*

The connector is finally ready to use, as shown in Figure 3-178.

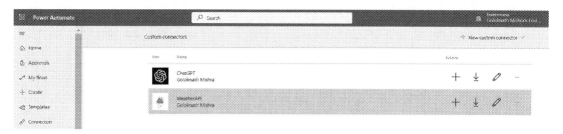

Figure 3-178. *The connector is ready to use*

Tips:

- Always name the flow something meaningful that identifies its use/feature.

- Always create flows in a solution after creating a meaningful name for the solution.

- Append your child flow names with the prefix Child to follow proper naming.

- Update the description of your flows with the creation date/update date, followed by the name of the person who edited it and a description of the change.

- It is good practice to use filtering rows/triggering conditions if they are available as part of the flow.

Summary

This chapter discussed different types of Cloud Flows. It also explained how to create, update, share, and migrate your flows. It explained the different controls and actions available to create flows, depending on your business case. It also discussed custom connectors. The next chapter explains Desktop Flows.

Answer a few questions based on your learnings:

1. What is Compose?

2. What is the difference between using Compose and using a variable?

Keywords

Action

Cloud Flow

Compose

Instant Flow

Scheduled Flow

Trigger

CHAPTER 4

Desktop Flow

The last chapter covered Cloud Flows. This chapter discusses Desktop Flows, which transformed Power Automate into a full-fledged RPA using its RPA capability.

This chapter covers how to install Desktop Flows and set them up, how to orchestrate Desktop Flows to run in attended and unattended modes, the actions available in Desktop Flows, and how to run, share, and ship Desktop Flows from one environment to another.

Desktop Flows enhance the existing robotic process automation (RPA) capabilities in Power Automate and help automate repetitive tasks.

When the Power Automate desktop is installed, a service called `UIFlowService` is also installed and set to start automatically. It runs as the new user `NTService\ UIFlowService`, which is created during installation.

An example of direct attended/unattended desktop connectivity to a cloud service is shown Figure 4-1.

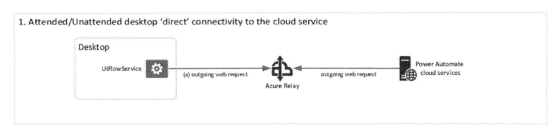

Figure 4-1. *BOT connected directly to cloud services*

Figure 4-2 shows attended/unattended desktop connected to the cloud service using an on-premise data gateway.

© Goloknath Mishra 2023
G. Mishra, *Deep Dive into Power Automate*, https://doi.org/10.1007/978-1-4842-9732-2_4

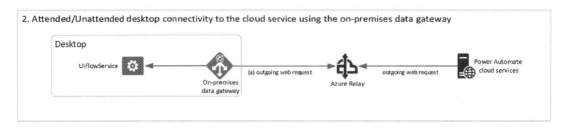

Figure 4-2. *BOT connected through an on-premise data gateway to cloud services*

When the on-premise data gateway service is installed separately, it acts as a communication gateway between UIFlowService and Azure Relay. By default, this on-premise data gateway service runs as user NTSERVICE\PBIEgwService. Azure Relay and Power Automate cloud services are both resources in Azure.

A desktop machine is registered by signing in to the on-premises data gateway or by registering inside Power Automate using the Direct Connectivity feature. This process generates a public and private key to be used for secure communication with this machine.

1. The machine registration request is sent by the desktop application to the Power Automate cloud services. The request contains the newly generated machine's public key. This key is stored along with the machine registration in the cloud.

2. When the request is completed, the machine is successfully registered and appears in the Power Automate web portal as a resource that can be managed. However, a flow cannot use the machine until a connection to it is established.

3. To establish a Power Automate connection in the web portal, users must select an available machine and provide the username and password credentials of the account.

Users can select any previously registered machine, including machines that have been shared with them. When a connection is saved, the credentials are encrypted using the public key associated with the machine and stored in this encrypted form.

The cloud service stores the encrypted user credentials for the machine. However, it can't decrypt the credentials because the private key only exists on the desktop machine. The user can delete this connection at any point, and the stored encrypted credentials will also be deleted.

1. When a Desktop Flow runs from the cloud, it uses a previously established connection selected in the Run a Flow Built with Power Automate for Desktop action.

2. When the Desktop Flow job is sent from the cloud to the desktop, it includes the encrypted credentials stored in the connection. These credentials are then decrypted on the desktop using the secret private key, and they're used to sign in as the given user account. Figure 4-3 shows this session credential lifecycle.

Session credential lifecycle

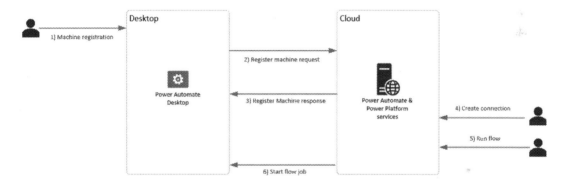

Figure 4-3. *Session credential lifecycle*

You can create a new solution to create a Desktop Flow or use an existing solution based on your business requirements. The example in this chapter creates a new solution.

Installing a Desktop Flow and Setting Up the Environment

This section begins by creating a Desktop Flow. You must first create a solution and add flow components, as shown in Figure 4-4.

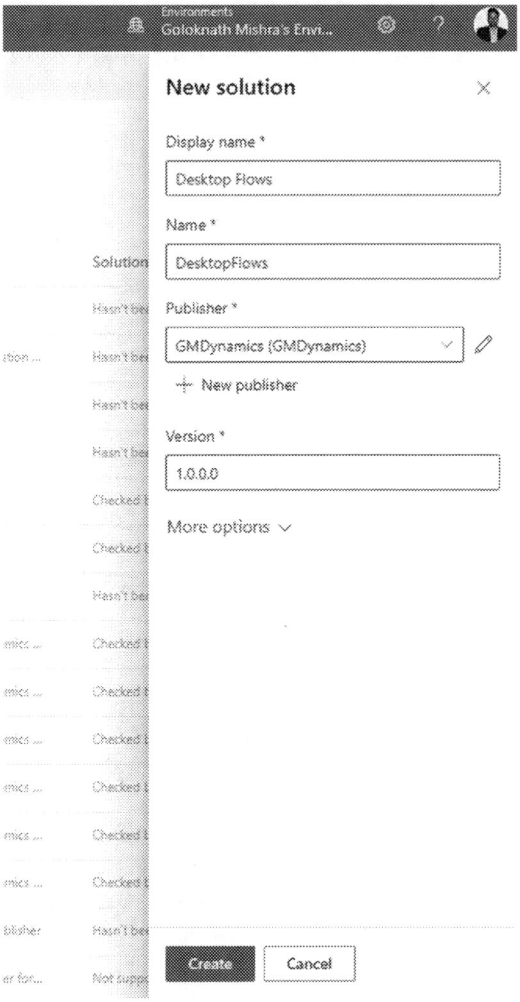

Figure 4-4. *A new solution has been created*

After you create a new solution, the screen will look like Figure 4-5, without any content.

Figure 4-5. *Empty solution*

To add an existing flow, navigate to Add Existing ➤ Automation ➤ Desktop Flow, as shown in Figure 4-6.

Figure 4-6. *Adding an existing flow*

If you want to create a new Desktop Flow, navigate to New ➤ Automation ➤ Desktop Flow. Click Desktop Flow, as shown in Figure 4-7.

Figure 4-7. *Creating a new Desktop Flow*

A new window will open to add a new Desktop Flow. Enter a name and click Launch App, as shown in Figure 4-8.

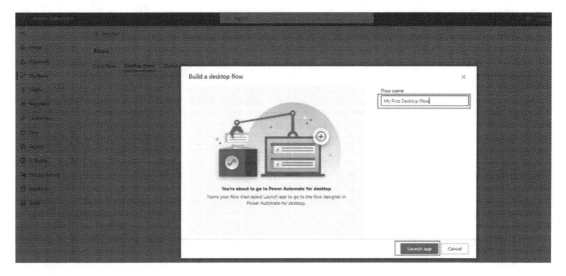

Figure 4-8. *Choose Launch App*

When you click Launch App, you will see the window in Figure 4-9, which will try
to open Power Automate Desktop if it's installed. Otherwise, you can install Power
Automate Desktop (PAD) by clicking Get the Latest Version, as highlighted in Figure 4-9.

Note   Windows 11 comes with a preinstalled version of Power Automate Desktop.

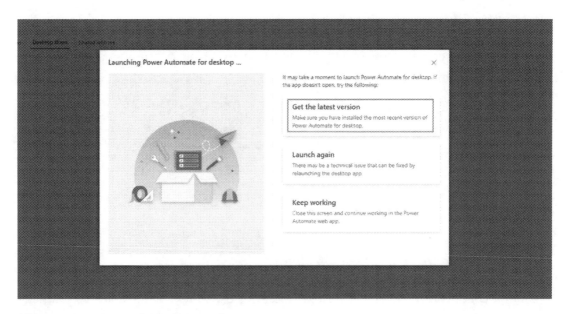

Figure 4-9. *Launching Power Automate*

The PAD software will download Power Automate to local the PC, as shown in Figure 4-10.

Figure 4-10. *Power Automate has been downloaded*

Double-click the file to install Power Automate Desktop. Click Next, as shown in Figure 4-11.

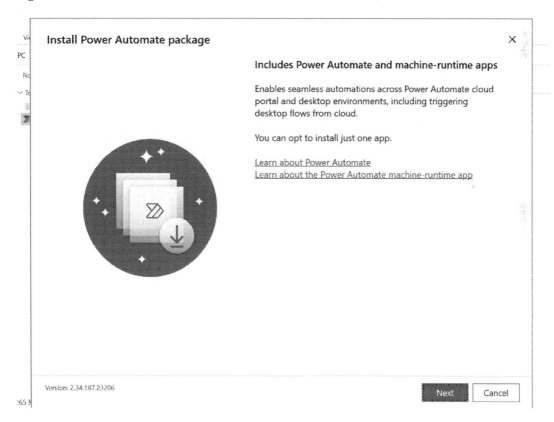

Figure 4-11. *Click Next to begin the installation process*

In the next screen, shown in Figure 4-12:

1. Uncheck the features that you don't want to install, such as Install Machine-Runtime App.

2. Check the Agreement box to agree to the conditions.

3. Click Install.

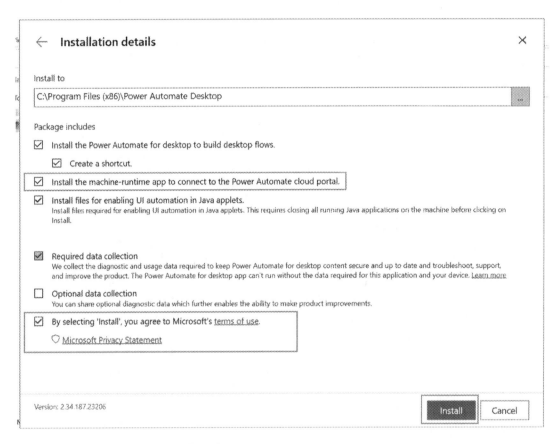

Figure 4-12. *Installation details*

The installer will display the progress tracker, as shown in Figure 4-13.

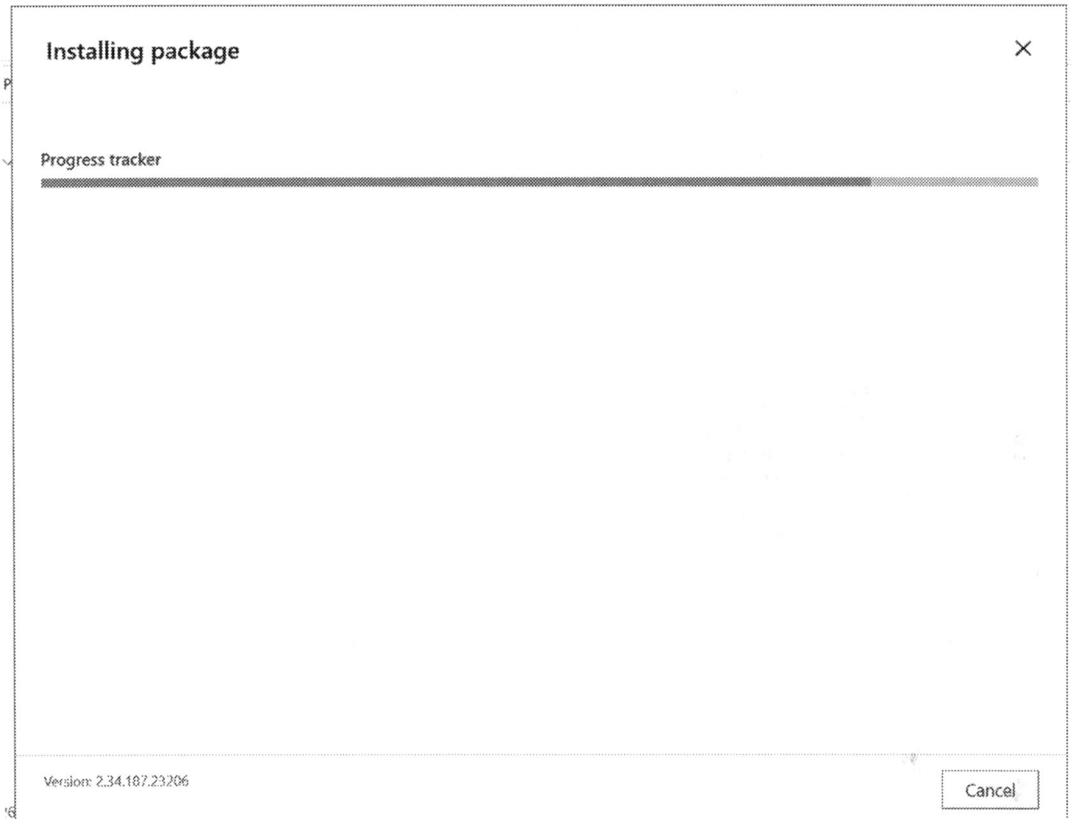

Figure 4-13. *The progress tracker*

Upon successful installation, the screen in Figure 4-14 will appear and you can click the highlighted links to enable the extensions in the respective browsers.

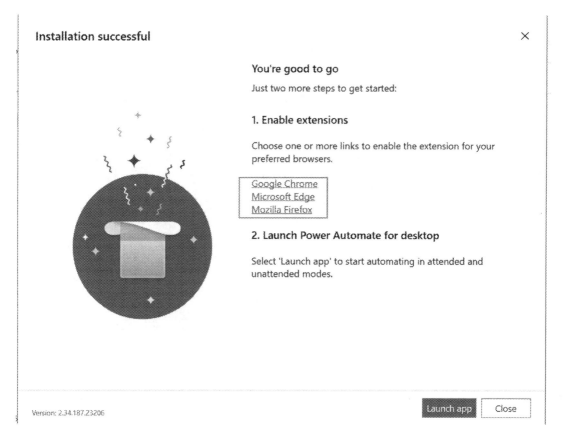

Figure 4-14. *Enable the extensions*

When you choose Google Chrome, the window in Figure 4-15 will open the Chrome Web Store. Click Add to Chrome.

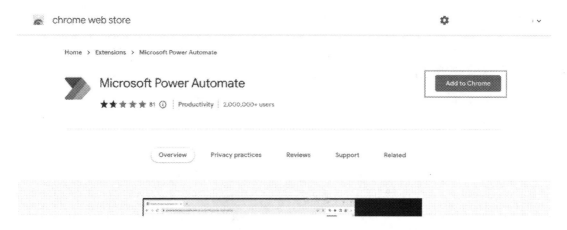

Figure 4-15. *Adding Power Automate to Chrome*

A confirmation dialog will appear. Click Add Extension, as highlighted in Figure 4-16.

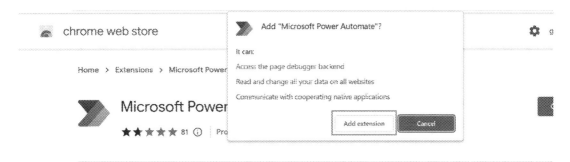

Figure 4-16. *Choose Add Extension*

This extension will be added to the browser. To confirm this, go to Google Extensions, as shown in Figure 4-17. If you want to remove the extension, click the Remove button.

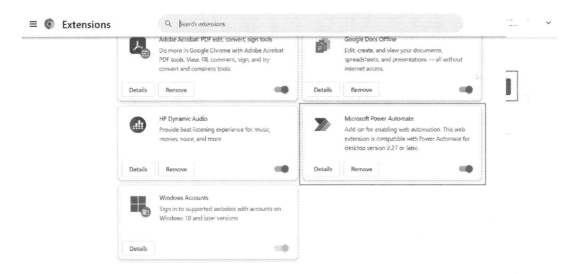

Figure 4-17. *Google Extensions shows that Power Automate has been added*

When you click Microsoft Edge, a window will open the Edge add-ons. Click Get, as shown in Figure 4-18.

Figure 4-18.   *Getting the Edge add-ons*

A confirmation dialog will appear, similar to the Google Chrome one. Click Add Extension, as highlighted in Figure 4-19.

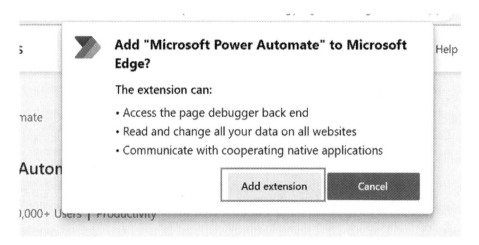

Figure 4-19.   *Adding Power Automate to Microsoft Edge*

This extension will be added to the browser. You can confirm this from the Installed Extensions window, as shown in Figure 4-20. If you want to remove it, simply click Remove.

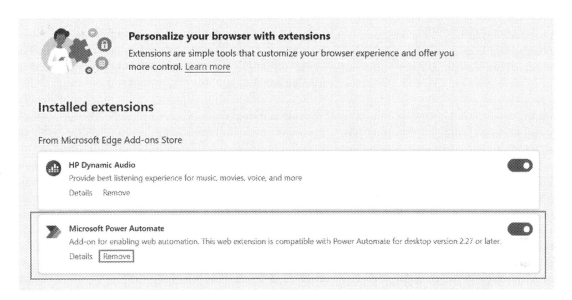

Figure 4-20. *Power Automate has been installed*

Now click Launch App, as shown in Figure 4-21.

Installation successful   ×

You're good to go

Just two more steps to get started:

1. Enable extensions

Choose one or more links to enable the extension for your preferred browsers.

Google Chrome
Microsoft Edge
Mozilla Firefox

2. Launch Power Automate for desktop

Select 'Launch app' to start automating in attended and unattended modes.

Version: 2.34.187.23206

Launch app   Close

Figure 4-21. *Launch Power Automate*

You now need to pass your credentials to log in to PAD, as shown in Figure 4-22.

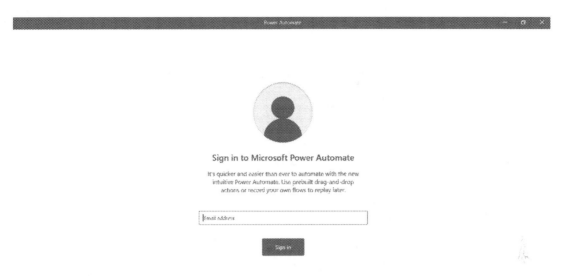

Figure 4-22. *Signing in to Power Automate*

After authentication, follow these steps:

1. Select the correct environment.

2. You can view your flows if you have any shared with you, as shown in Figure 4-23.

3. You can click +New Flow to create a new flow.

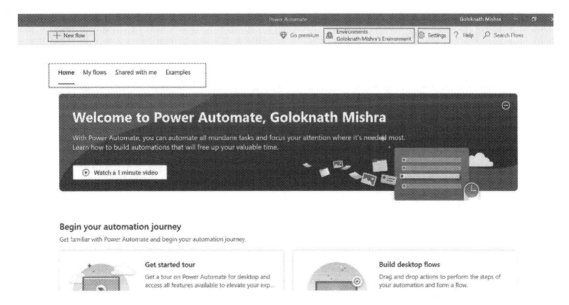

Figure 4-23. *Viewing existing flows*

When you click Settings, as shown in Figures 4-24 and 4-25, you will see the different options.

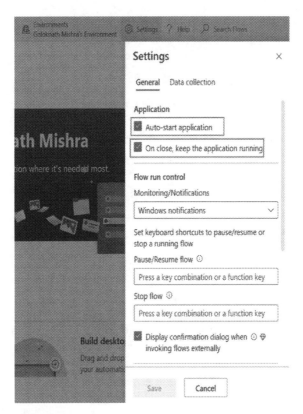

Figure 4-24. *Different settings*

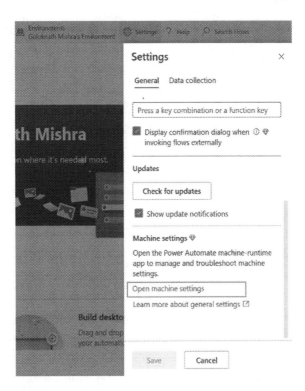

Figure 4-25. *More settings*

When you click Open Machine settings, you will see the Machine Settings area, as shown in Figure 4-26. Select the environment in which you want to register the machine.

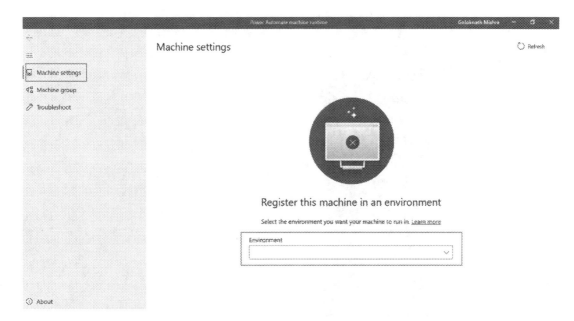

Figure 4-26. *Select the environment in which you want to register the machine*

Select Machine Group and enter the relevant environment, as shown in Figure 4-27.

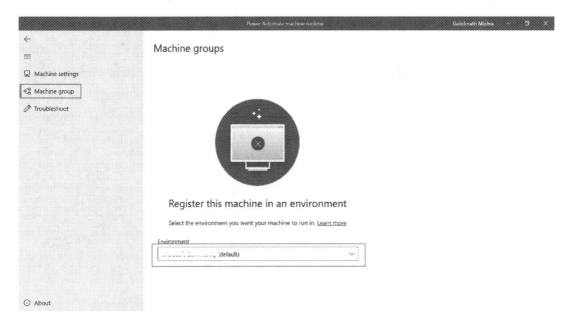

Figure 4-27. *Machine Group setting*

If you select the Troubleshoot option, you will see the account the service is running in. You can export the machine logs for troubleshooting purposes, as shown in Figure 4-28.

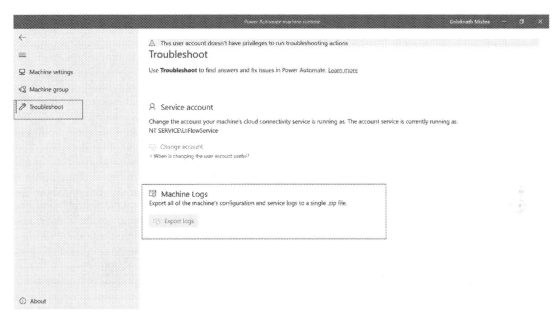

Figure 4-28. *Troubleshooting options*

When you click the + New Flow option, a dialog will open, where you name the flow and then click Create. See Figure 4-29.

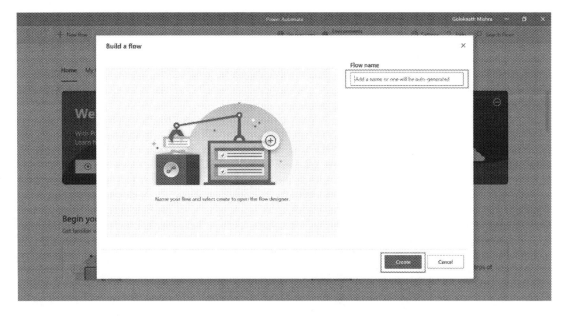

Figure 4-29. *Naming the new flow*

Now you can launch PAD from the solution. Once the Desktop Flow has been added, a window will prompt you to open PAD, as shown in Figure 4-30. Click Open Power Automate.

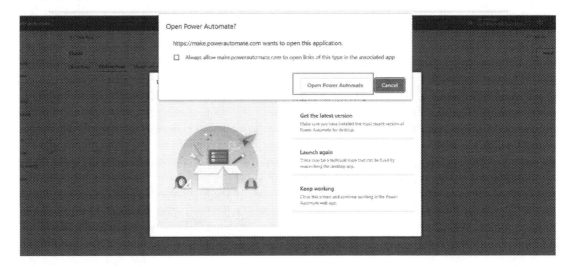

Figure 4-30. *Prompt for launching Power Automate*

A blank Desktop Flow will open with name provided as the flow name, as shown in Figure 4-31.

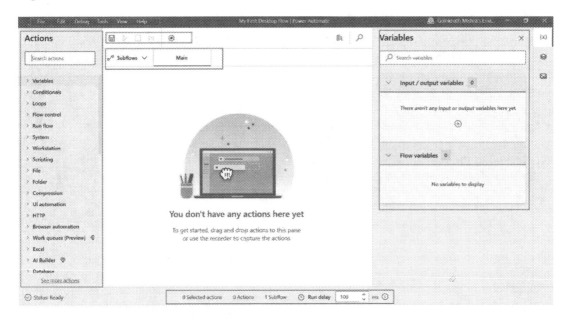

Figure 4-31. *A blank Desktop Flow opens*

Based on the Flow Designer UI navigation, the left side displays the flow's actions with options to search. The center pane is called the *workspace* and it will contain the main flow and any subflows, as shown in Figure 4-32. The right pane displays the flow variables and the top pane displays the toolbar.

Once you have saved the flow, you will see your flow under the Desktop Flow in the Power Automate Portal.

Figure 4-32. *You can see your flow under the Desktop Flow*

You can see this same flow inside the Power Automate Desktop app, under My Flows, as shown in Figure 4-33.

Figure 4-33. *To find the flow in Power Automate, go to My Flows*

Now open the Desktop Flow to create your first Desktop Flow and search for the Display Message action. Drag and drop the Display Message action onto the workspace area. See Figure 4-34.

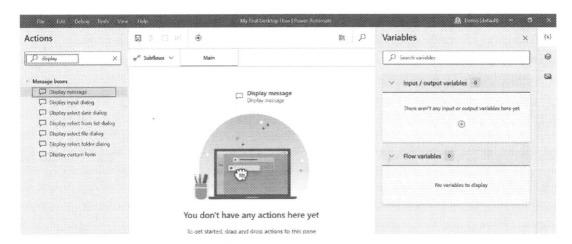

Figure 4-34. *Find the Display Message action*

When you place the Display Message action in the workspace area, a dialog will open, where you define the properties of the Display Message action, as shown in Figure 4-35.

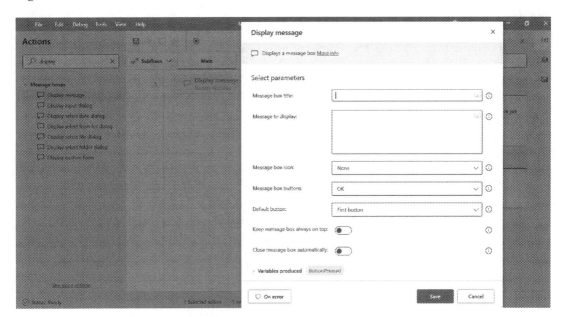

Figure 4-35. *Display Message action*

Fill in the required information, as shown in Figure 4-36.

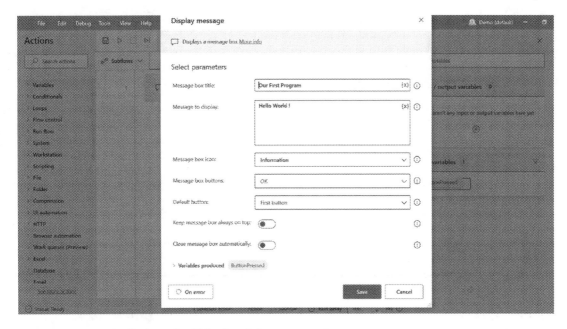

Figure 4-36. *Defining the Display Message action*

Click Save, which will generate the flow variable automatically. Click Run to see the results. See Figure 4-37.

Figure 4-37. *The Display Message action has been defined*

The action displays Hello World, as shown in Figure 4-38.

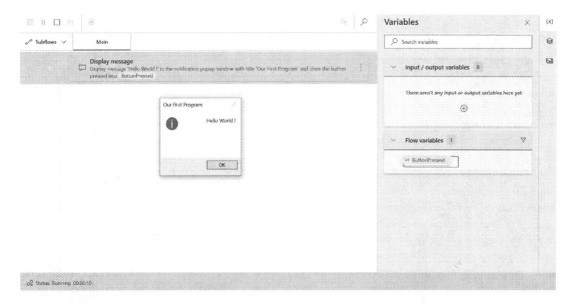

Figure 4-38. *The Display Message action displays the Hello World text*

Using Hosted Machines

Hosted machines allow you to build, test, and run attended and unattended Desktop Flows without providing or setting up any physical machines. Figure 4-39 illustrates the differences between machines and machine groups.

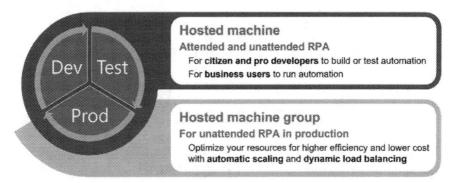

Figure 4-39. *Machines vs. machine groups*

To create and use hosted machines you should have the following:

- A valid and working Intune and Azure Active Directory tenant.

- Intune device type enrolment restrictions are set to Allow Windows (MDM) platform for corporate enrolment.

Follow these steps to create a new hosted machine:

1. Navigate to Monitor ➤ Machine ➤ Hosted Machine, as highlighted in Figure 4-40.

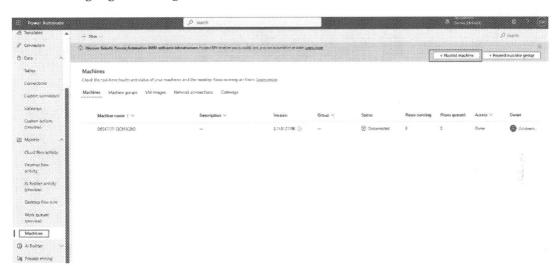

Figure 4-40. *Creating a new hosted machine*

A page will appear, where you can create a new hosted machine, as shown in Figure 4-41. Select a name for the hosted machine and add a description; then click Next.

Figure 4-41. *Name the hosted machine*

If you have an VM image available, you can use it. Otherwise, use the default settings.

Tip   The image needs to be replicated in the same Azure region as the hosted machine.

When you click + New VM Image, you will see an option to select the name along with options to use it with a hosted machine, a hosted machine group, or both.

As shown in Figure 4-42, I choose Hosted Machine but I don't have an image available.

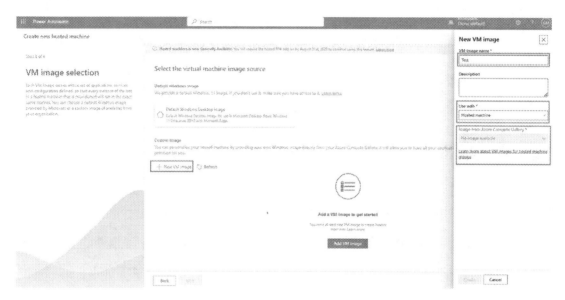

Figure 4-42. *Picking the source of the virtual machine*

I selected the default Windows 11 Enterprise VM, as shown in Figure 4-43. Once you pick your image, click Next.

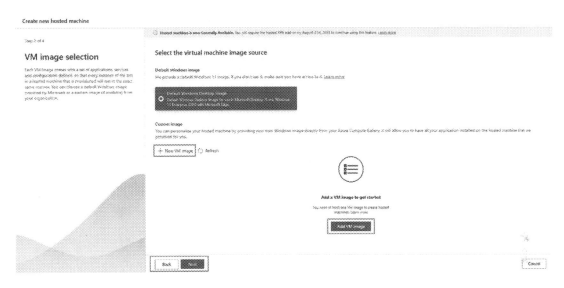

Figure 4-43. *I chose the Windows 11 Enterprise VM*

If you want to add a custom network setup, you can do by clicking + New Network Connection, as shown in Figure 4-44. This is optional.

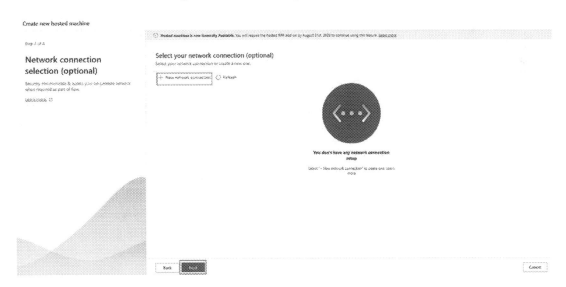

Figure 4-44. *Add a custom network setup*

When I try to add a new network, I see that I don't have an Azure virtual network, as shown in Figure 4-45.

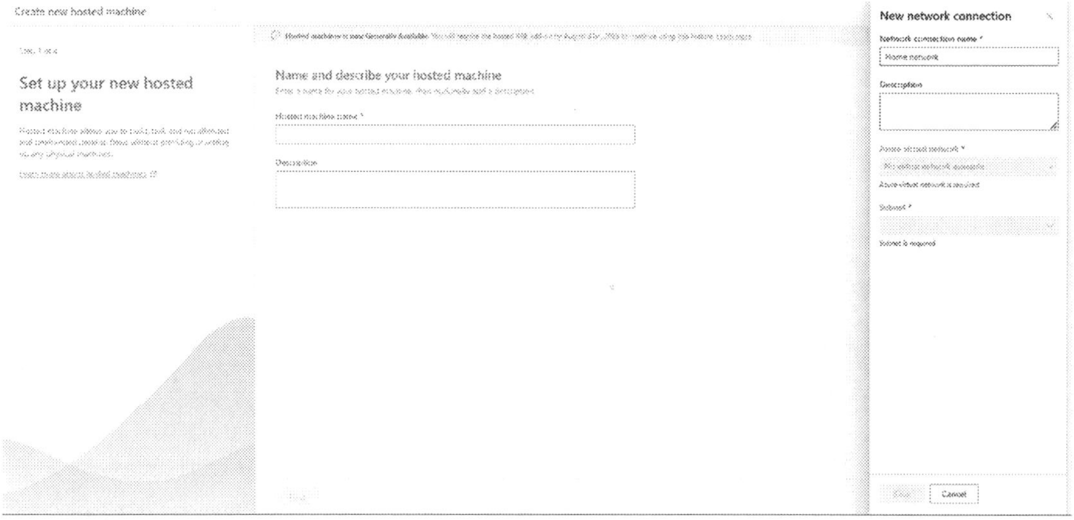

Figure 4-45. *There is no Azure virtual network*

In this case, just click Next. The default network and VM image will then be selected, as shown in Figure 4-46. Click Create.

Figure 4-46. *The default settings are used*

Figure 4-47 shows the provisioning process for the VM.

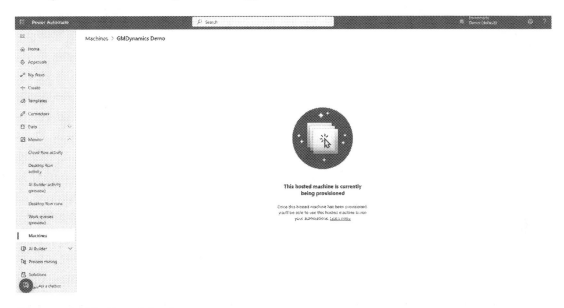

Figure 4-47. *Provisioning process*

Once it's provisioned, you can see the machine, as shown in Figure 4-48.

Figure 4-48. *You can now see the machine*

If you want to create a hosted machine group instead, click Hosted Machine Group, as highlighted in Figure 4-49.

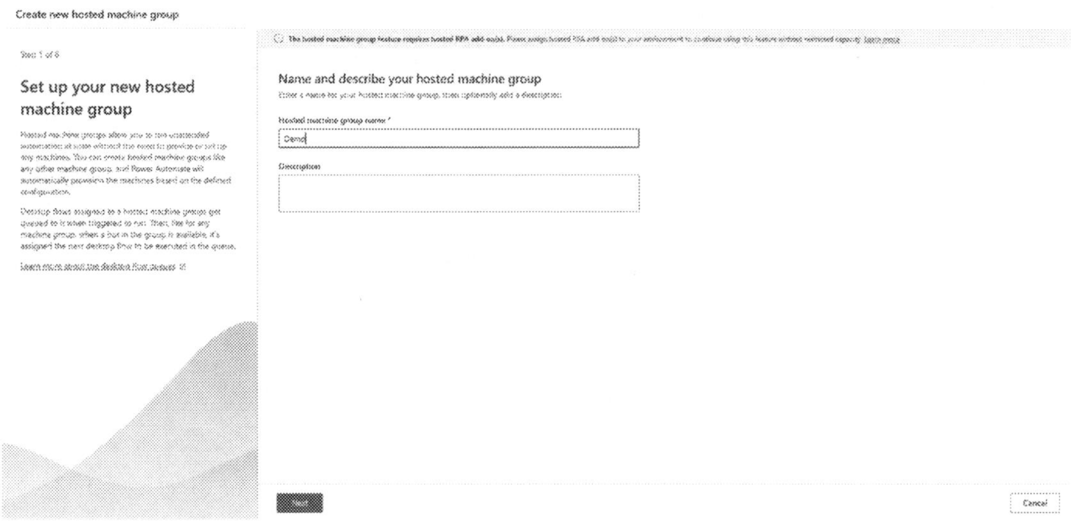

Figure 4-49. *Create a hosted machine group*

When you click Next, select the Reuse Session button. See Figure 4-50.

Figure 4-50. *Choose to reuse the session*

When you click Next again, you can assign the maximum number of bots you want to run on this machine group. See Figure 4-51.

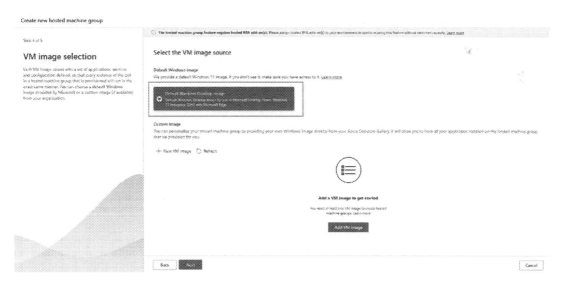

Figure 4-51. *Set the maximum number of bots to run*

Select the VM image, as shown in Figure 4-52.

Figure 4-52. *Select the VM image*

Now choose how you want to connect to your bots, as shown in Figure 4-53. You can:

- Use your work or school account

- Create and use a local account

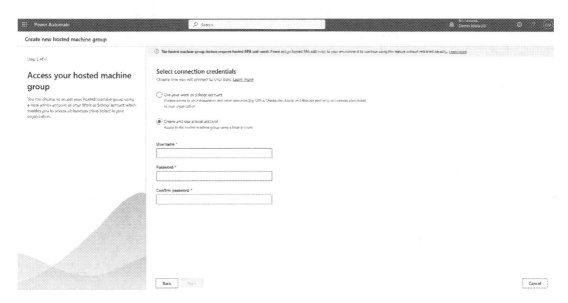

Figure 4-53. *Choose how you want to connect to your bots*

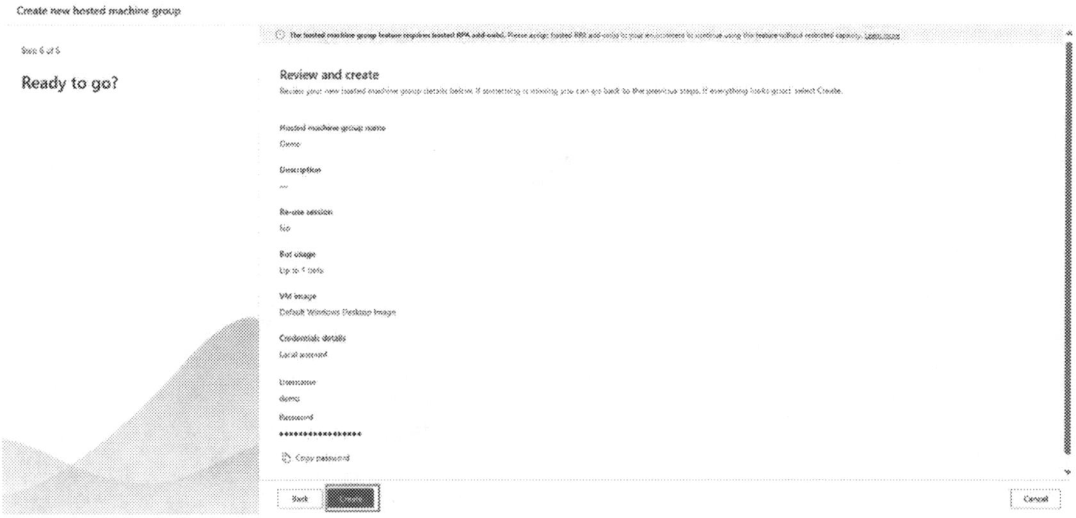

Figure 4-54. *Review the settings and click Create*

Once the hosted machine groups have been created, you can see their status, as shown in Figure 4-55.

Figure 4-55. *Machine groups status*

When you click Share, you can share the hosted machine group, as highlighted in Figure 4-56.

Figure 4-56. *Share the hosted machine group*

When you click Settings, you can select the max number of bots, whether to reuse sessions, and whether to enable maintenance mode. See Figure 4-57.

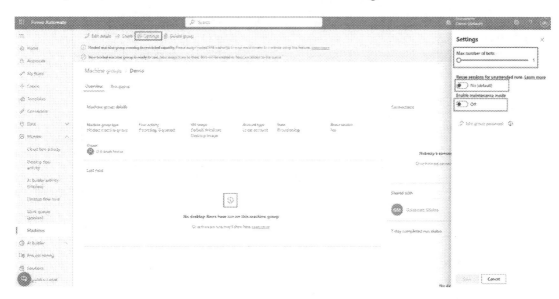

Figure 4-57.   *The settings area*

You can view your hosted machine group under Machine Groups, as shown in Figure 4-58.

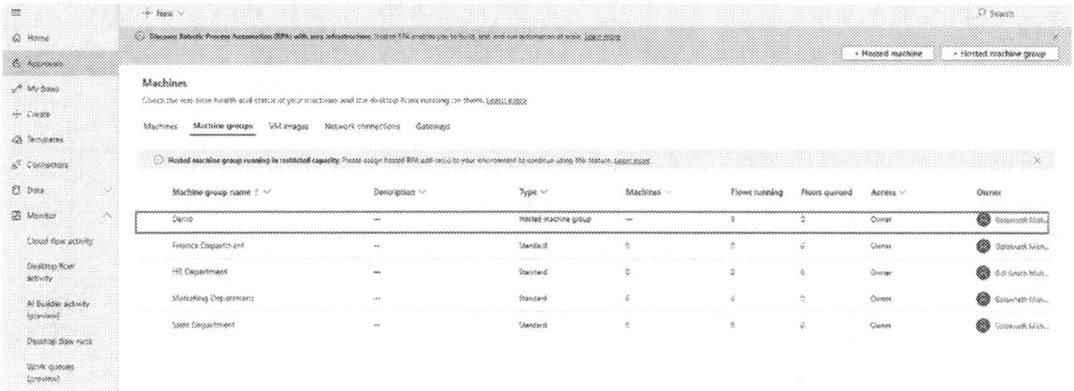

Figure 4-58.   *Your hosted machine group appears under Machine Groups*

You can create new machine groups by clicking +New within the Machine Group area, as highlighted in Figure 4-59.

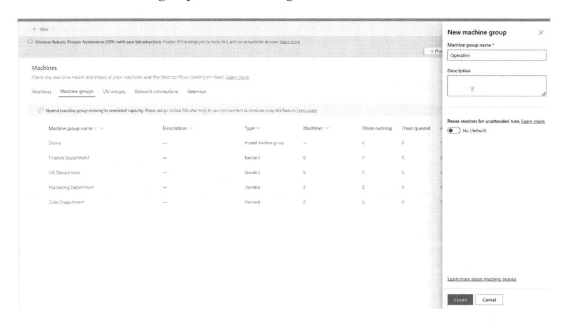

Figure 4-59. *Creating a new machine group*

Name the machine group, as shown in Figure 4-60.

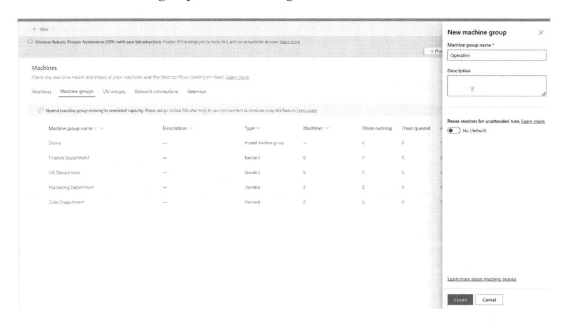

Figure 4-60. *Naming the new machine group*

Once you have created a new machine group, choose Add Machine to add machines to it, as shown in Figure 4-61.

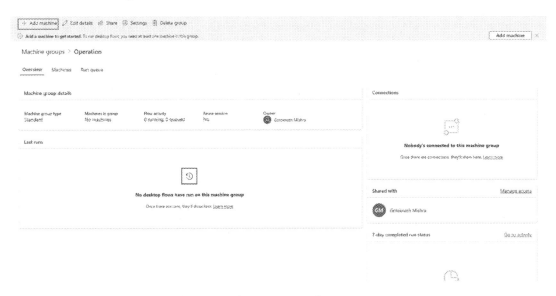

Figure 4-61. *Adding machines to the new machine group*

Running Desktop Flows

Desktop Flows can be triggered from a Cloud Flow. Just create an instant flow in the created solution, as shown in Figure 4-62.

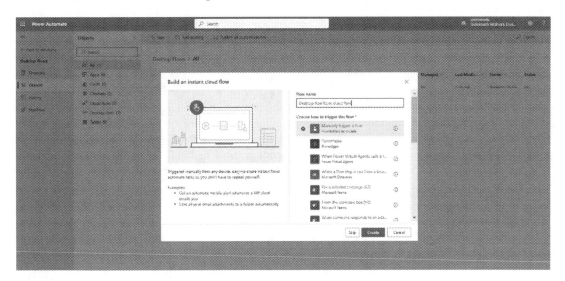

Figure 4-62. *Creating an instant flow*

Search for the Run a Flow Built with Power Automate for Desktop action, as highlighted in Figure 4-63.

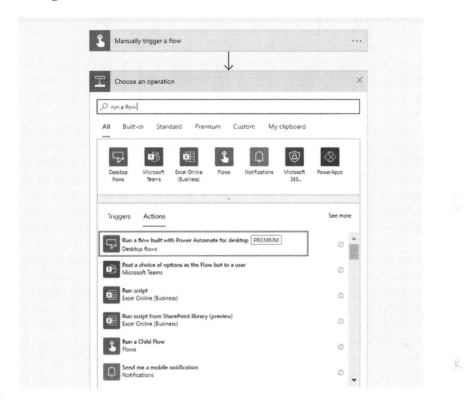

Figure 4-63. *The Run a Flow Built with Power Automate for Desktop action*

Then provide the required information, including credentials to set up the connection. See Figure 4-64.

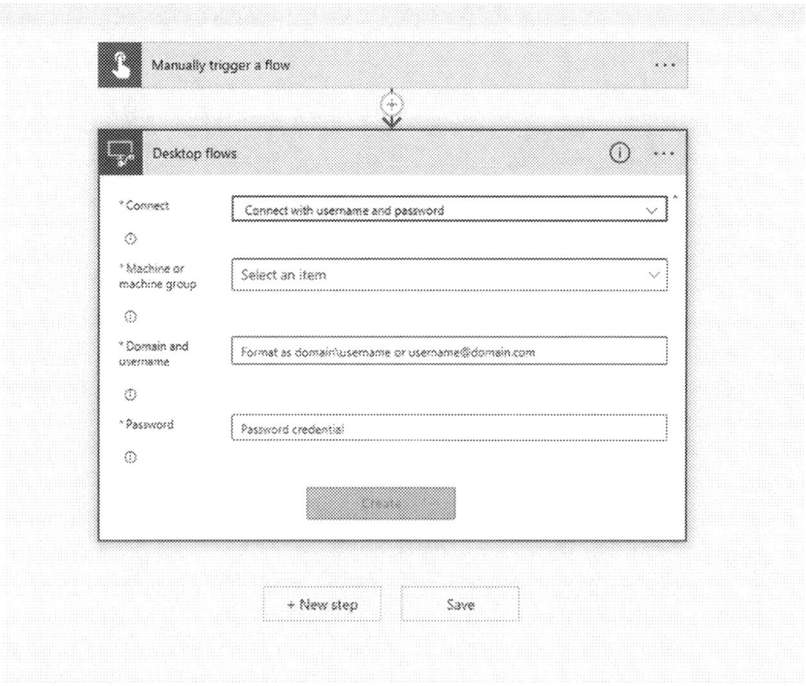

Figure 4-64. *Provide credentials*

There are three ways you can connect, as shown in Figure 4-65.

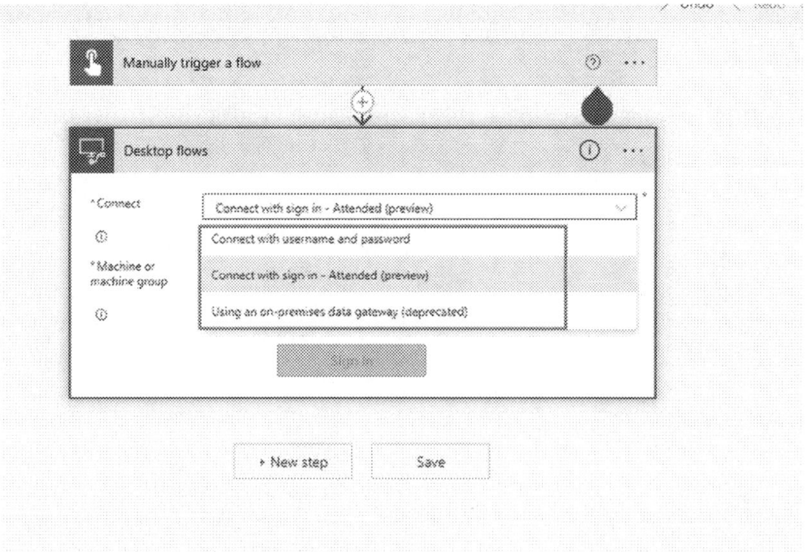

Figure 4-65. *Three ways to connect*

Once a connection has been established, you can select the Desktop Flow you want to run from the Cloud Flow and Run mode. The flow can be attended or unattended. See Figures 4-66 and 4-67.

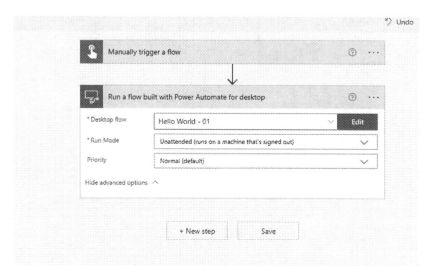

Figure 4-66. *Selecting an unattended Desktop Flow*

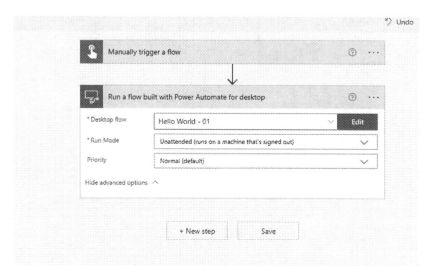

Figure 4-67. *Selecting an attended Desktop Flow*

Figure 4-68 shows the flow running.

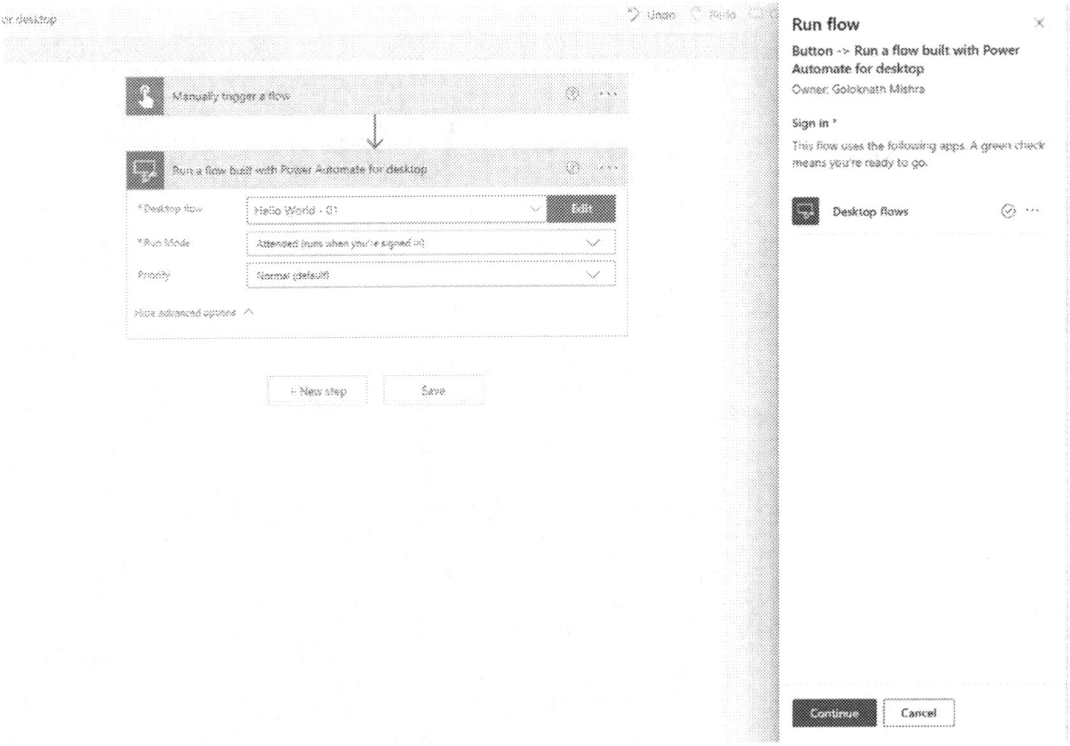

Figure 4-68. *The flow is running*

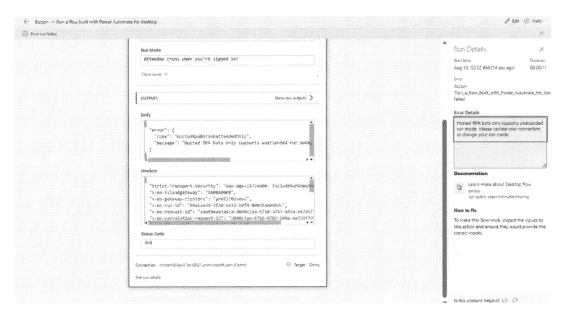

Figure 4-69. *An error has occurred*

When you select Hosted Machine, you cannot use the attended run mode. When you change this to unattended, it will run successfully.

You can also select Machine instead of Hosted Machine to run it in attended mode. Note these requirements:

- Unattended Desktop Flows require an available machine with all users signed out.

- Locked Windows user sessions will prevent unattended Desktop Flows from running.

- Unattended Desktop Flows can't run with elevated privileges.

Click Desktop Flow in Power Automate and then click Details, as shown in Figure 4-70.

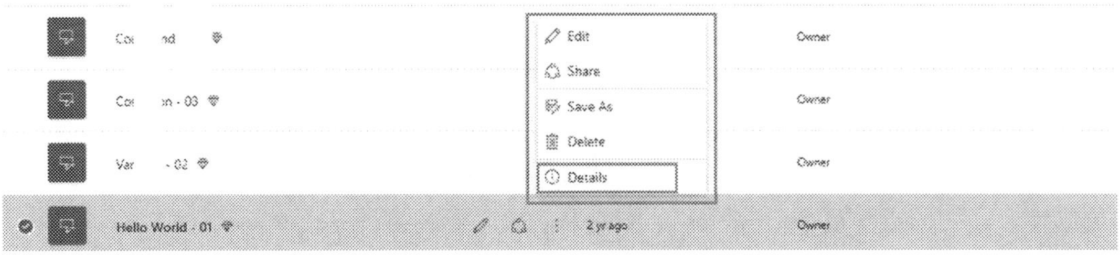

Figure 4-70. *Choose Details to display the Desktop Flow details*

When you click Details, it will display the flow run status, as shown in Figure 4-71.

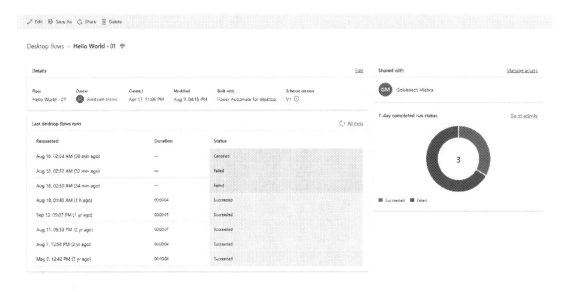

Figure 4-71. *The status of the flow run*

When you click on an individual run status, it is as highlighted, as shown in Figure 4-72.

Figure 4-72. *Viewing an individual run*

This will display the flow run status with detailed information about its parameters, as shown in Figure 4-73.

Figure 4-73. *Detailed information about the individual run*

Click Go to Activity and then choose 7-Day Completed Run Status, as shown in Figure 4-74.

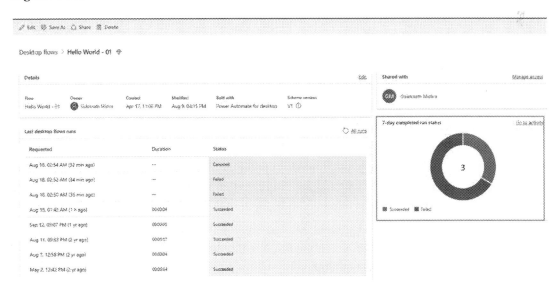

Figure 4-74. *Choose 7-Day Completed Run Status*

Figure 4-75 shows the status.

Figure 4-75. *The 7-Day Completed Run Status*

Your Data loss prevention (DLP) policy can be enforced from the Power Platform Admin Center (`https://aka.ms/ppac`). DLP policies help protect your organizational data from being shared with a list of connectors that you define. See Figure 4-76.

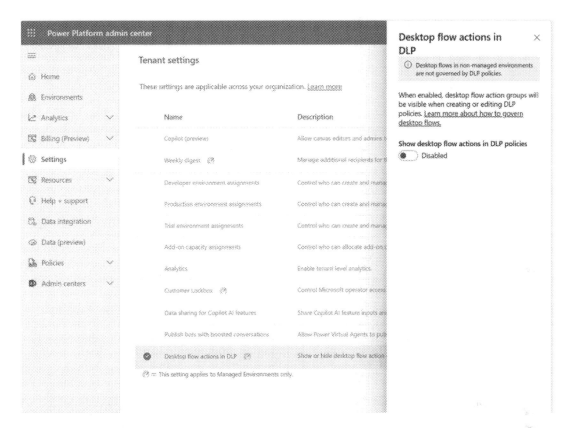

Figure 4-76. *Setting up DLP*

Actions in Power Automate Desktop

In Power Automate Desktop (PAD), you can search for certain variables, as shown in Figure 4-77.

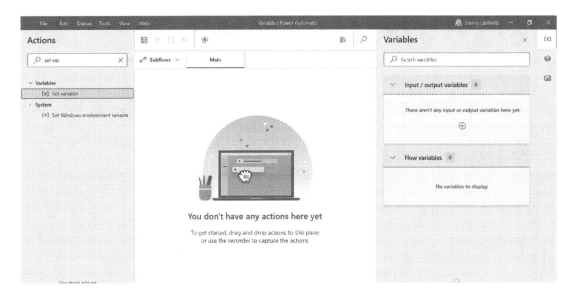

Figure 4-77. *Searching for variables*

When you create a variable, it's called NewVar, as shown in Figure 4-78. Double-click NewVar to change the name and enter a value for the variable.

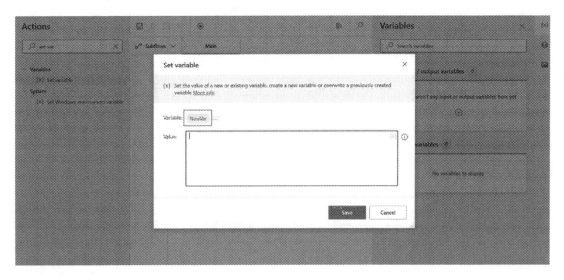

Figure 4-78. *Naming the new variable*

Figure 4-79 shows a new variable being created. Variables must start and end with % and can't contain spaces.

Update the variable name, Value and click Save.

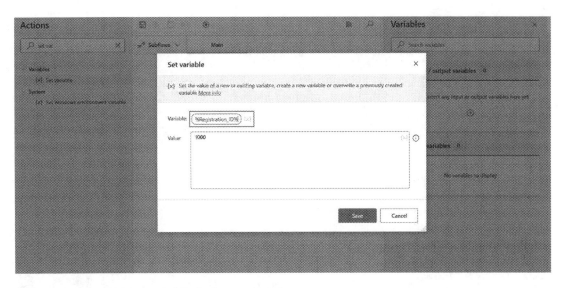

Figure 4-79. *New variable being created*

After clicking Save, you will notice that the new variable appears in the Variables section as well as the Set Variable area in the workspace. See Figure 4-80.

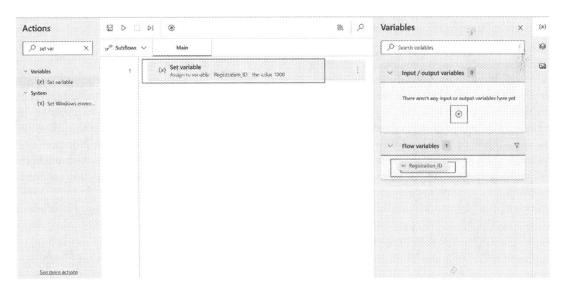

Figure 4-80. *The new variable has been added*

You can also increase the value of a variable, as shown in Figure 4-81.

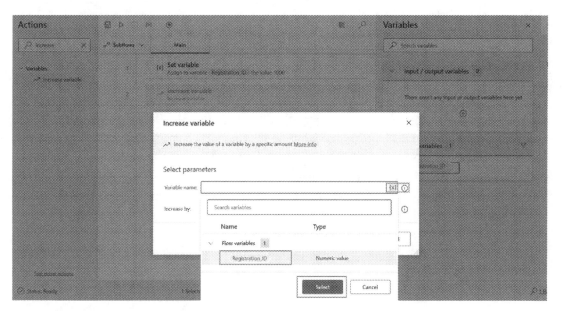

Figure 4-81. *Increasing the value of a variable*

Click {x} to select the variable, as shown in Figure 4-82.

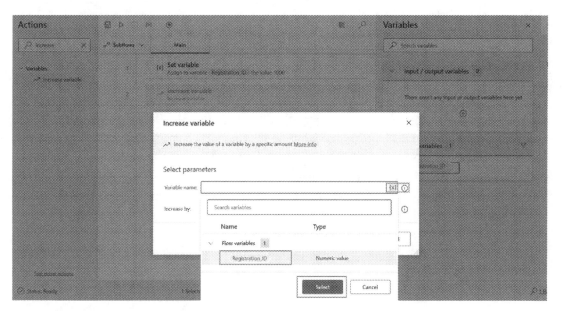

Figure 4-82. *Find the variable you want to edit*

Enter the variable's name and then increase it by two, as shown in Figure 4-83.

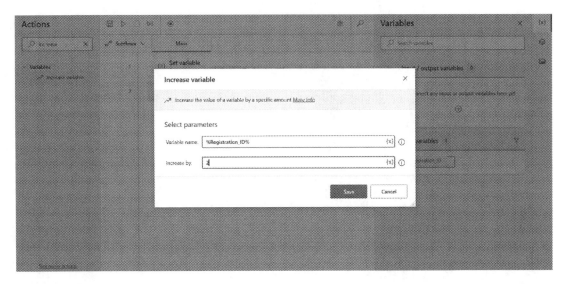

Figure 4-83. *Increasing the variable by two*

To see the outcome, use the display message, which also generated a new variable. You can modify that variable as well, as shown in Figure 4-84.

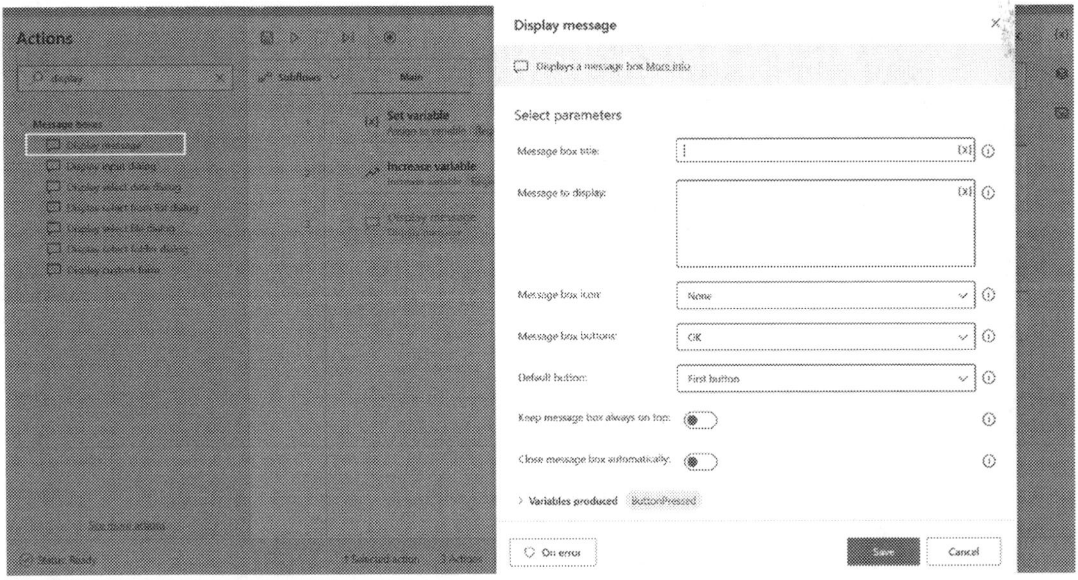

Figure 4-84. *The Display Message variable*

Once you edit the variable, click Save. See Figure 4-85.

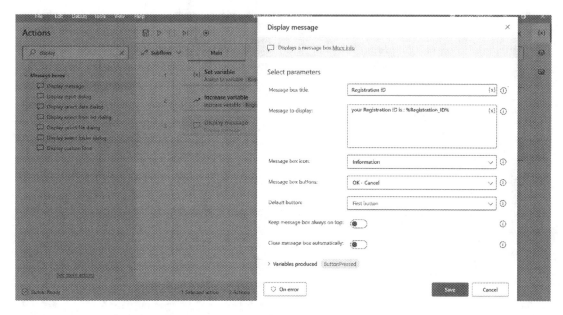

Figure 4-85. *Saving the changes to the variable*

Enter the required details, as shown in Figure 4-86, and then click On Error.

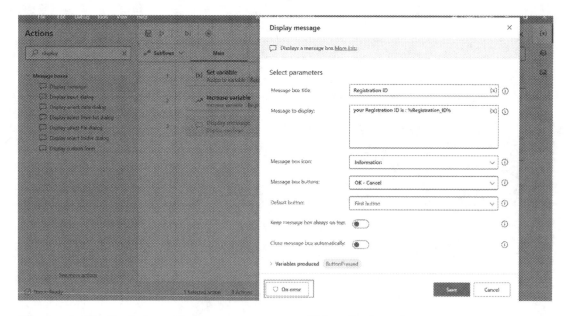

Figure 4-86. *Defining what error message will be displayed*

Configure the action to perform when there is an error. For example, you can set a rule, retry, or display custom message, as shown in Figure 4-87.

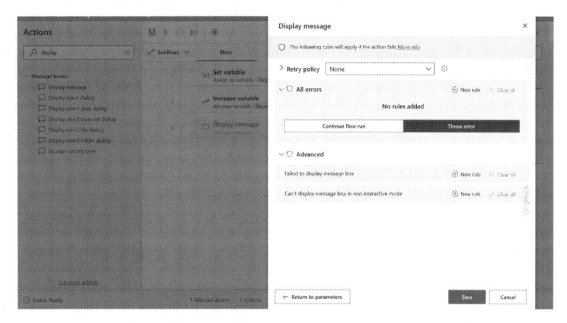

Figure 4-87. *Defining the action for the error message*

Now you have two variables. Click Save and Run, as shown in Figure 4-88.

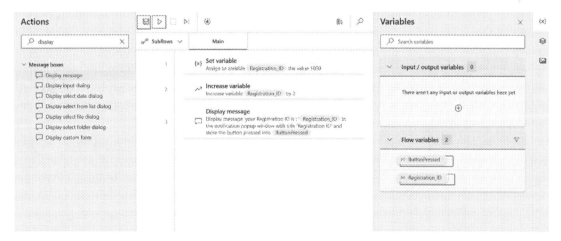

Figure 4-88. *Click Save and Run*

The result is shown in Figure 4-89.

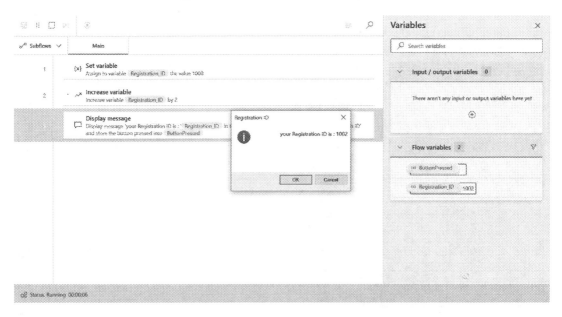

Figure 4-89. *The result of clicking Save and Run*

Now you'll see how to create an input variable. First choose Input, as shown in Figure 4-90. Figure 4-91 shows the process of adding details for this variable.

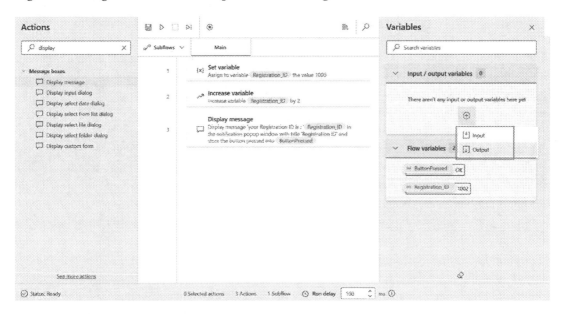

Figure 4-90. *Creating an input variable*

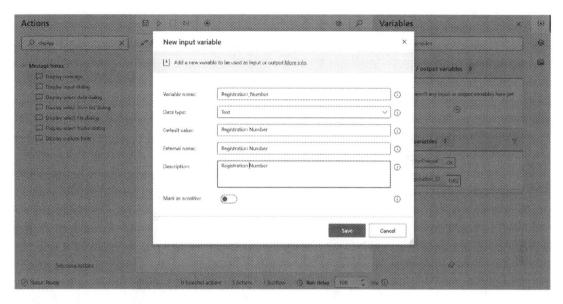

Figure 4-91. *Defining the input variable*

After the entering the details, the input variable will be created, as shown in Figure 4-92.

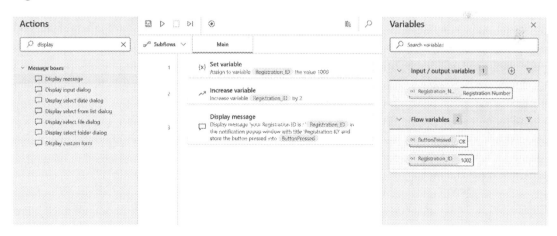

Figure 4-92. *The input variable has been created*

Now you can use the Generate Random Number function, as shown in Figure 4-93.

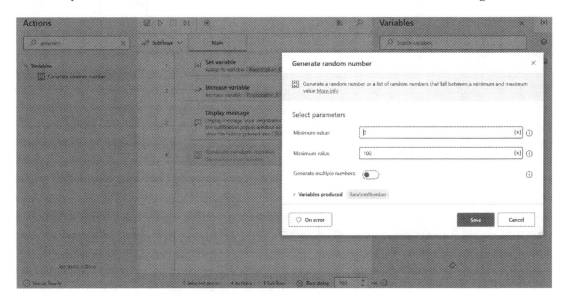

Figure 4-93. *The Generate Random Number function*

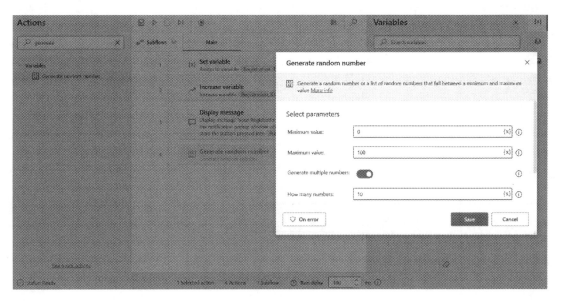

Figure 4-94. *Choose Generate Multiple Numbers*

Name the new variable `SecretCode`, as shown in Figure 4-95.

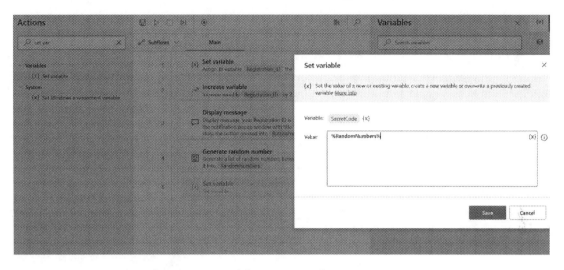

Figure 4-95. *Name the new variable SecretCode*

The secret code is generated, as shown in Figure 4-96.

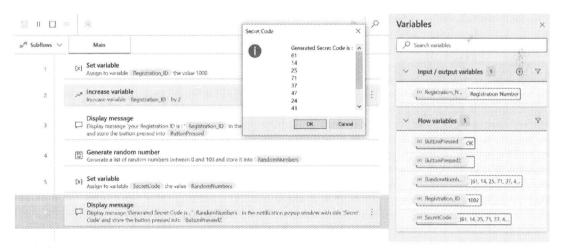

Figure 4-96. *Generating the secret code*

Choose the Display Custom Form action shown in Figure 4-97, which displays the data in the forms.

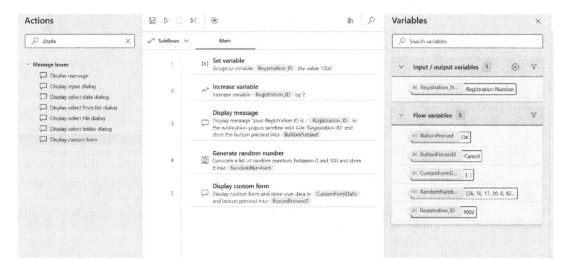

Figure 4-97. *Choose the Display Custom Form action*

To clear the data on the form, you can use the eraser icon, as shown in Figure 4-98.

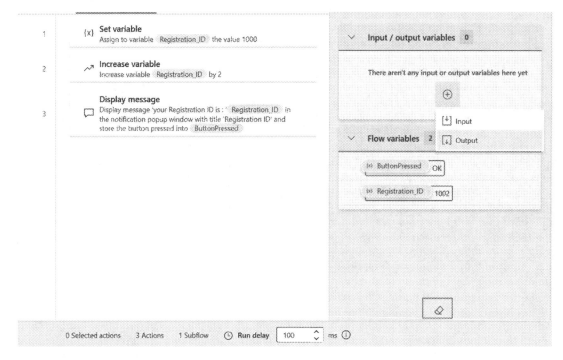

Figure 4-98. *Use the eraser icon to clear the form data*

In the next scenario, you can see whether the student passed in the exam or not:

- If Mark > 500, Qualified with Distinction

- If Mark >= 300, Passed the exam

- Else failed

You can implement that feature in Power Automate Desktop by following these code steps:

- Set the variable to initialize the variable `Mark = null`.

- Display the input dialog to capture the mark entered by the user.

- Feed the user's input into the `Mark` variable using `Set Variable`.

- Display the message to confirm the entered mark.

- `If Mark > 500`, then display the `Student Qualified with Distinction` message.

- `Else if Mark > 300`, then display the `Student Passed the Exam` message.

- `Else` display the `Student Failed in the Exam` message.

- `End`

First, you need to add a label descriptor to define the flow, as shown in Figure 4-99.

Figure 4-99. *Add a label descriptor*

Enter the Mark variable using Set Variable and rename it, as shown in Figure 4-100.

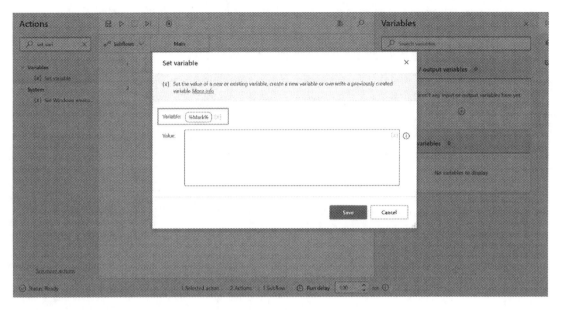

Figure 4-100. *Renaming the variable*

Also set the default value to null, as shown in Figure 4-101.

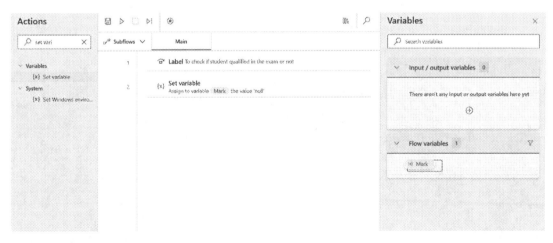

Figure 4-101. *Set the default value to null*

Access the Display Input Dialog window and enter the required information, as shown in Figure 4-102.

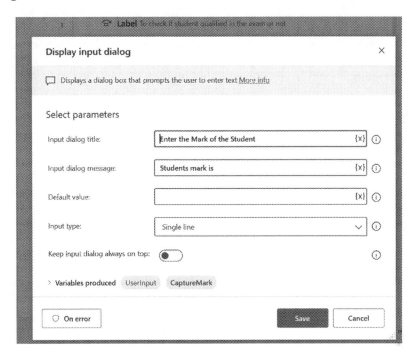

Figure 4-102. *Enter the required information*

Then set the variable with the input from the user, as shown in Figure 4-103.

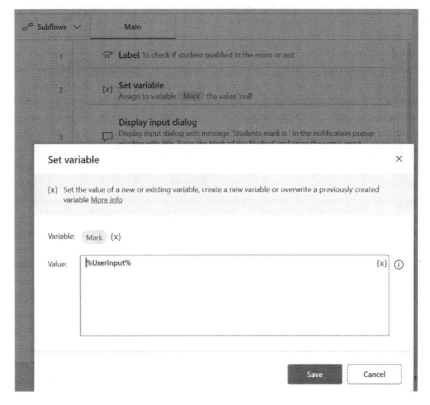

Figure 4-103. *Set the variable based on the user's input*

Add the display message to confirm, as shown in Figure 4-104.

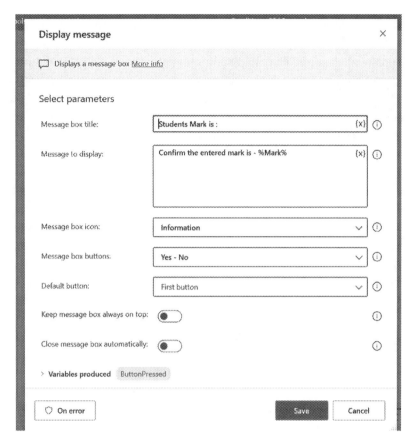

Figure 4-104. *Adding a display message to confirm the entry*

Next, add the if block with the required details, as shown in Figure 4-105.

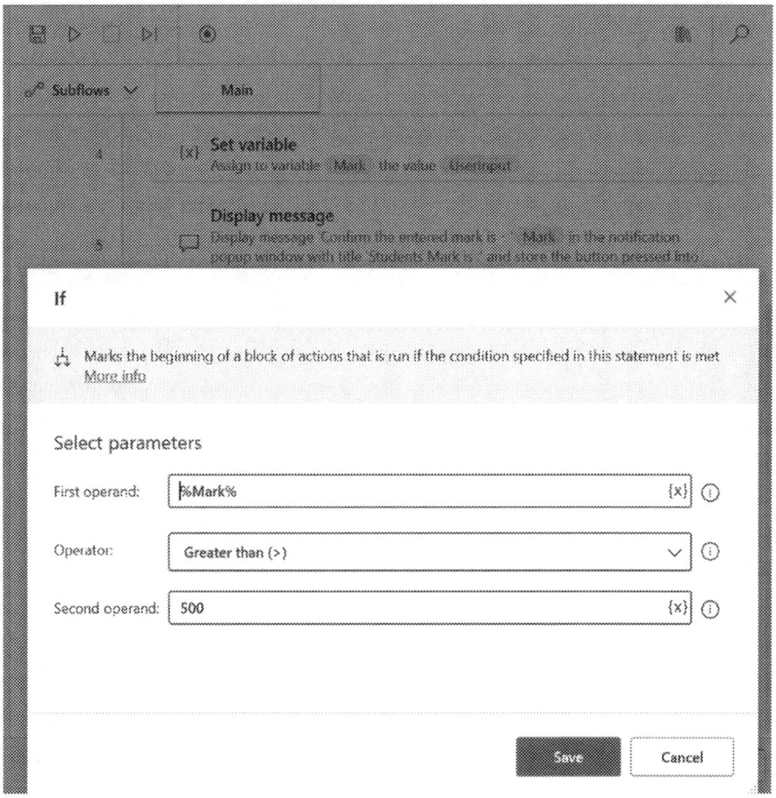

Figure 4-105. *Add the if block using the required details*

Inside the if block, add the display message to tell the students whether they passed with distinction.

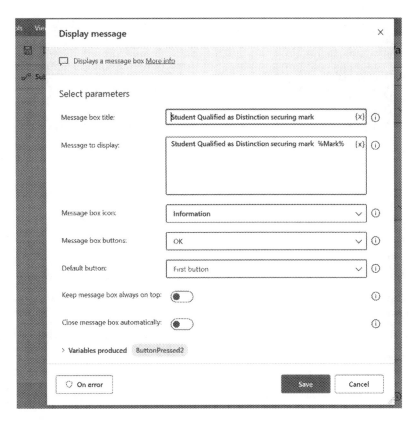

Figure 4-106. *Message to tell students if they passed*

Then add the else if block with the required details, as shown in Figure 4-107.

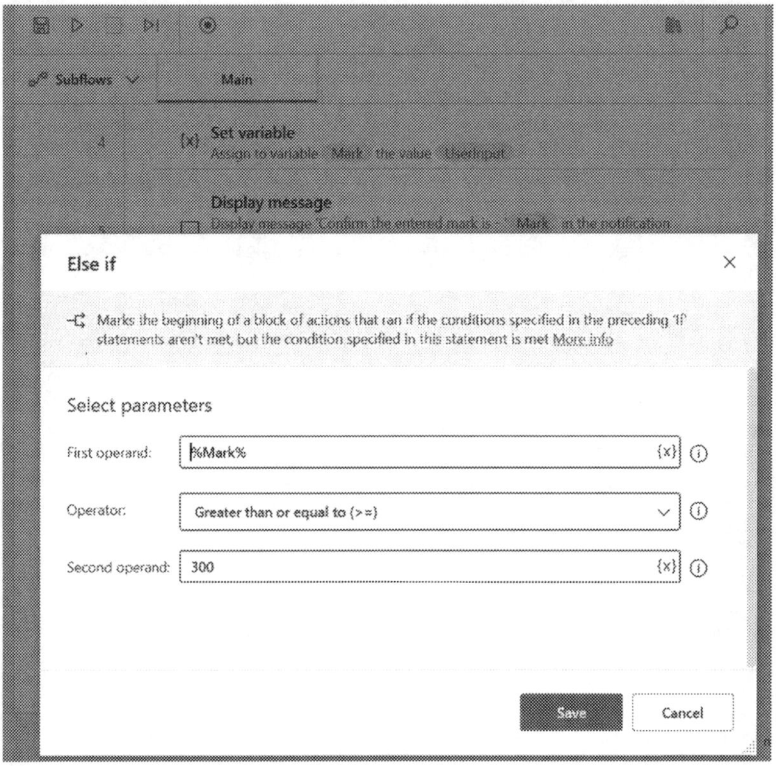

Figure 4-107. *Adding the else if block*

Add a display message for the Else If block, as shown in Figure 4-108.

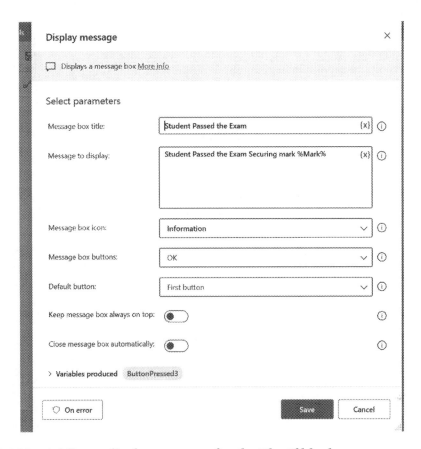

Figure 4-108. *Adding a display message for the Else If block*

Then add the Else block followed by the display message, as shown in Figure 4-109.

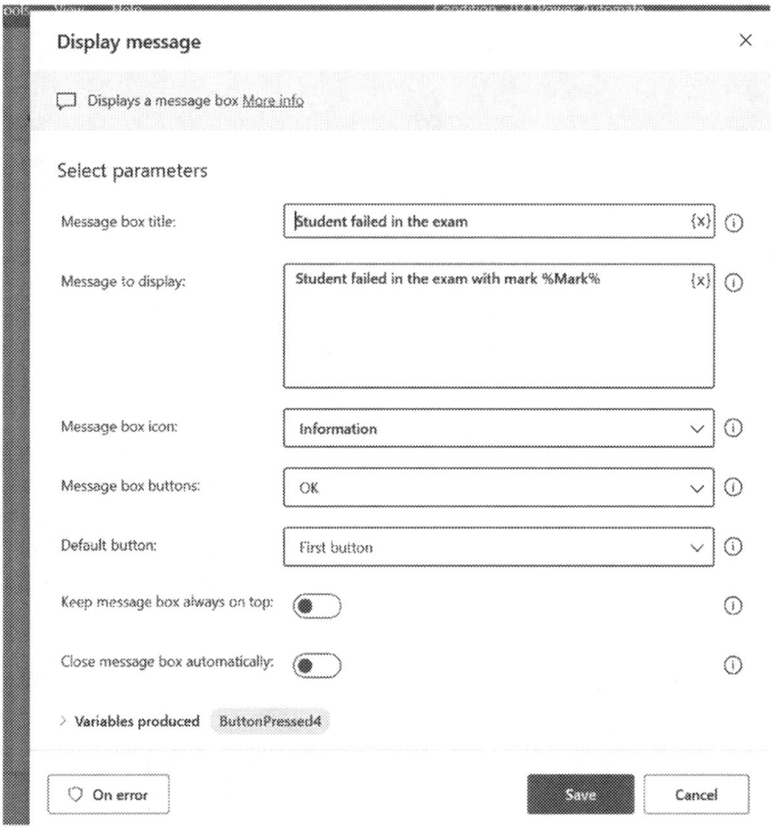

Figure 4-109. *Add the display message*

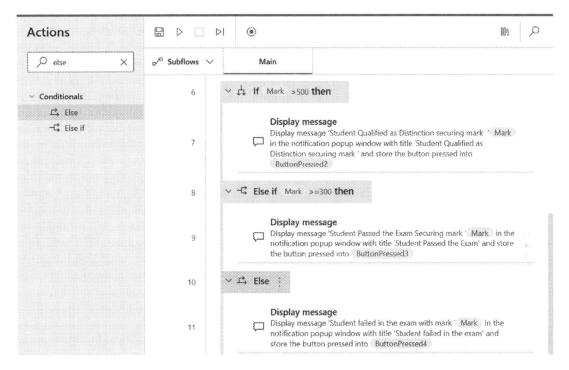

Figure 4-110. *The code so far*

Add an End block to close the control, as shown in Figure 4-111.

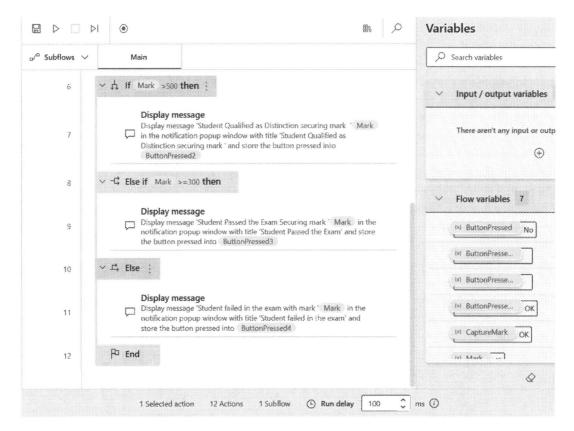

Figure 4-111. *Adding the End block to close the control*

Figure 4-112 shows of the whole flow, end to end.

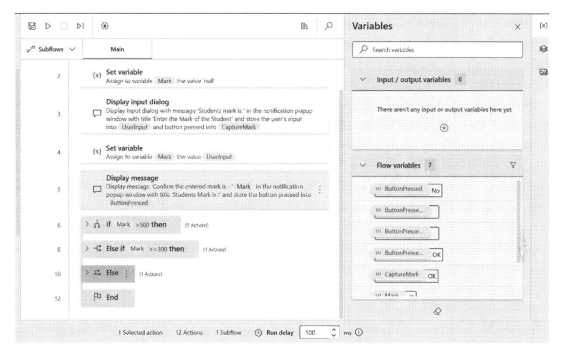

Figure 4-112. *The entire flow*

Click the Run button. A prompt will appear, where you enter the score (the mark), as shown in Figure 4-113.

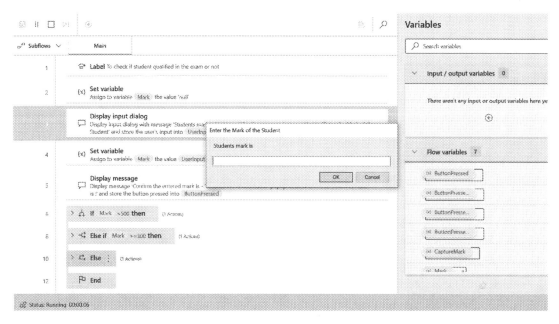

Figure 4-113. *Enter the student's score/mark*

Based on the flow definition, a prompt will appear, as shown Figure 4-114.

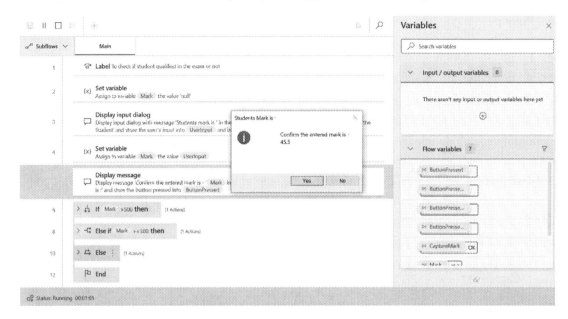

Figure 4-114. *Confirm the mark that you entered*

Once the mark of 45.5 is confirmed, the failed message will appear, as shown in Figure 4-115.

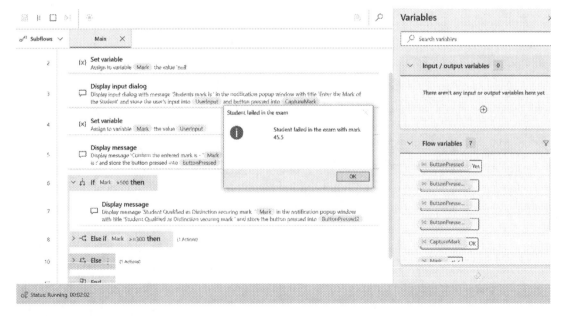

Figure 4-115. *The program shows that the student failed*

If you were to enter a score of 500.6, the passed with distinction message would be displayed, as shown in Figure 4-116.

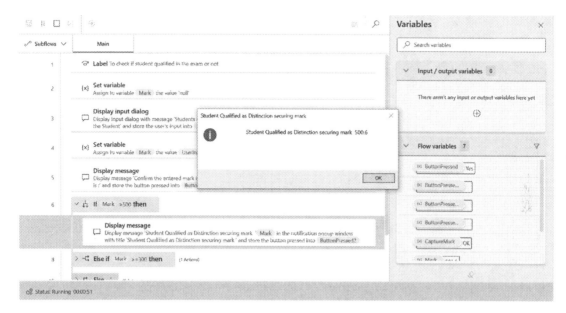

Figure 4-116. *The passed with distinction message is displayed this time*

Follow these steps to create a loop function:

1. Initiate a variable called counter, as shown in Figure 4-117.

Figure 4-117. *Initiating the counter variable*

A flow variable counter is generated, as shown in Figure 4-118.

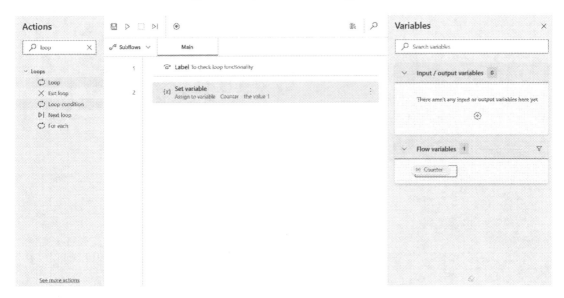

Figure 4-118. *A flow variable counter is generated*

Add the Loop action, as shown in Figure 4-119. Define the Start From, End to, and Increment by parameters.

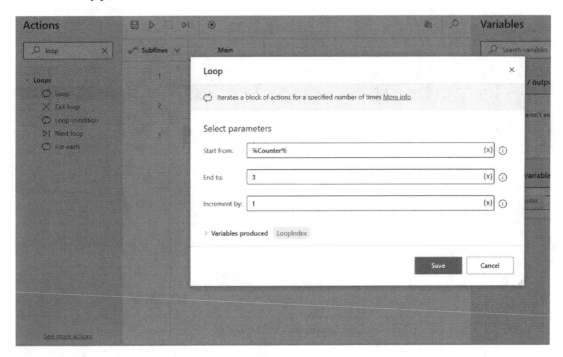

Figure 4-119. *Defining the loop's parameters*

The loop action will be created, as shown in Figure 4-120.

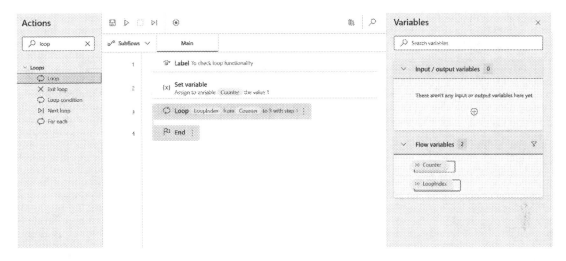

Figure 4-120. *The loop action is created*

Create a new variable called Counter_Loop and set it as an increment of the Counter variable, as shown in Figure 4-121.

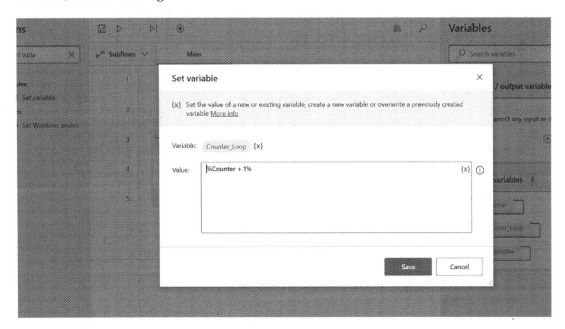

Figure 4-121. *Setting the Counter_Loop variable*

Add a `display message` action inside the loop, as shown in Figure 4-122.

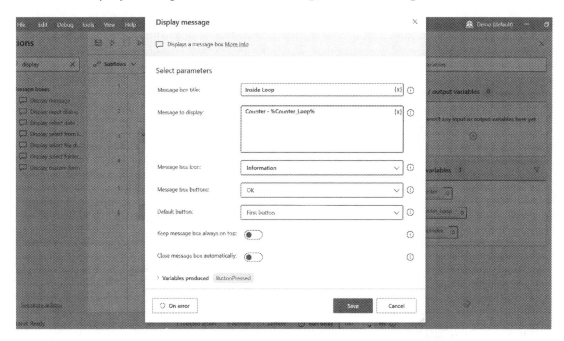

Figure 4-122. *Adding a display message action inside the loop*

After these steps, the flow will look like Figure 4-123.

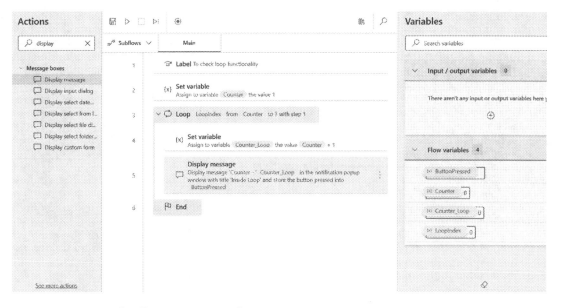

Figure 4-123. *The flow process so far*

Add a display message action outside the loop, as shown in Figure 4-124.

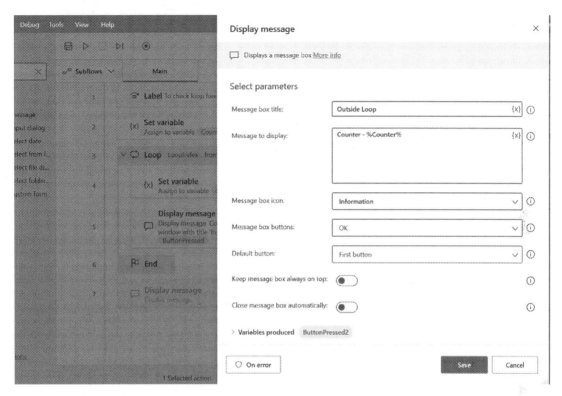

Figure 4-124. *A display message action outside the loop*

Counters should be set to zero initially, as highlighted in Figure 4-125.

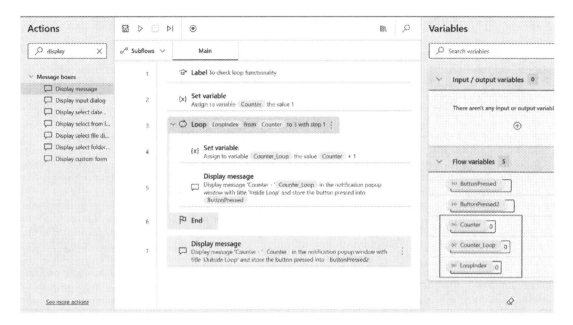

Figure 4-125. *Set the counters to zero*

Debugging a Desktop Flow

Figure 4-126 displays the Debug menu options.

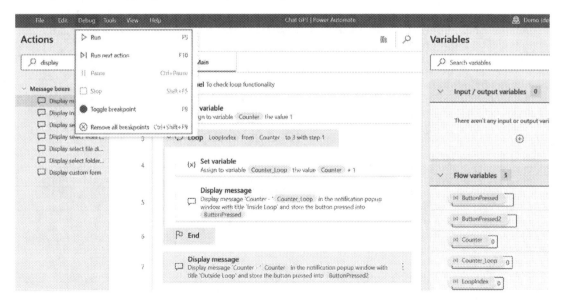

Figure 4-126. *The Debug menu options*

You can add breakpoints, as shown in Figure 4-127, by clicking near the numbers.

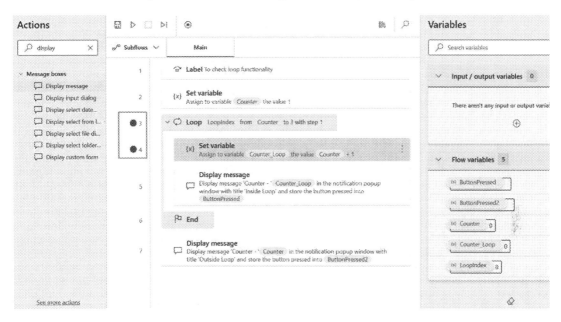

Figure 4-127. *Adding breakpoints*

Click the Run button. The execution will pause at the first breakpoint and `counter` will update to 1, as highlighted in Figure 4-128.

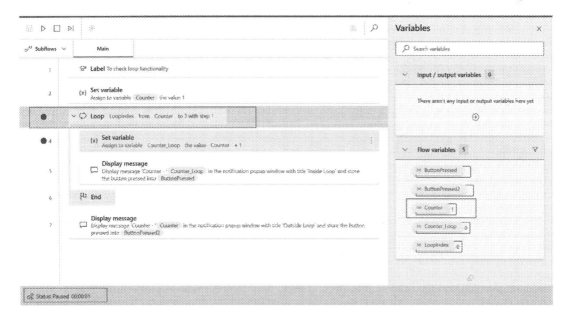

Figure 4-128. *The execution pauses at the first breakpoint*

Click F10 to run the next action item. The LoopIndex is updated to 1, as shown in Figure 4-129.

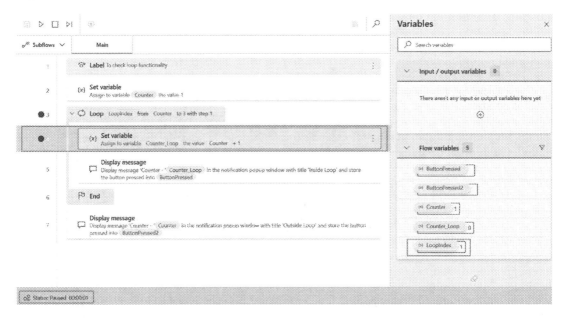

Figure 4-129. *LoopIndex is updated to 1*

Now Counter_Loop will update to counter + 1 (in other words, 2). See Figure 4-130.

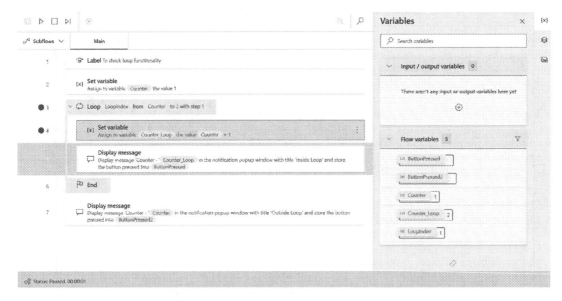

Figure 4-130. *The Counter_Loop will update to 2*

When you press F10 again, the message will display as shown in Figure 4-131.

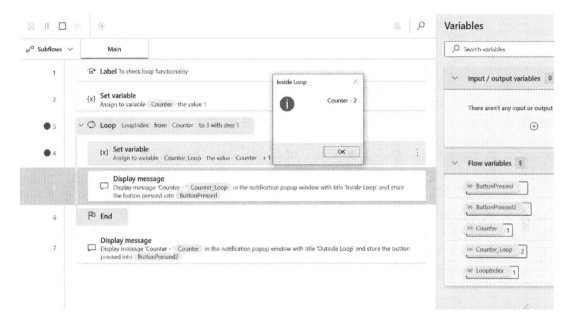

Figure 4-131. *The message displays the counter increment again*

The execution will continue until the loop index is set to 4 (after executing three times), as shown in Figure 4-132.

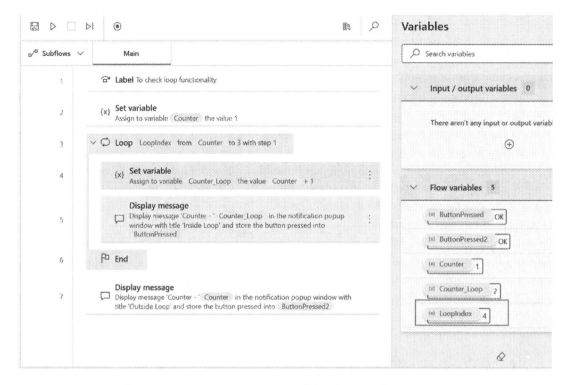

Figure 4-132. *The execution continues until the loop index is set to 4*

To clear the value, click the eraser icon under the flow variable, as shown in Figure 4-133.

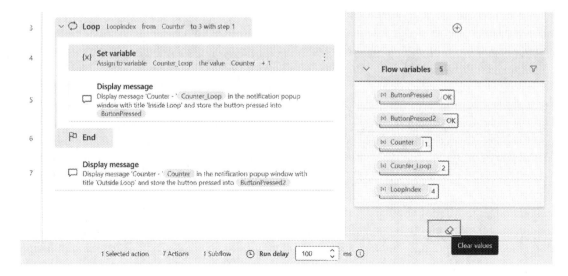

Figure 4-133. *Click the eraser icon to clear the values*

When you clear the values, the variables will be set to blank and the clear value icon will be disabled, as shown in Figure 4-134.

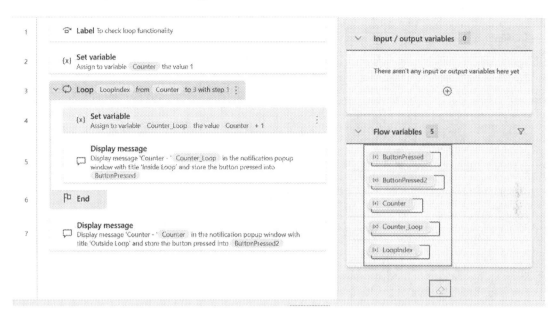

Figure 4-134. *The variables are now set to blank*

Similarly, you can add a loop condition, as shown in Figure 4-135.

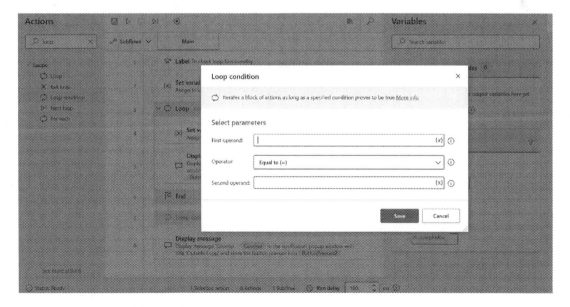

Figure 4-135. *Adding a loop condition*

Update the counter to 6 to see the difference in execution of the loop and the loop condition, as shown in Figure 4-136.

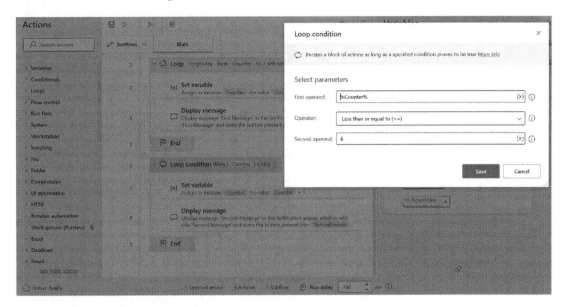

Figure 4-136. *Setting counter to 6*

The entire flow is shown in Figure 4-137.

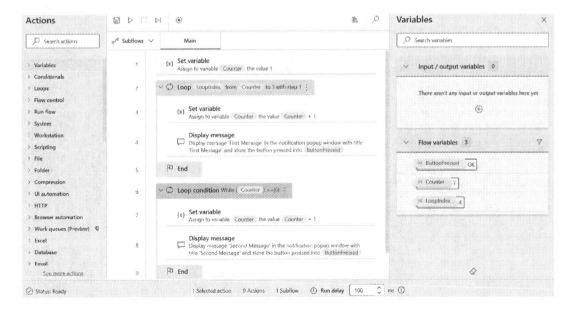

Figure 4-137. *The entire flow*

Now consider the for each loop, along with the file and folder operations.
Figure 4-138 shows files in two different folders.

Figure 4-138. *Files in two different folders*

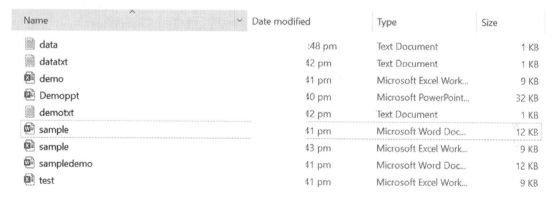

Figure 4-139. *The sample document*

Create the Set Variable action to set the file path, as shown in Figure 4-140.

Figure 4-140. *Creating the Set Variable action*

Access the Get Files in Folder action next, which contains the File_Path variable as the folder. Add a filter (if any). Since this example has no filter, an asterisk (*) is selected. Choose Include Subfolders if you have subfolders. See Figure 4-141.

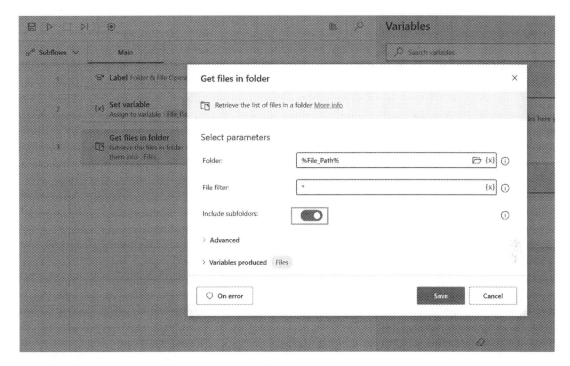

Figure 4-141. *The Get Files in Folder settings*

If you expand the Advanced area, you can see the Sort By parameter, as shown in Figure 4-142.

Get files in folder   ×

📋 Retrieve the list of files in a folder More info

∨ Advanced

Fail upon denied access to any   ⬤◯   ⓘ
subfolder:

Sort by: | Name   ∨ | ⓘ

Descending: ◯⬤   ⓘ

Then by: | No sort   ∨ | ⓘ

Descending: ◯⬤   ⓘ

♡ On error   Save   Cancel

Figure 4-142. *Options for sorting the files*

The current flow is shown in Figure 4-143.

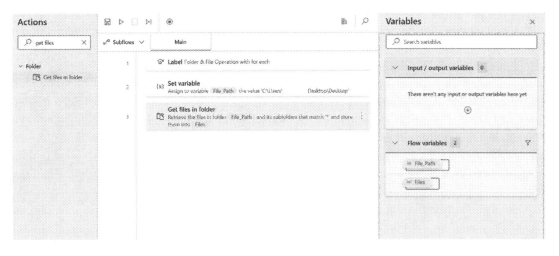

Figure 4-143. *The entire flow*

Now you'll add a child flow, by using Subflows ➤ New Subflow, as shown in
Figure 4-144.

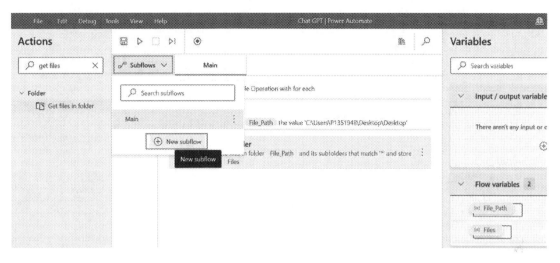

Figure 4-144. *Adding a subflow*

Rename the subflow and then pass the duplicate file path, getting input from the user if the path doesn't exist, as shown in Figure 4-145.

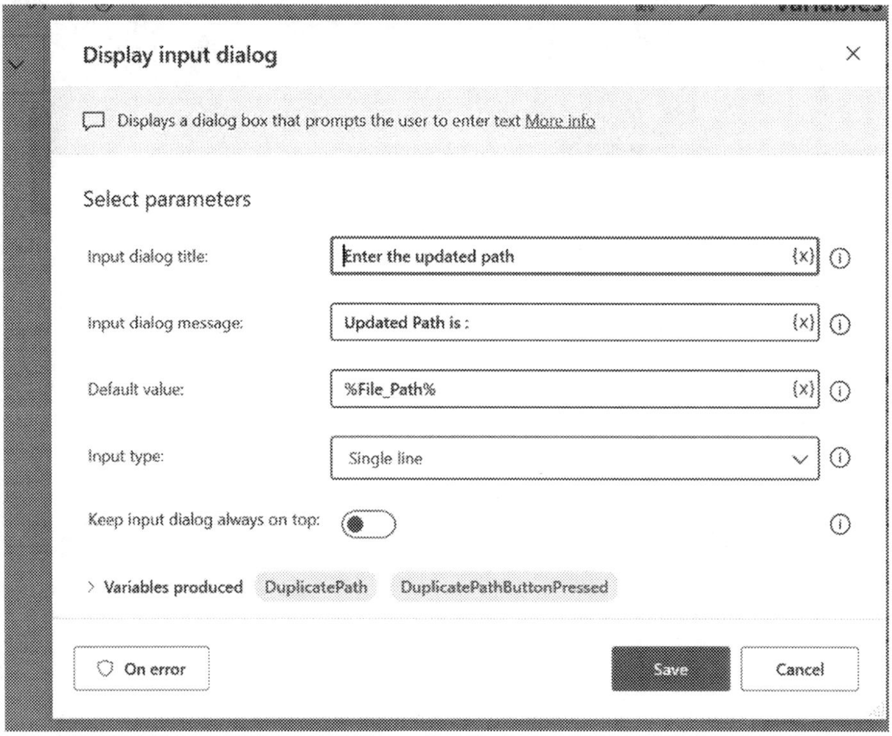

Figure 4-145. *Enter the updated path*

The current flow, with the main flow and the subflow, is shown in Figure 4-146.

Figure 4-146. *The current flow*

Now run the subflow by parsing a backup path using On Error, as shown in Figure 4-147.

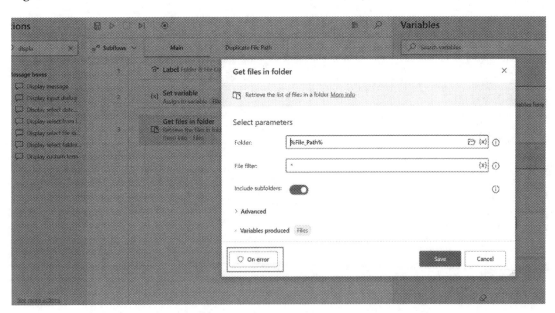

Figure 4-147. *Choose On Error*

When you click On Error, you'll see Figure 4-148, where you can set the retry count. I set the fixed retry count to 1. I also selected Throw Error and added a new rule (choose New Rule ➤ Run Subflow). In the Advanced field, find Folder Doesn't Exist, as shown in Figure 4-148. Once you are happy with the settings, update the variable accordingly.

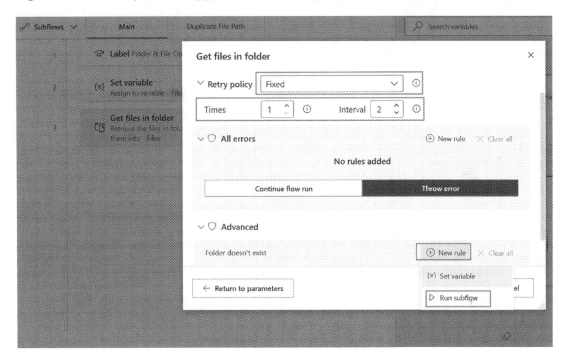

Figure 4-148. *Setting the retry count*

Select the Duplicate File Path subflow, as shown in Figure 4-149.

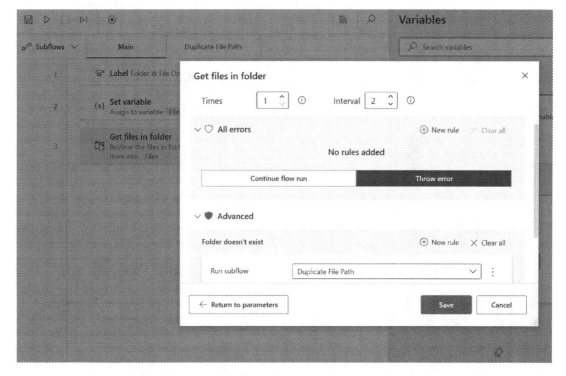

Figure 4-149. *Choose Duplicate File Path*

If any of the steps have an error, you can bypass them using Continue Flow Run, as highlighted in Figure 4-150.

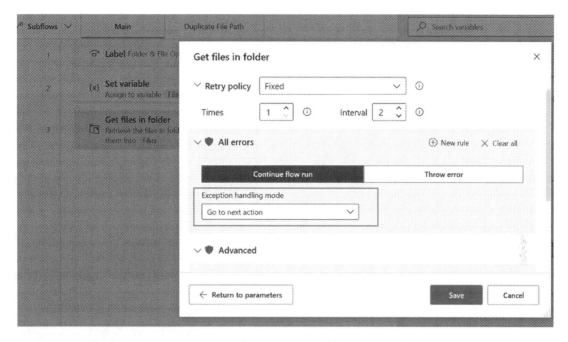

Figure 4-150. *If there is an error, the action will be skipped*

Click Save. You'll then see an icon of the handles in the main flow.

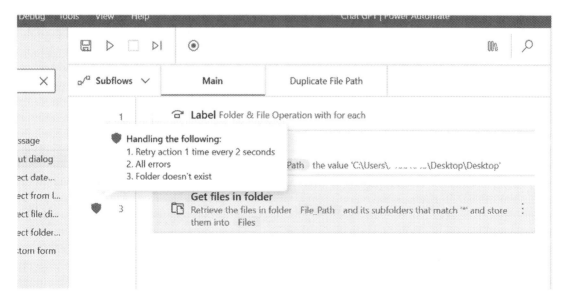

Figure 4-151. *The icon shows the full process*

After executing the flow, you can click Flow Variables to see the list of files, as shown in Figure 4-152. You can see more details when you click More.

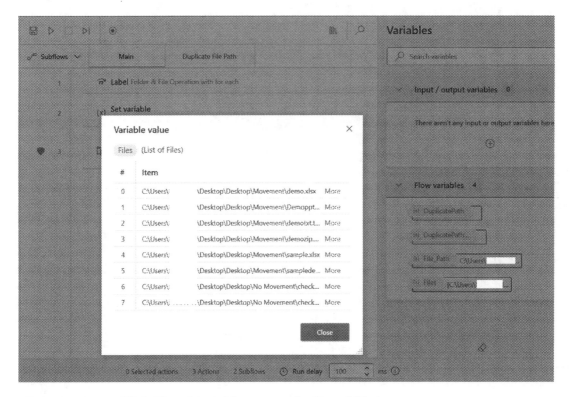

Figure 4-152. *Click Flow Variables to see the list of files*

Then you can add a For Each action and pass the value, as shown in Figure 4-153.

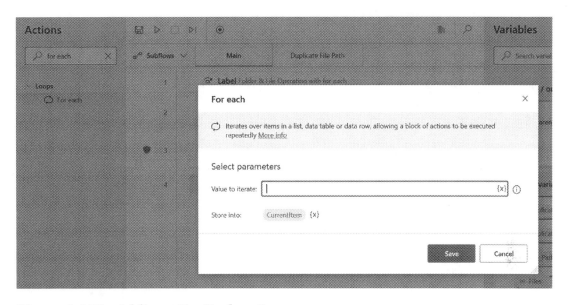

Figure 4-153. *Adding a For Each action*

Rename the variable to something that's easy to understand, as shown in Figure 4-154.

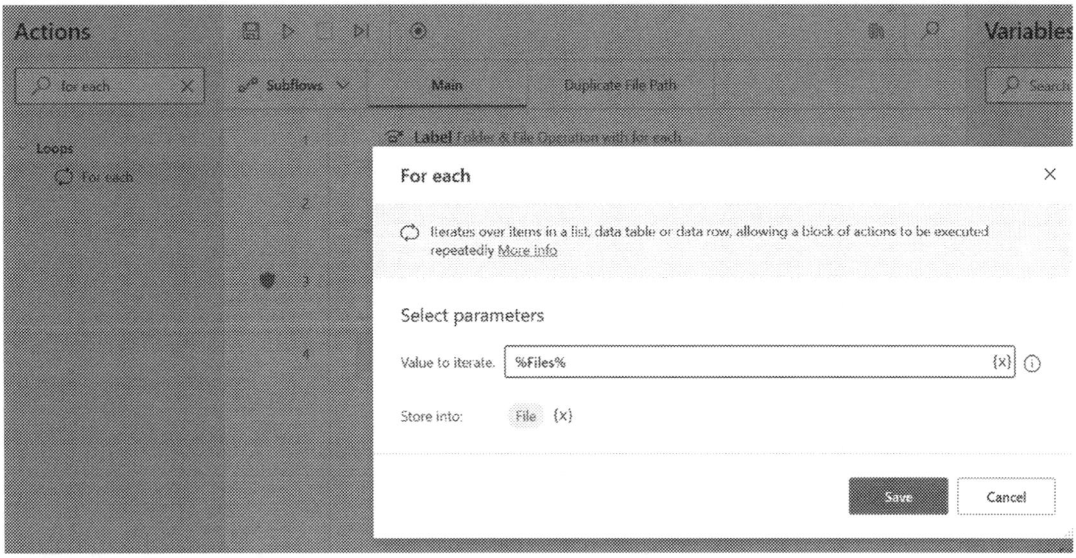

Figure 4-154. *Renaming the variable*

The flow is shown in Figure 4-155.

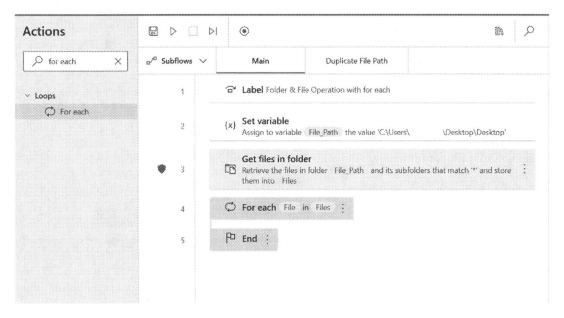

Figure 4-155. *The current flow*

To get the file extension, use the Get Subtext action, as shown in Figure 4-156.

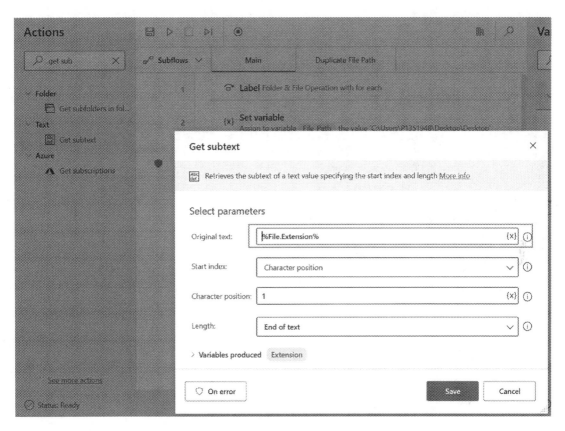

Figure 4-156. *Using the Get Subtext action*

To require a specific case, use the Change Text Case action, as shown in Figure 4-157.

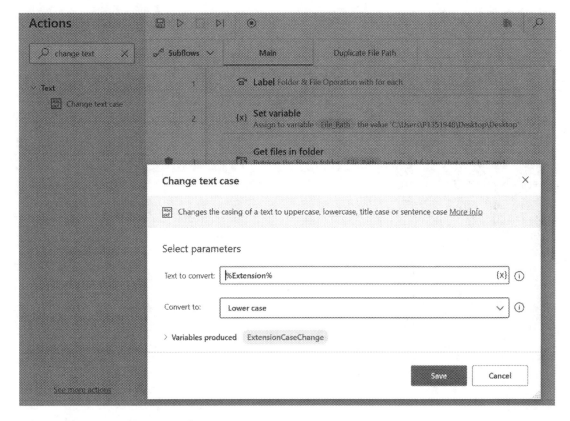

Figure 4-157. *Changing the text case*

Add a new action to define the extension as an xlsx file, as shown in Figure 4-158.

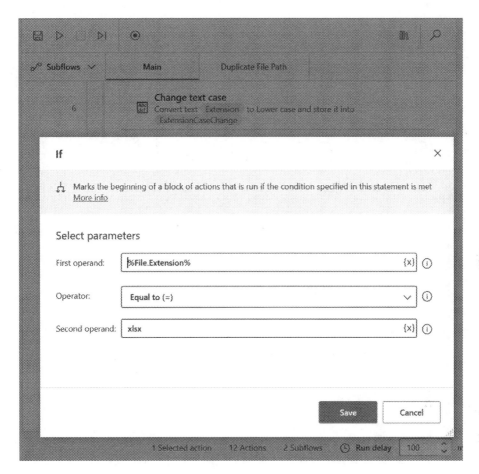

Figure 4-158. *Defining the extension as an xlsx file*

Create a new folder, as shown in Figure 4-159.

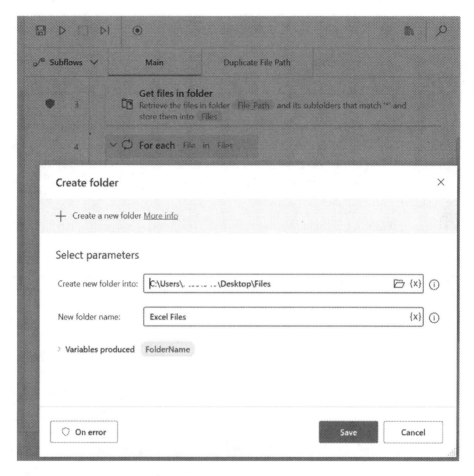

Figure 4-159. *Creating a new folder*

Use the Move File function to move the files into the new folder, as shown in Figure 4-160.

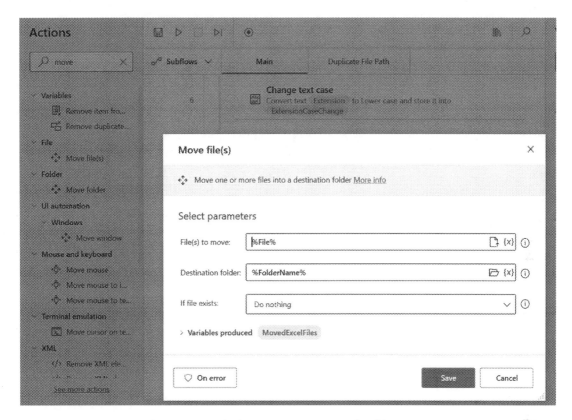

Figure 4-160. *Use the Move File function to move the files*

The final flow is shown in Figure 4-161.

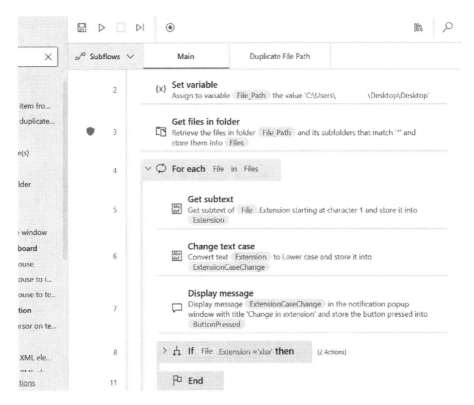

Figure 4-161. *The final flow*

After executing the flow, a new folder is created and the Excel files are moved. See Figure 4-162.

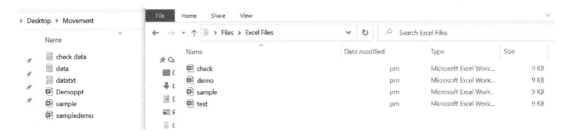

Figure 4-162. *The new folder has been created and the Excel files have been moved*

Now you use a premium feature to learn how to connect a SharePoint/OneDrive. Create a blank folder called demo in your OneDrive, as shown in Figure 4-163.

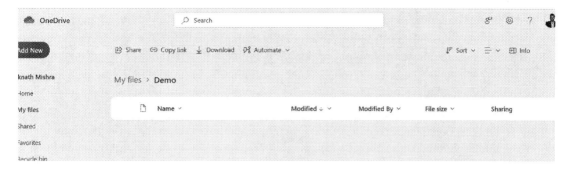

Figure 4-163. *Create a blank folder called demo*

Select the SharePoint/OneDrive action, as highlighted in Figure 4-164.

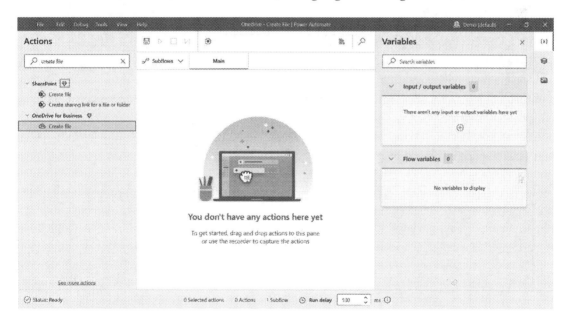

Figure 4-164. *Select the SharePoint/OneDrive action*

Now create a file in OneDrive using Power Automate Desktop so you can test the Create File actions.

Once you drag the action into the workspace, the system will prompt you to pass your credentials to create a connection with OneDrive. This is called a *connection reference*. See Figure 4-165.

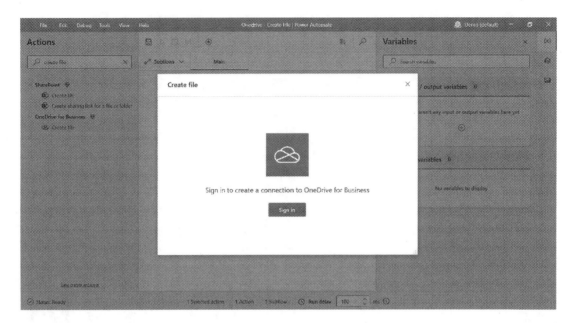

Figure 4-165. *Sign in to create a connection with OneDrive*

Once you have been authenticated, you will see the connection reference in the top-right corner of the Create File action, as highlighted in Figure 4-166.

Figure 4-166. *The connection reference appears in the top-right corner of the Create File action*

When you double-click that connection reference, you will see your connection reference and you can add new ones, as highlighted in Figure 4-167.

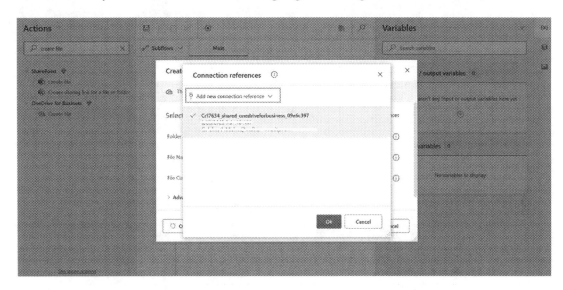

Figure 4-167. *Viewing and adding connection references*

Pass the folder path shown in Figure 4-168 (use the Demo folder if you created it).

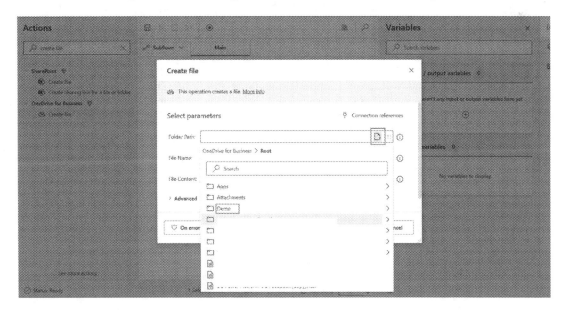

Figure 4-168. *Pass the folder path*

This example uses the PAD.txt file, as shown in Figure 4-169.

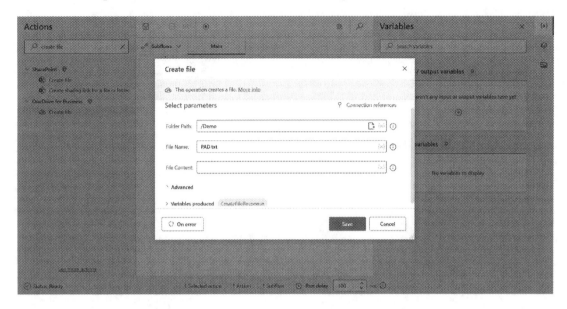

Figure 4-169. *Naming the file*

When you click Save, you will get the error shown in Figure 4-170, because this file is empty.

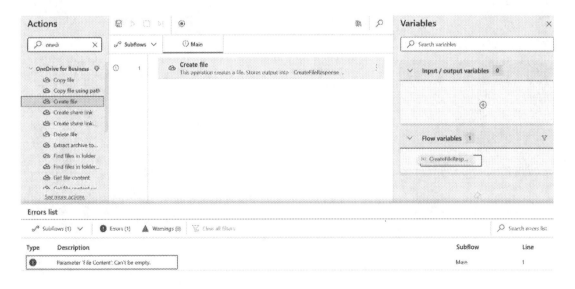

Figure 4-170. *The file cannot be empty*

File contents should be binary in nature. So, you need to convert the input file to binary. Use the convert file to binary data action to do that. See Figure 4-171.

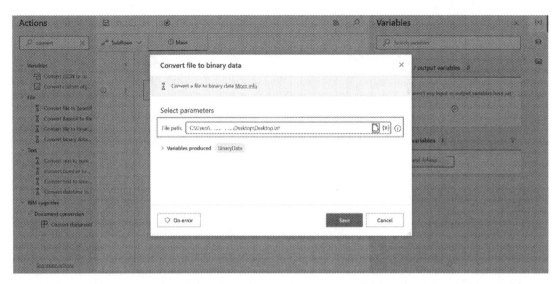

Figure 4-171. *Converting the file to binary data*

The output and the timeout period I added are shown in Figure 4-172.

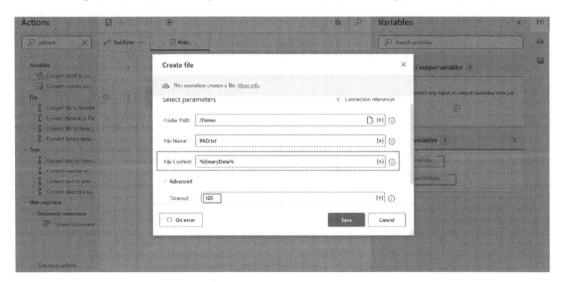

Figure 4-172. *The file contents and settings*

Save and execute the flow, as shown in Figure 4-173.

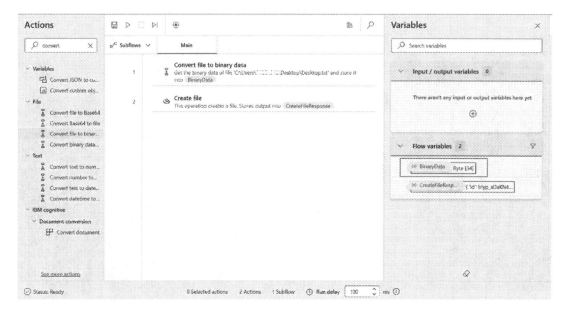

Figure 4-173. *Save and execute the flow*

The flow executed successfully and created a file in OneDrive, as shown in
Figure 4-174.

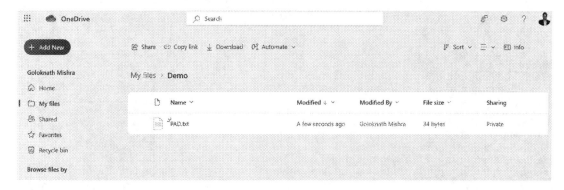

Figure 4-174. *The PAD.txt file was successfully created*

Excel and Email Automation

Now set a new variable to store the path of an Excel file, as shown in Figure 4-175.

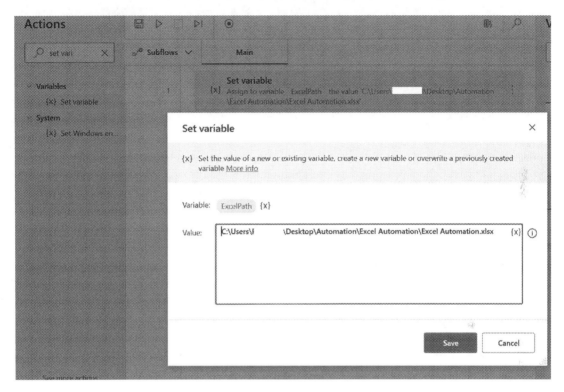

Figure 4-175. *Create a path for an Excel file*

Launch Excel with all the relevant field information, as shown in Figure 4-176.

277

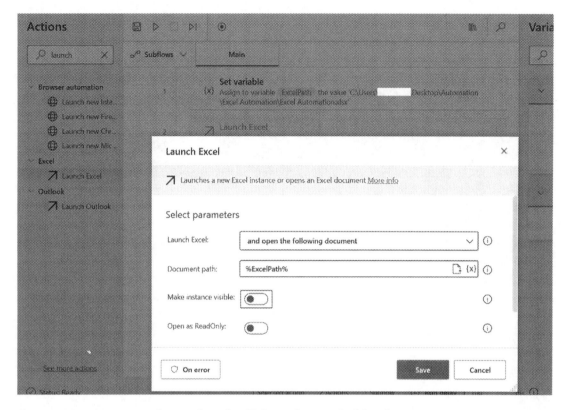

Figure 4-176. *Launch Excel with all the relevant field information*

Set the active Excel worksheet from which the data will be read using Set Active Excel Worksheet, as shown in Figure 4-177.

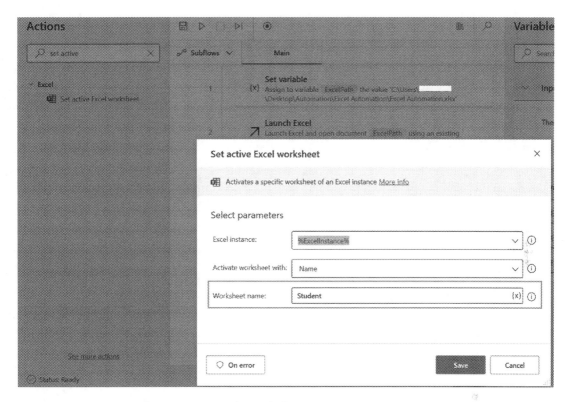

Figure 4-177. *Set the active Excel worksheet*

Then add the Read from Excel Worksheet action, selecting the highlighted fields, as shown in Figure 4-178.

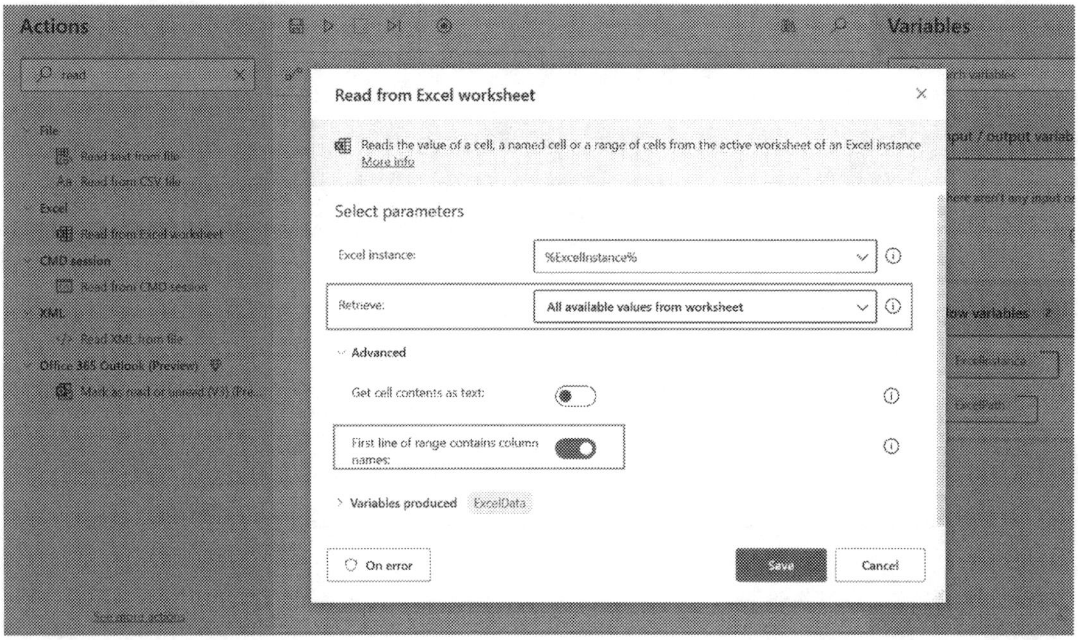

Figure 4-178. *Add the Read from Excel Worksheet action*

Close Excel, as shown in Figure 4-179,

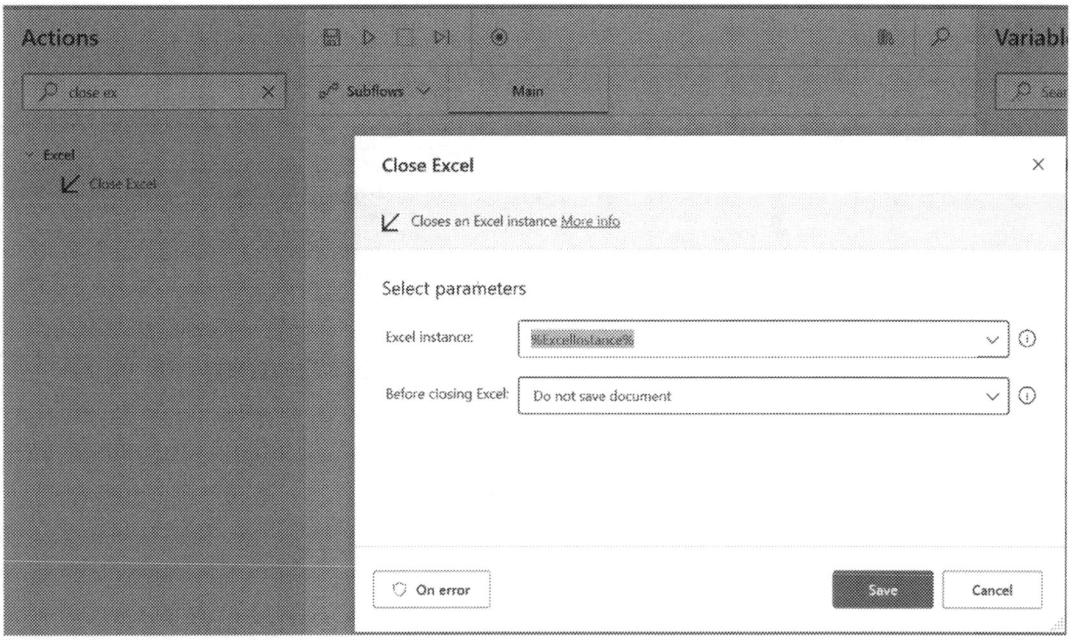

Figure 4-179. *Closing Excel*

Run the flow, as shown in Figure 4-180, which will update the variables.

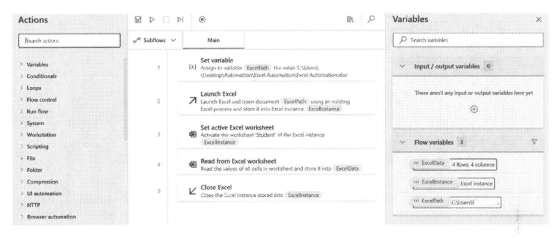

Figure 4-180. *The current flow*

The variable pulled the information from Excel, as shown in Figure 4-181.

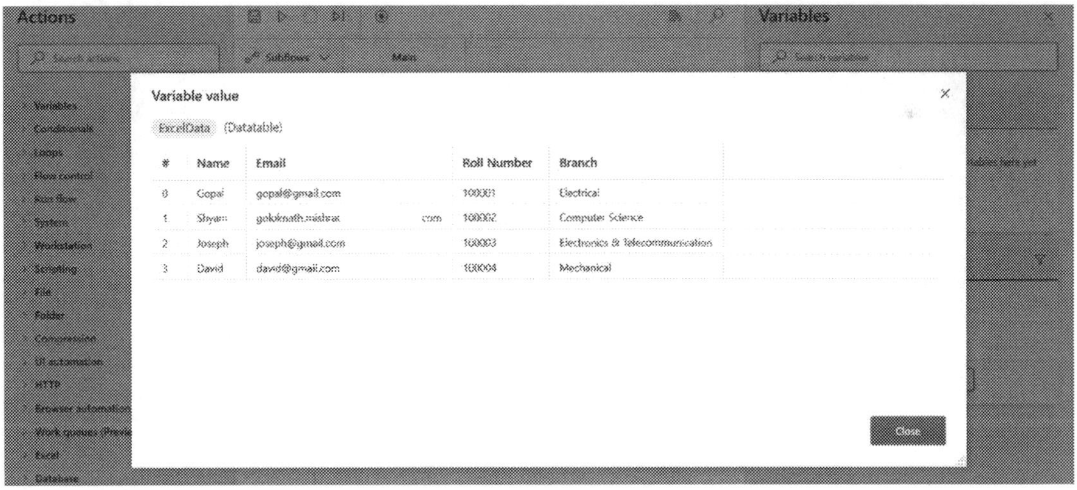

Figure 4-181. *The variable pulled the information from Excel*

Loop though all the email IDs using For Each, as shown in Figure 4-182.

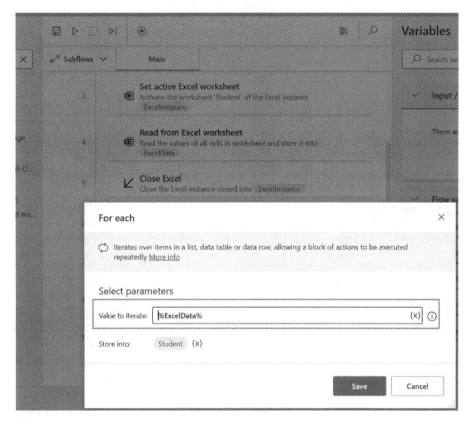

Figure 4-182. *Loop though the email IDs*

Dynamically select the email IDs from Excel. Then use the Send an Email action to dynamically trigger an email. See Figure 4-183.

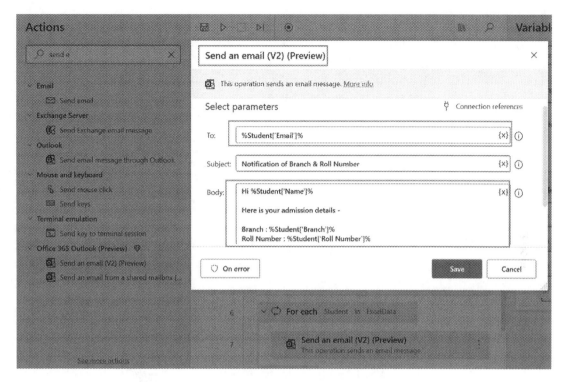

Figure 4-183. *Setting up the email that will be triggered*

Figure 4-184 shows the flow, end to end.

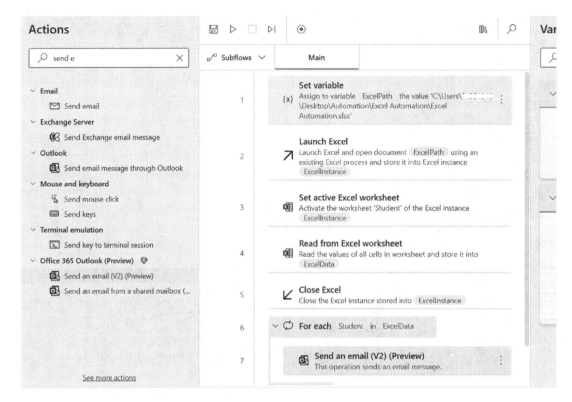

Figure 4-184. *The flow, end to end*

The output is shown in Figure 4-185.

Notification of Branch & Roll Number

ⓘ This message was sent with Low importance

GM Goloknath Mishra
     To: Goloknath Mishra

Hi Shyam Here is your admission details - Branch : Computer Science Roll Number : 100002 Regards, Admin

↩ Reply   ↪ Forward

Figure 4-185. *The output of this action*

Web Automation

To set up web automation, first call the Set Variable action to define the URL, as shown in Figure 4-186.

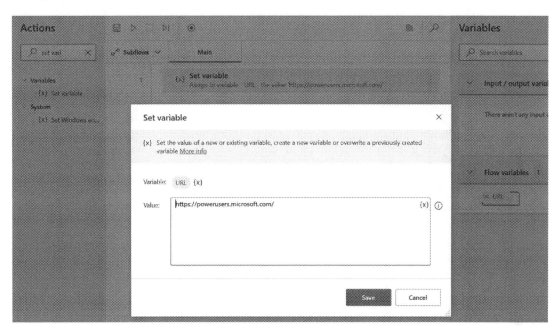

Figure 4-186. *Call the Set Variable action to define the URL*

Then start the recorder by clicking the Record button, as highlighted in Figure 4-187.

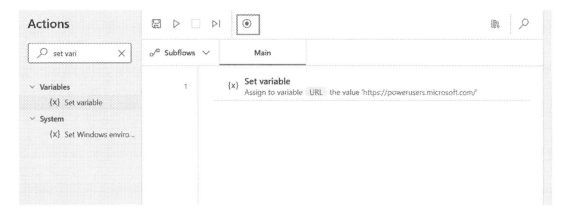

Figure 4-187. *Start the recorder by clicking the Record button*

You can also start recording by choosing Tools ➤ Recorder, as shown in Figure 4-188.

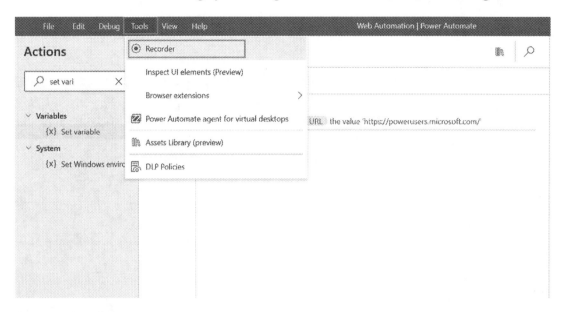

Figure 4-188. *Start the recorder by choosing Tools, Recorder*

When you start the recorder, the window will open in Figure 4-189. Click the Record button to start the recording.

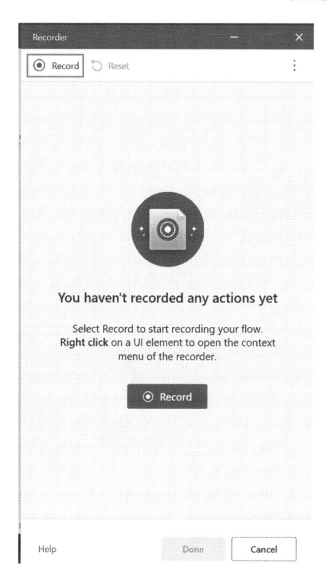

Figure 4-189. *Click the Record button to start recording*

The actions will be captured, as shown in Figure 4-190.

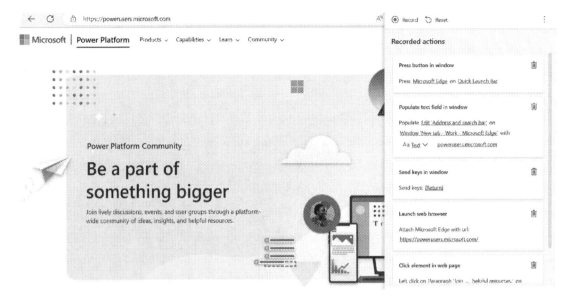

Figure 4-190. *The actions will be captured*

To extract content from the website, follow the steps shown in Figure 4-191.

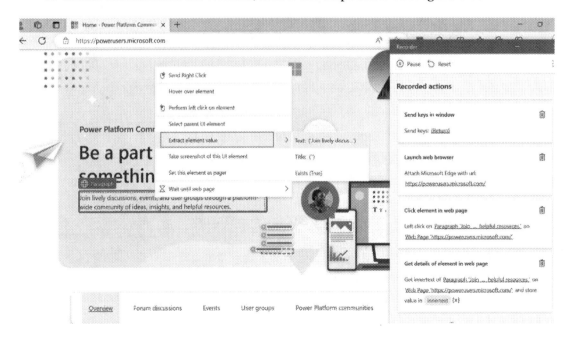

Figure 4-191. *Extracting content from the website*

When you click Done, the script is generated for the recorded action, as shown in Figure 4-192.

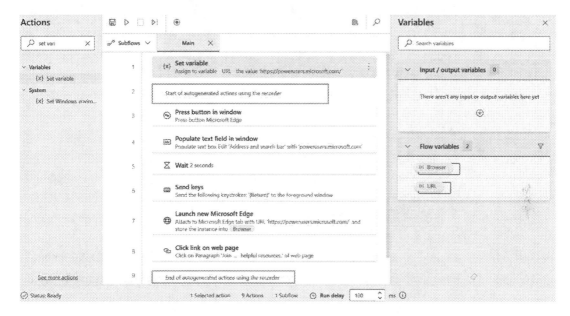

Figure 4-192. *Script for the recorded action*

Refine the necessary steps. If you want to add any UI elements, you can do so using Add UI Elements. See Figure 4-193.

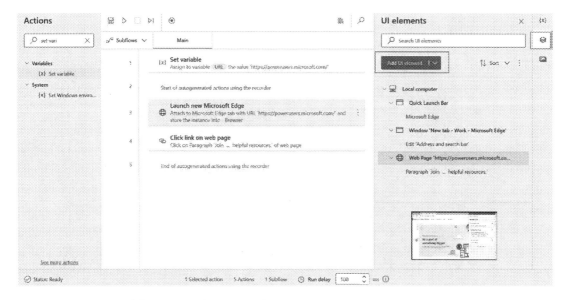

Figure 4-193. *Add any UI elements if you want*

Update the URL in the generated script, as shown in Figure 4-194.

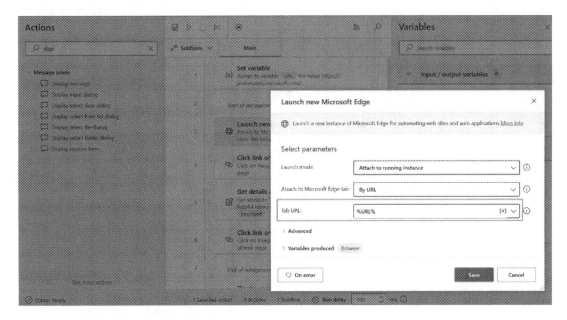

Figure 4-194. *Update the URL*

To display the extracted text, define the Display Message action as %innertext%, as shown in Figure 4-195.

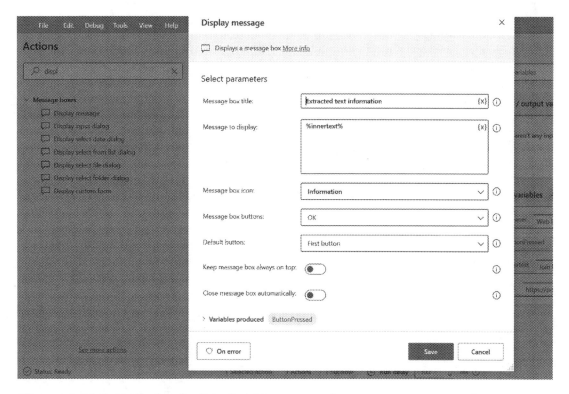

Figure 4-195. *Defining the Display Message action*

The full flow of the web automation is shown in Figure 4-196.

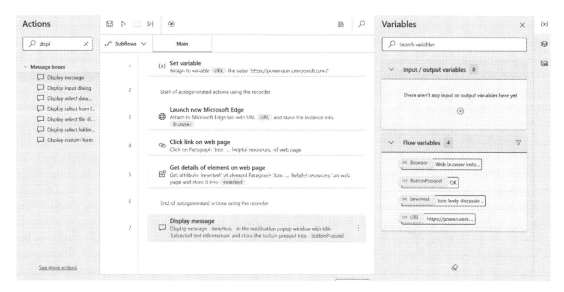

Figure 4-196. *The full flow of the web automation*

When the flow runs, it will extract the text from the website, as shown in Figure 4-197.

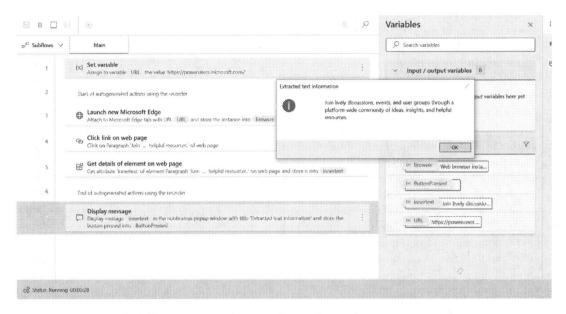

Figure 4-197. *The flow extracts the text from the website*

Now, install the Contoso Invoicing application from the Microsoft documentation and create a desktop shortcut.

Open a new recorder and start recording an operation, such as a data entry process for the application, as shown in Figure 4-198.

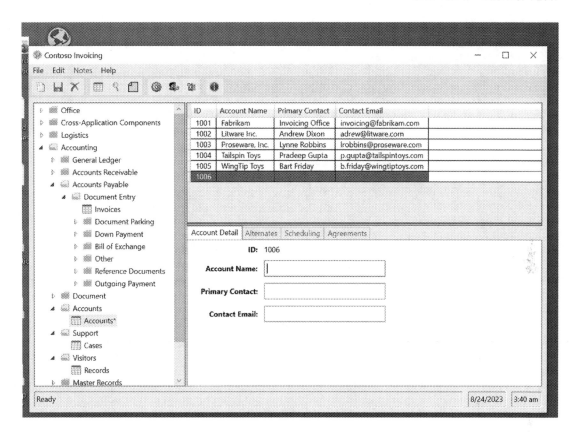

Figure 4-198. *Recording a data entry process for the application*

Record the steps and accept user input using the Display Input Dialog window, as shown in Figure 4-199.

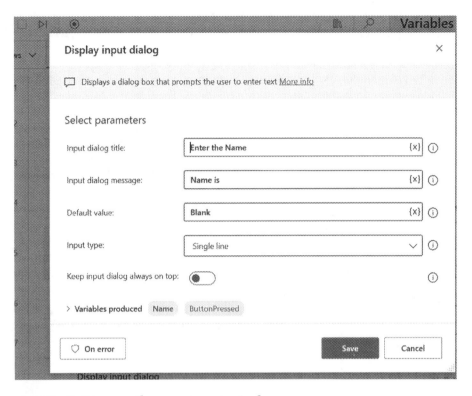

Figure 4-199. *Setting up the user input window*

The final flow after the recording will generate the script, as shown in Figures 4-200 and 4-201.

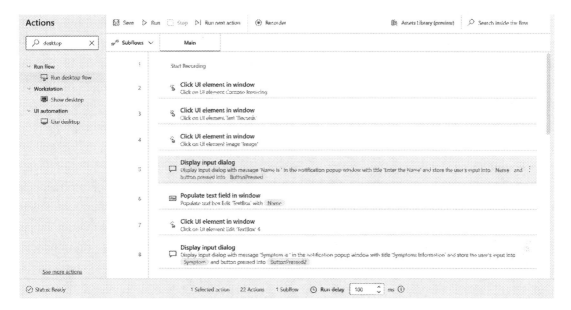

Figure 4-200. *The final flow generates the script*

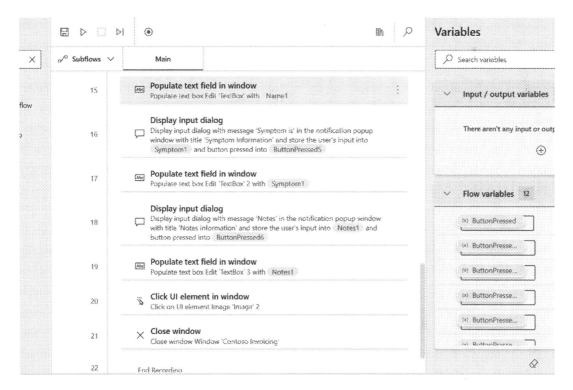

Figure 4-201. *The final flow generates the script*

When you run the flow, it will display a dialog box where users must enter the required data, as shown in Figure 4-202.

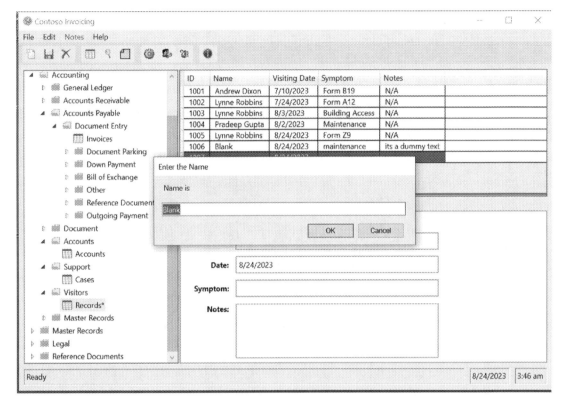

Figure 4-202. *Users must enter the name here*

Summary

This chapter discussed the Desktop Flow, including its architecture. It also explained how to configure different machines and hosted machines with groups.

Answer a few questions based on your learnings:

1. What is the difference between a machine and a hosted machine?

2. What is OCR?

3. What is the difference between a Cloud Flow and a Desktop Flow?

Keywords

Machine

Machine groups

Hosted Machine

Desktop flows

PAD

Attended flows

Unattended flows

Power Automate Desktop

OCR

CHAPTER 5

Business Process Flow

The previous two chapters covered the Cloud Flow and the Desktop Flow, which help with operational process improvement and execution.

This chapter discusses the Business Process flow, which provides visual guidance to get your desired outcome in a streamlined way. The chapter discusses how to create a Business Process Flow, along with its features and functionalities.

What Is a Business Process Flow?

Business Process Flows provide a visual guide for people to see the current progress of the work. Typically, Business Process Flows define the steps that people need to follow to get a desired outcome in a streamlined way.

Business Process Flows define these stages and steps, which are displayed in a control at the top of the form. The following standard tables can also use Business Process Flows:

- Account
- Appointment
- Campaign
- Campaign Activity
- Campaign Response
- Competitor
- Contact
- Email
- Entitlement
- Fax

© Goloknath Mishra 2023
G. Mishra, *Deep Dive into Power Automate*, https://doi.org/10.1007/978-1-4842-9732-2_5

- Case

- Invoice

- Lead

- Letter

- Marketing List

- Opportunity

- Phone Call

- Product

- Price List Item

- Quote

- Recurring Appointment

- Sales Literature

- Social Activity

- Order

- User

- Task

- Team

All custom tables can use Business Process Flows. To enable a custom table for a Business Process Flow, select the Business Process Flows check box (columns will be created) in the table definition.

Tip   You can't disable a Business Process Flow once it's been enabled for any custom entity.

The limitations of Business Process Flows are as follows:

- There is a maximum of ten activated Business Process Flow processes per table.

- Each process can contain maximum 30 stages.

- Multi-table processes can contain a maximum of five tables.

- If a solution includes a Business Process Flow table, that table must be manually added to the solution before you export it. Otherwise, the Business Process Flow table won't be included in the solution package.

You can use Business Process Flows offline if the following conditions are met:

- The Business Process Flow is used from a Power Apps app.

- The Power Apps app is enabled for offline use.

- The Business Process Flow has a single table.

Standard Business Process Flow

The "Phone to Case Process" Business Process Flow is a standard Business Process Flow that's created when you create a model-driven app using the case entity. Choose Identify ➤ Research ➤ Resolve, as shown in Figure 5-1.

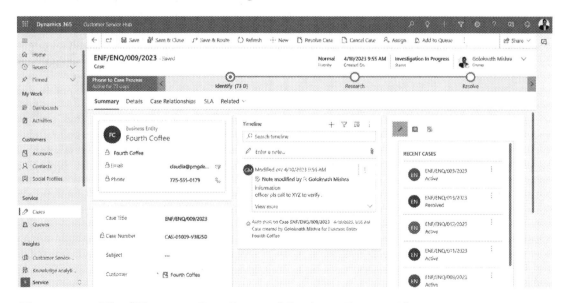

Figure 5-1. *The "Phone to Case Process" Business Process Flow*

The "Lead to Opportunity" Business Process Flow is a standard Business Process Flow that's created when you create a model-driven app using the lead entity. You do so by choosing Qualify ➤ Develop ➤ Propose ➤ Close, as shown in Figure 5-2.

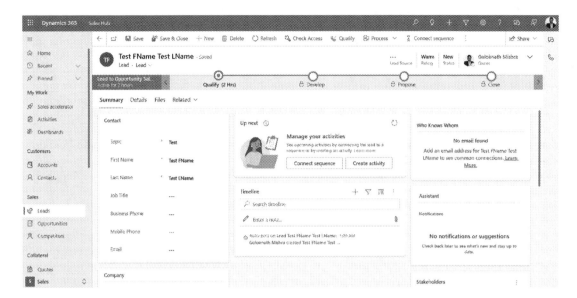

Figure 5-2. *The "Lead to Opportunity" Business Process Flow*

The "Sales Process" Business Process Flow is a standard Business Process Flow that's created when you create a model-driven app using the opportunity entity. You do this by choosing Qualify ➤ Develop ➤ Propose ➤ Close, as shown in Figure 5-3.

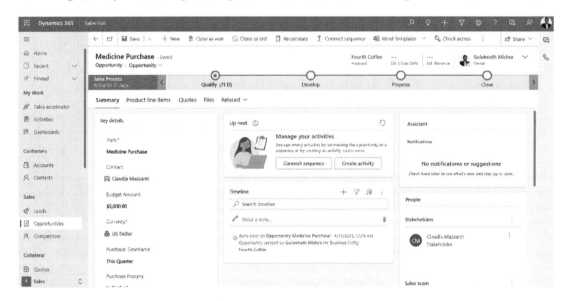

Figure 5-3. *The "Sales Process" Business Process Flow*

Creating a Business Process Flow

Always create a Business Process Flow in the solution so that it will be easy to migrate the solution from one environment to another. First create a blank solution by navigating to Solution and clicking +New, as shown in Figure 5-4.

Figure 5-4.   *Creating a blank solution*

Navigate to +New ➤ Automation ➤ Process ➤ Business Process Flow, as shown in Figure 5-5.

Figure 5-5.   *Creating a Business Process Flow*

The Campaign table doesn't have a Business Process Flow, so let's add a Business Process Flow to it. See Figure 5-6.

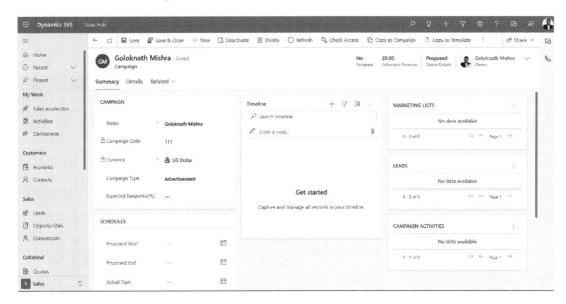

Figure 5-6. *Adding a Business Process Flow*

Enter the name and table name on which Business Process Flow will be built, as shown in Figure 5-7.

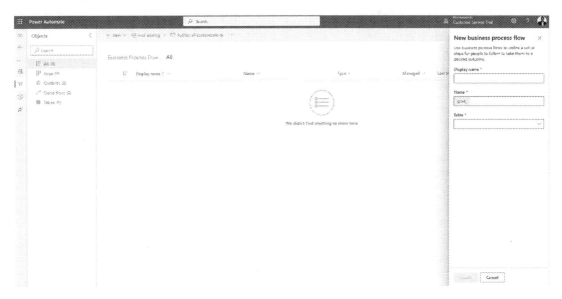

Figure 5-7. *Enter a name and table name*

As highlighted in Figure 5-8, fill in the required details and click Create.

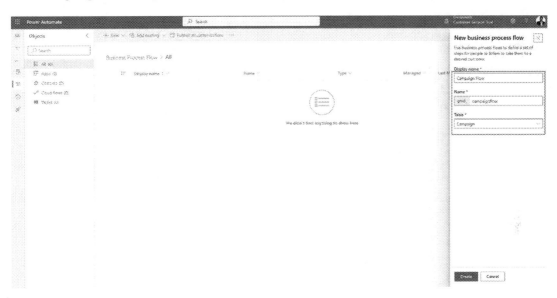

Figure 5-8. *Fill in the required details and click Create*

The system will display a stage with components, as shown in Figure 5-9.

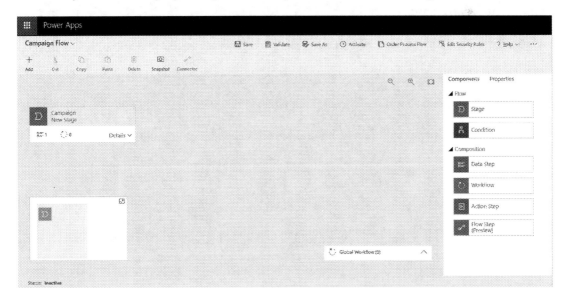

Figure 5-9. *The stage shows the components of the table*

Click Properties to change the stage name and then click Apply, as shown in Figure 5-10.

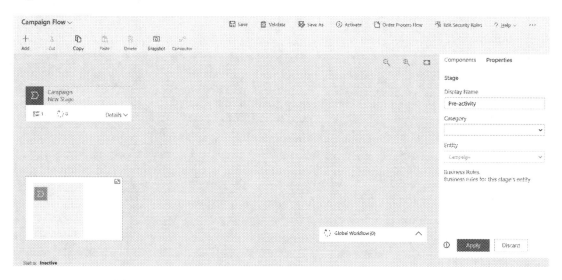

Figure 5-10. *Changing the stage name*

Select a Stage from the Components list and drag it to the + sign, as shown in Figure 5-11.

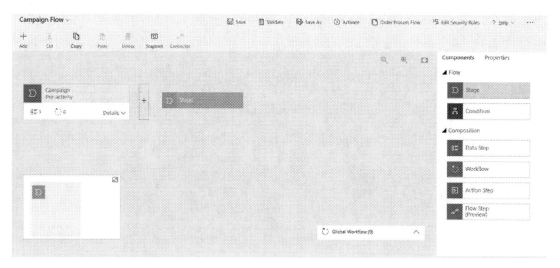

Figure 5-11. *Adding a stage*

Similarly add all the other stages, as shown in Figure 5-12.

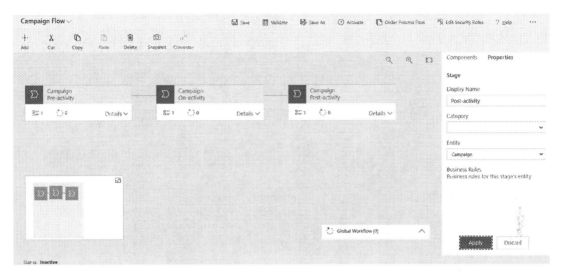

Figure 5-12. *Adding multiple stages*

Then add steps for each stage by selecting the Data field and the Step name, as shown in Figure 5-13.

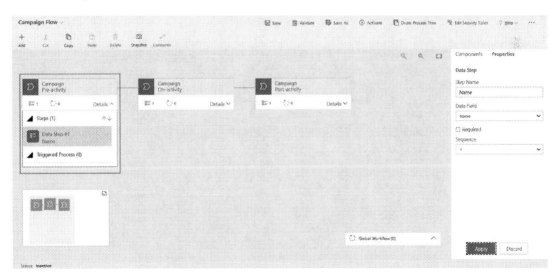

Figure 5-13. *Select the Data field to add steps*

To add an additional step, drag Data Step to the + sign on the Data stage. See Figure 5-14.

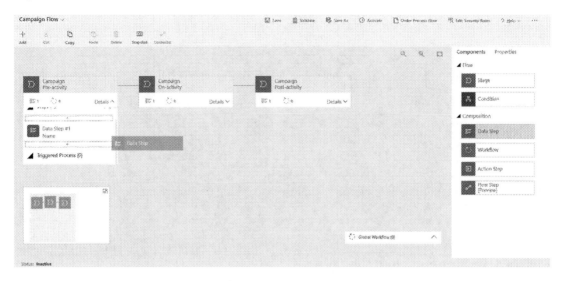

Figure 5-14. *Drag Data Step to the + sign on the Data stage*

Fill in the step name and the data field. Then select the Required checkbox if you want to make the step mandatory. See Figure 5-15.

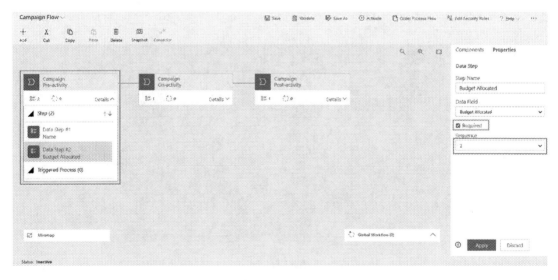

Figure 5-15. *Making the step mandatory*

Follow this same process to add more steps as needed. See Figure 5-16.

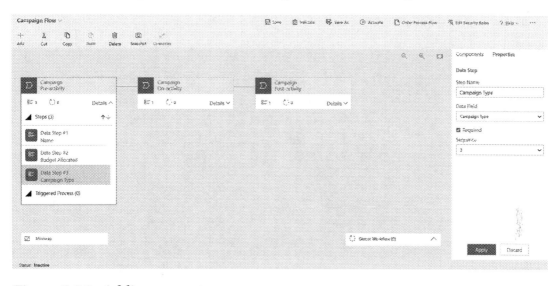

Figure 5-16. *Adding more steps*

Similarly, add steps to stage 2, as shown in Figure 5-17.

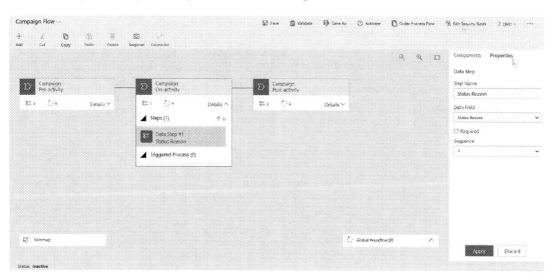

Figure 5-17. *Adding steps to stage 2*

Add steps to stage 3, as shown in Figure 5-18.

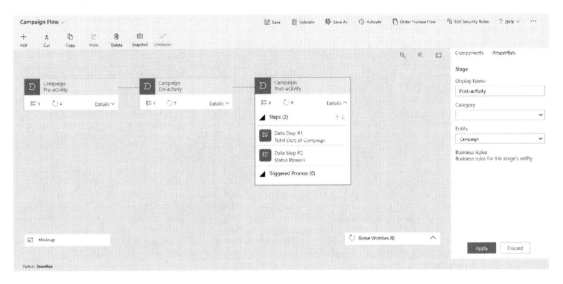

Figure 5-18. *Adding steps to stage 3*

You can add another table as well. As shown in Figure 5-19, Campaign Response has been added to Campaign. Click Save followed by Validate and Activate.

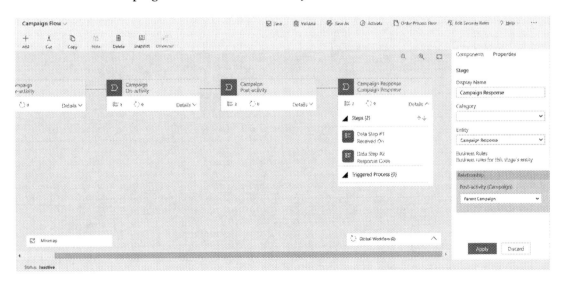

Figure 5-19. *Adding the Campaign Response table*

Create a solution of model-driven app that contains the campaign and add the newly created process to the solution, as shown in Figure 5-20.

Figure 5-20. *Creating a model-driven app that contains the campaign*

Open the model-driven app and click Edit to add the Business Process Flow and display it on top of the Campaign table. See Figure 5-21.

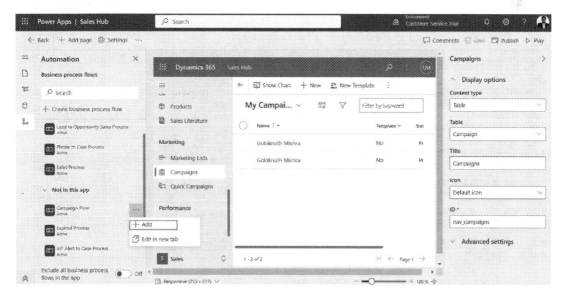

Figure 5-21. *Adding the new Business Process Flow to the Campaign table*

As shown in Figure 5-22, the campaign flow has been added to the model-driven app.

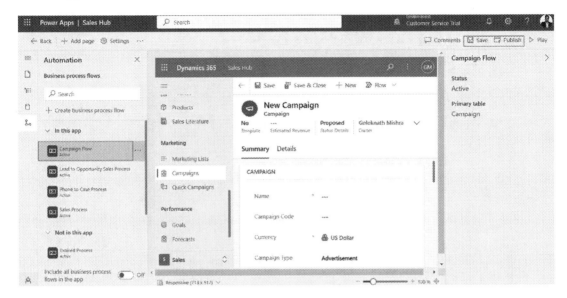

Figure 5-22. *The new campaign has been added to the model-driven app*

The classic UI you can use to add Business Process Flows is as shown in Figure 5-23.

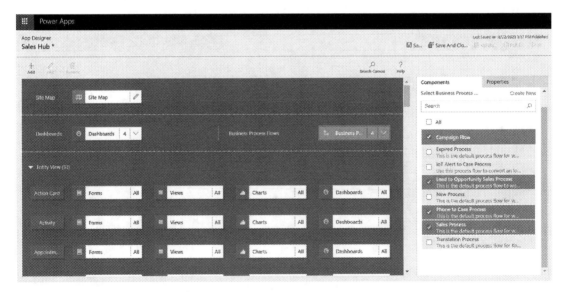

Figure 5-23. *The classic UI*

Click Save and Publish to see the Business Process Flow on top of the Campaign table, as shown in Figure 5-24.

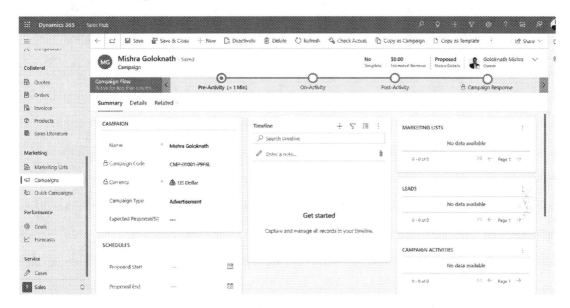

Figure 5-24. *The Business Process Flow is on top of the Campaign table*

Click each next stage to move ahead. See Figures 5-25 through 5-28.

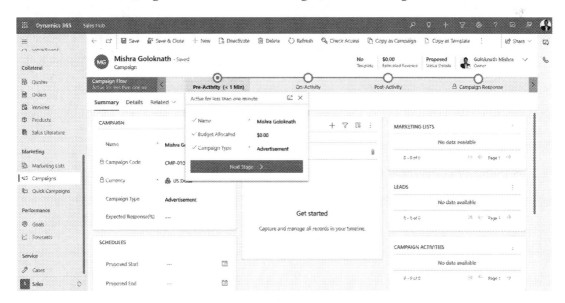

Figure 5-25. *Click through each stage to move ahead*

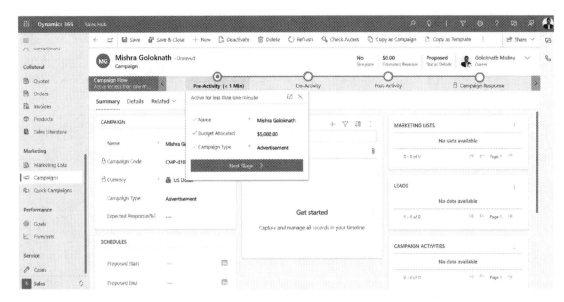

Figure 5-26. *Click through each stage to move ahead*

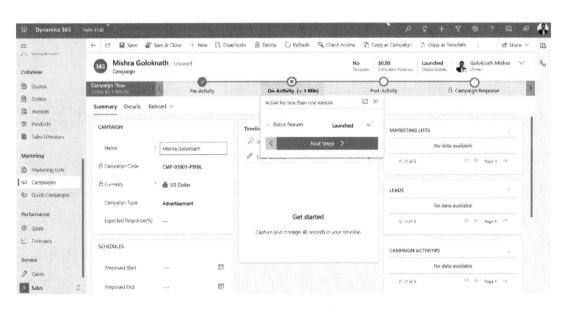

Figure 5-27. *Click through each stage to move ahead*

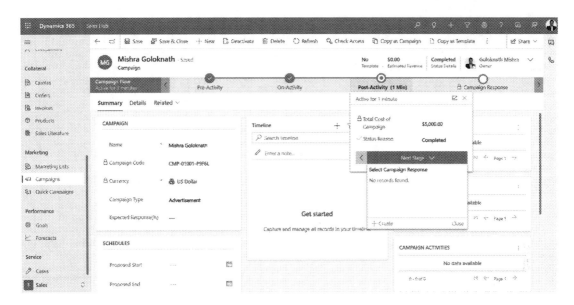

Figure 5-28. *Click through each stage to move ahead*

As you click ahead in each stage, the Business Process Flow acts as a visual indicator at the top. In the last stage, click Finish, as shown in Figure 5-29.

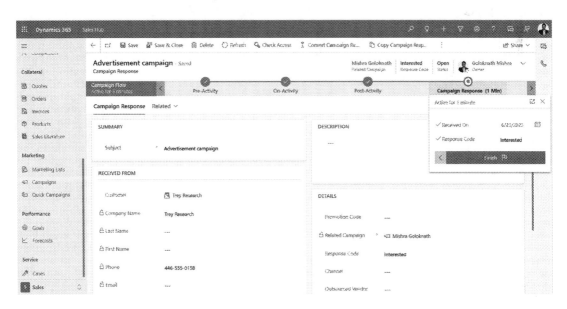

Figure 5-29. *Click Finish*

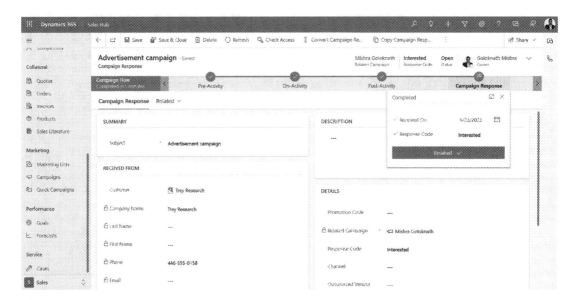

Figure 5-30. *Finishing the process*

Switch and Conditional Branching of Business Process Flows

There is a standard Phone to Case Process BPF (Business Process Flow), but you can also build a second BPF for this. See Figure 5-31.

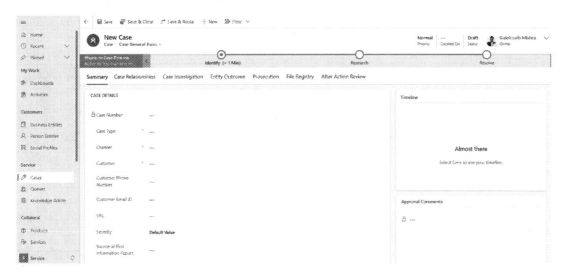

Figure 5-31. *Building a second BPF*

Name the second Business Process Flow Create to Closure, as shown in Figure 5-32.

Figure 5-32. *The second BPF is called Create to Closure*

Enter the steps for the first stage, Case Create, as shown in Figure 5-33.

Figure 5-33. *The first stage is called Case Create*

To add conditional branching, drag the condition component to the desired place between the stages. See Figure 5-34.

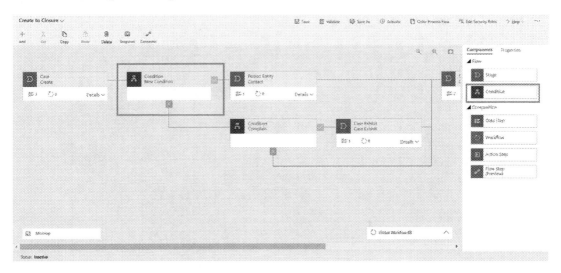

Figure 5-34. *Adding a condition*

Let's add a condition: If the case type complains, Case Exhibit will display and fill in the information. See Figure 5-35.

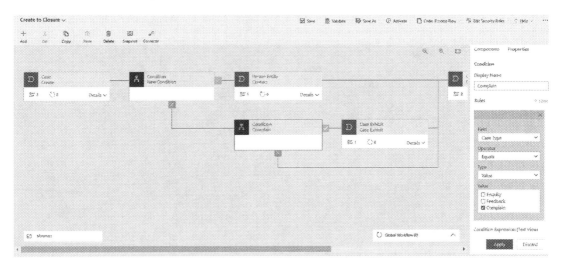

Figure 5-35. *Adding a condition*

Executing Workflows and Power Automate Flows from BPFs

You can execute Power Automate flows from a BPF by adding a flow step, as shown in Figure 5-36.

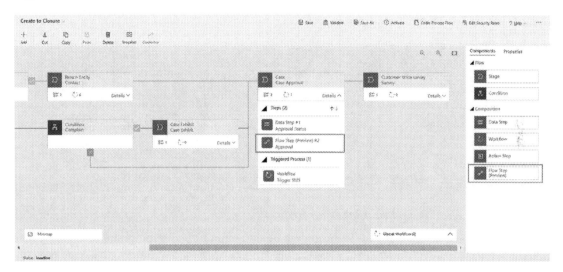

Figure 5-36. *Adding a flow step*

Then fill in the required information, including a name and flow name. In the current case, it's Approval Flow, as shown in Figure 5-37.

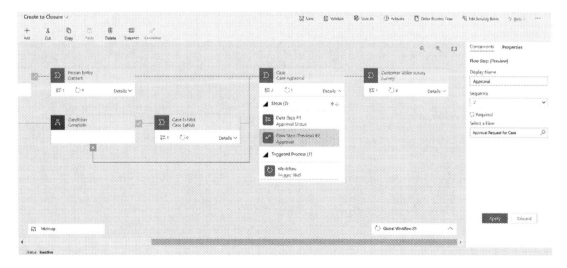

Figure 5-37. *Provide the required information*

You can execute the workflow from the BPF by adding a workflow step, as shown in Figure 5-38.

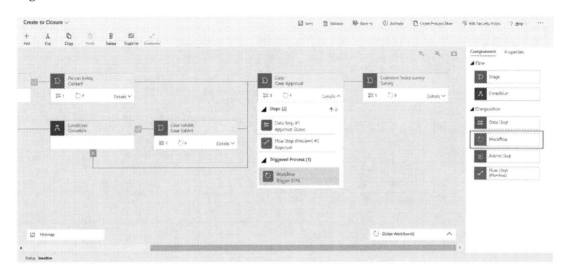

Figure 5-38. *Executing the workflow from a BPF*

Based on the current use case, you need to trigger SMS through the workflow, which should be on-demand in nature. See Figure 5-39.

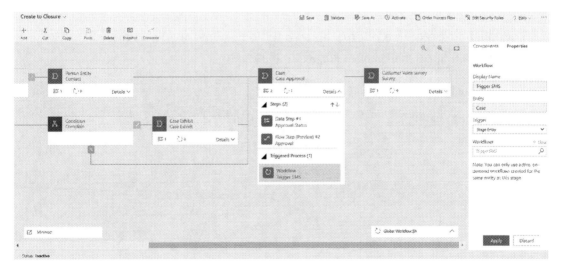

Figure 5-39. *Triggering SMS through the workflow*

When the BPF is ready, click Save and Validate, as shown in Figure 5-40. Then click the Activate button.

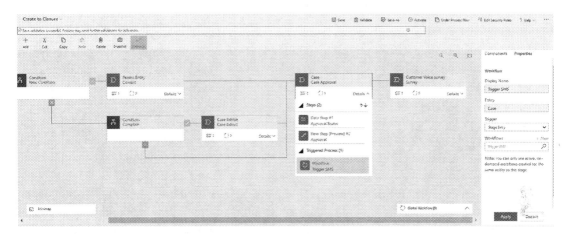

Figure 5-40. *Choose Save and Validate*

Renaming, Ordering, and Assigning Security Roles to BPFs

You can assign BPFs based on security roles, by using the Edit Security Role feature shown in Figure 5-41.

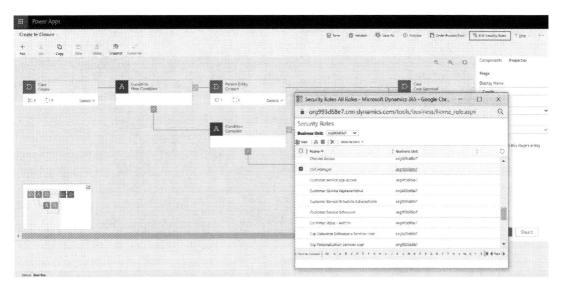

Figure 5-41. *The Edit Security Role feature*

Now Case has two Business Process Flows, so you can select the order of the BPFs using the Order Process Flow button. See Figure 5-42.

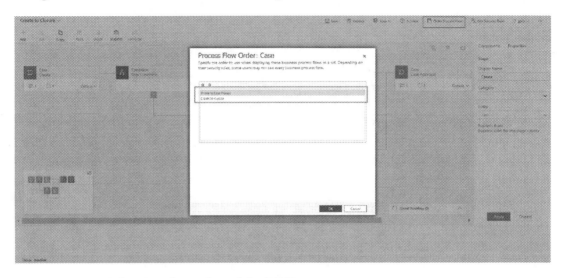

Figure 5-42. *Selecting the order of the BPFs*

You can rename the BPF by expanding the workflow, as shown in Figure 5-43.

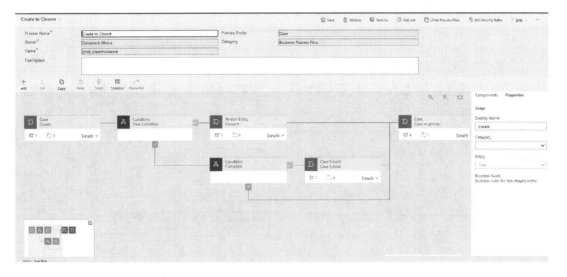

Figure 5-43. *Renaming your BPFs*

Then click Validate and activate the flow, as shown in Figure 5-44.

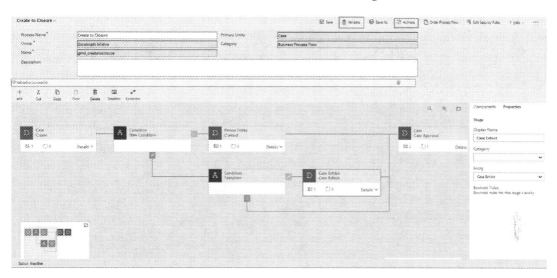

Figure 5-44.   *Activating the flow*

Once the BPF is activated, you will see the Deactivate button instead of the Activate button. See Figure 5-45.

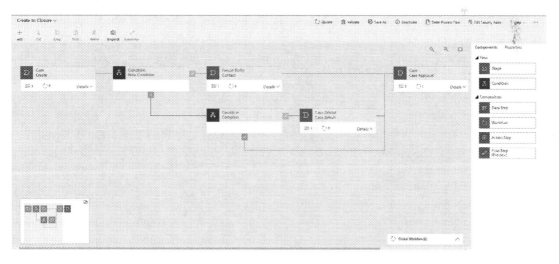

Figure 5-45.   *The Deactivate button replaces the Activate button*

Add the new Business Process Flow to the app, as shown in Figure 5-46.

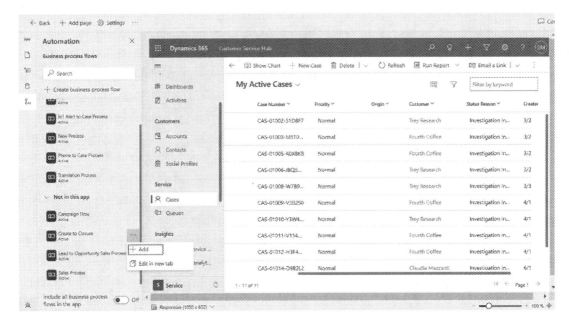

Figure 5-46. *Adding the new Business Process Flow to the app*

Choose Save and Publish so that the changes will take effect. See Figure 5-47.

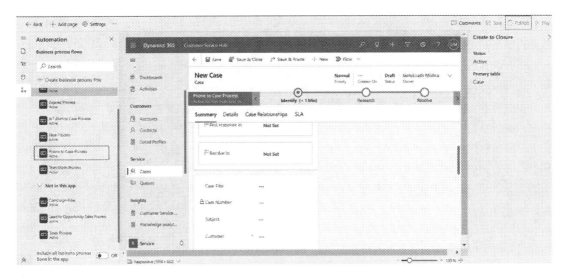

Figure 5-47. *Choosing Save and Publish*

Next, navigate to the Case form it displays the out-of-the-box for the Phone to Case process. See Figure 5-48.

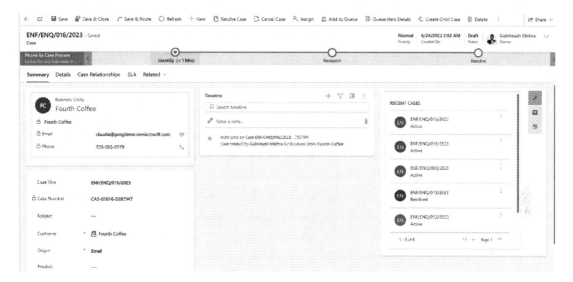

Figure 5-48. *Out-of-the-box the Phone to Case process form*

Then click Process and choose Switch Process, as shown in Figure 5-49.

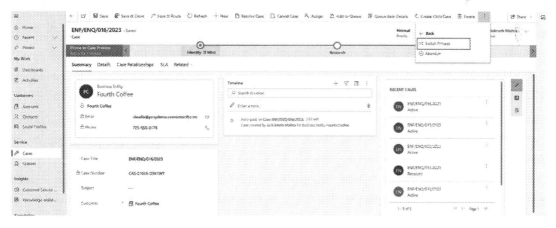

Figure 5-49. *Choose Switch Process here*

A dialog will pop up showing both flows to switch, as shown in Figure 5-50.

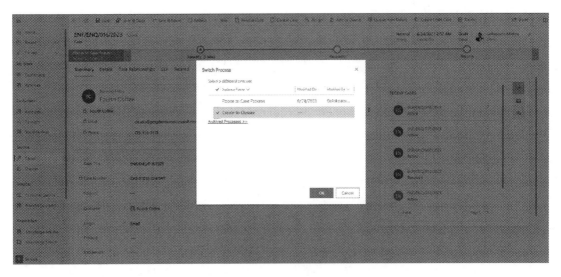

Figure 5-50. *The flows that will be switched are shown here*

Click OK to switch the BPF; the second BPF will display. See Figure 5-51.

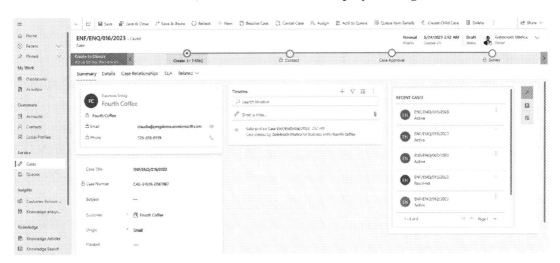

Figure 5-51. *The second BPF now appears*

Use Figures 5-52 through 5-58 to complete each stage.

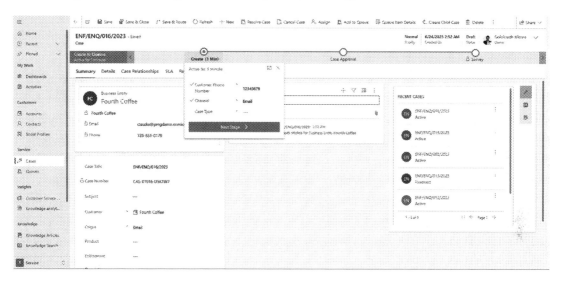

Figure 5-52. *Complete each stage*

When the Case Type is Enquiry, it displays the case approval stage, as shown in Figure 5-53.

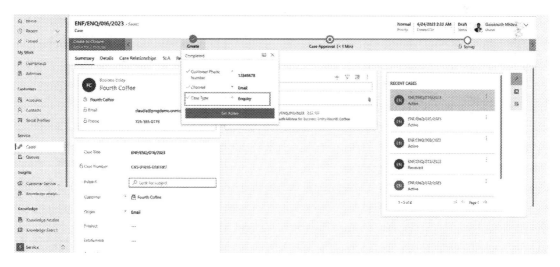

Figure 5-53. *The case type is Enquiry*

When the case type is Complain, the BPF asks to enter the Case Exhibit, as shown in Figure 5-54.

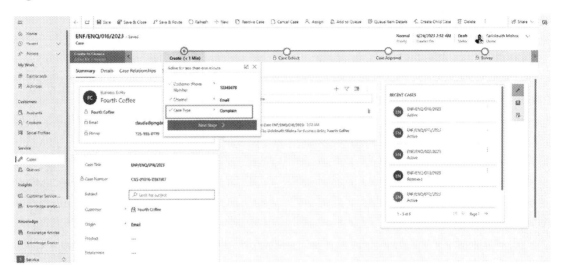

Figure 5-54. *The case type is Complain*

Click Next Stage to enter the case exhibit. See Figure 5-55.

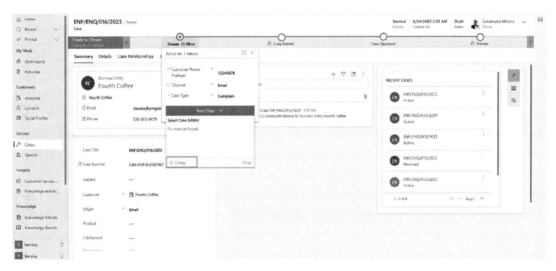

Figure 5-55. *Click Next Stage to enter the case exhibit*

Enter the case exhibit, as shown in Figure 5-56.

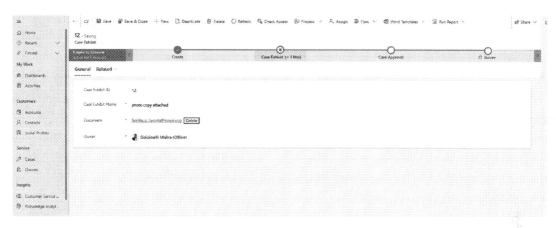

Figure 5-56. *Entering the case exhibit*

Click Next in the Case Exhibit stage. The BPF will bring it back to the case form for approval. Click Run Flow to run the approval flow. See Figure 5-57.

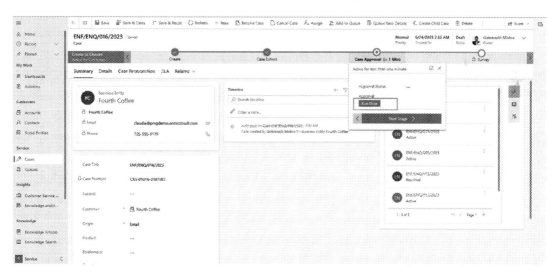

Figure 5-57. *Run Flow approval*

Once the approval flow runs successfully, the approval status will change to approved. See Figure 5-58.

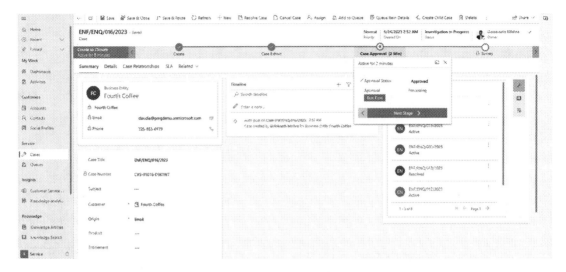

Figure 5-58. *The approval status changes to approved*

This is how you can benefit from a Business Process Flow.

Summary

This chapter discussed how to create Business Process Flows, how to create Power Automate flows in a Business Process Flow, how to use branching in Business Process Flows, and how to add on-demand workflows to a Business Process Flow.

Answer a few questions based on your learnings:

1.   Each process can contain how many stages?

2.   How do you add branching to a Business Process Flow (BPF)?

Keywords

BPF

Branching

Business Process Flow

Workflow

CHAPTER 6

Process Advisor

Previous chapters explained what automation is, what RPA is, and what Power Automate is. You also learned about the different types of flows—Cloud Flows, Desktop Flows, and Business Process Flows. Many businesses still find it difficult to know when they need to do automation and what the suitable criteria are for automation. This chapter covers when and where flow utilization is required and how to optimize the flow.

Using Process Advisor

Process Advisor allows you to find underperforming business processes that need to be optimized. Process Advisor offers the following capabilities to improve process efficiency:

- Task mining
- Process mining

You must satisfy the following prerequisites before you can begin using Process Advisor:

- You should have Microsoft Dataverse along with an environment in Microsoft Power Platform.

- You should have the Environment Maker security role in the Power Platform Admin Center.

- For task mining, download the Power Automate desktop application.

- For process mining, download the Microsoft Minit desktop application.

© Goloknath Mishra 2023
G. Mishra, *Deep Dive into Power Automate*, https://doi.org/10.1007/978-1-4842-9732-2_6

Process Mining vs. Task Mining

In this section, you learn the differences between process mining and task mining. After that, you will dive deeply into both of these topics. Table 6-1 compares process mining to task mining.

Table 6-1. *Process Mining vs Task Mining*

Process Mining	Task Mining
Discovers inefficiencies in organization-wide processes	Discovers tasks happening on the desktop
Enables you to gain a deep understanding of your processes using event log files by system of recording. Displays a process map with data and parameters to recognize performance issues.	Provides insight by recording and collecting user action data to see how processes are performed, find common mistakes while performing tasks, and identify tasks that can be automated.
Process-oriented	User-oriented
See the actual steps needed to perform your organization's operation process and remove any guesswork.	Understand what employees do when performing each task on their desktops.
Save time and money by optimizing processes.	Identify and eliminate unnecessary actions in process tasks.
Detect noncompliant processes and/or tasks.	Identify the most common actions through user interactions.
Discover automation opportunities.	Automate tasks that will accelerate processes and reduce human errors.

The next section takes a closer look at process mining and the circumstances under which you might want to use it.

Process Mining

Process mining in Process Advisor is a valuable tool for businesses seeking to improve their operational efficiency and make better decisions. The benefits of process mining can be classified as follows:

- Improves operational efficiency

- Enhances customer experience

- Optimizes resources

- Ensures compliance

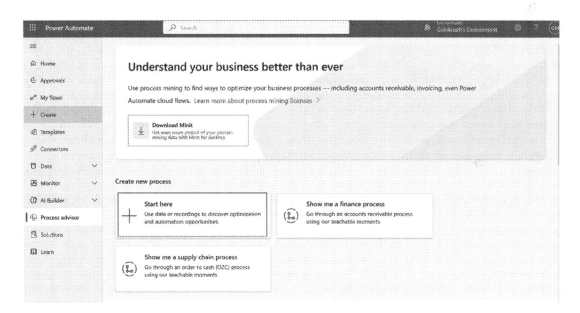

Figure 6-1.   *Click Start Here to begin process mining*

Click Start Here, as highlighted in Figure 6-1, to start a new process.

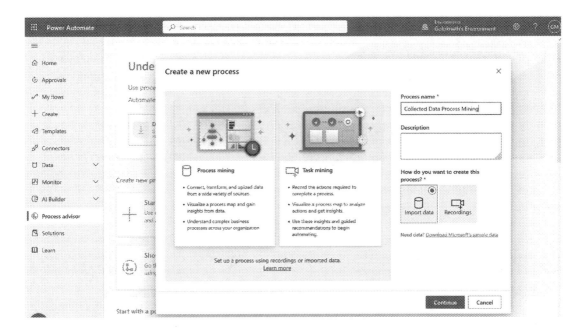

Figure 6-2. *Choose Import Data here*

A dialog will appear, as shown in Figure 6-2. Select the Import Data button to create the process and then name it. Then click Continue.

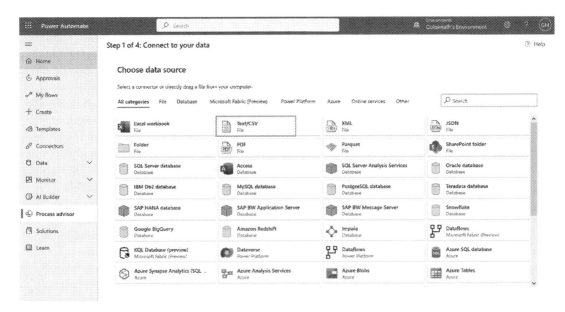

Figure 6-3. *Choose a data source (Text/CSV in this case)*

The system will display categories from which you choose the source. In this example case, the source is a CSV file, so choose Text/CSV, as shown in Figure 6-3.

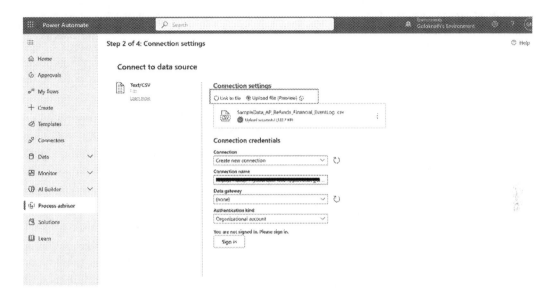

Figure 6-4. *Choose Upload File to upload the CSV file*

Next select Upload File to upload the collected data CSV (see Figure 6-5). Then click Sign-In.

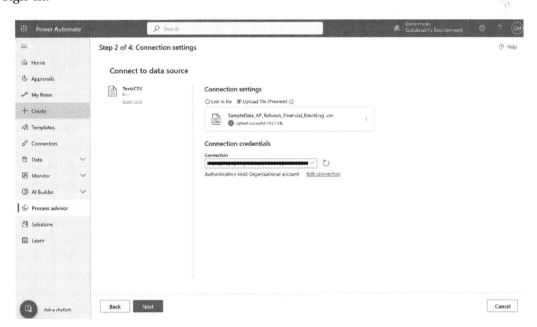

Figure 6-5. *Connecting to the data source*

After the sign-in is successful, a connection will be established, as shown in
Figure 6-5. Click Next, as shown in Figure 6-6.

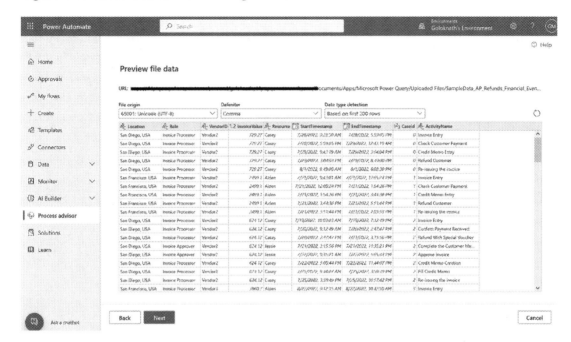

Figure 6-6. *Click Next*

Process Advisor will display the preview file data in a Power Query window, as shown
in Figure 6-7. Click Next if you want to transform the data.

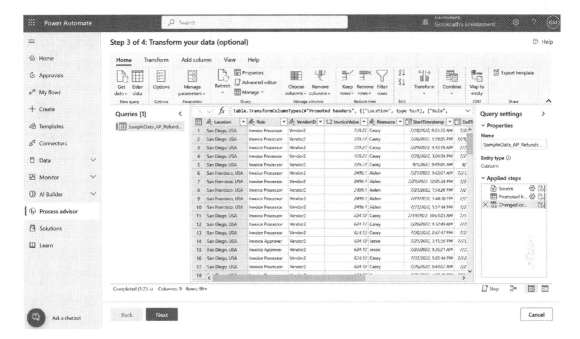

Figure 6-7. *The preview file is shown in a Power Query window*

Next, you need to map the data and then click Save and Analyze, as shown in Figure 6-8.

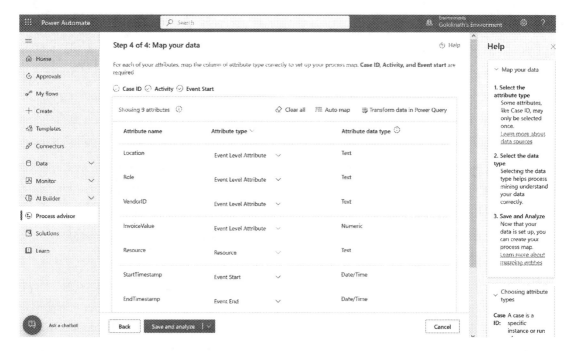

Figure 6-8. *Mapping your data*

The system will start analyzing and will prepare a report, as shown in Figure 6-9.

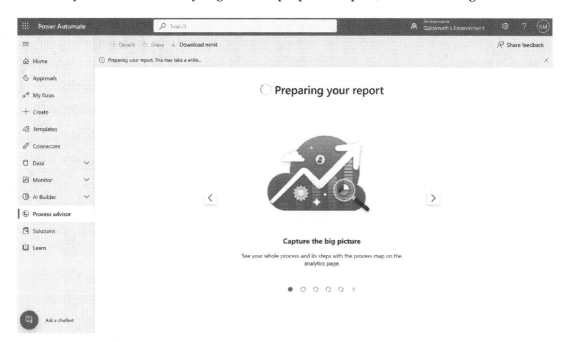

Figure 6-9. *Preparing your report*

A summary of the report is shown in Figure 6-10.

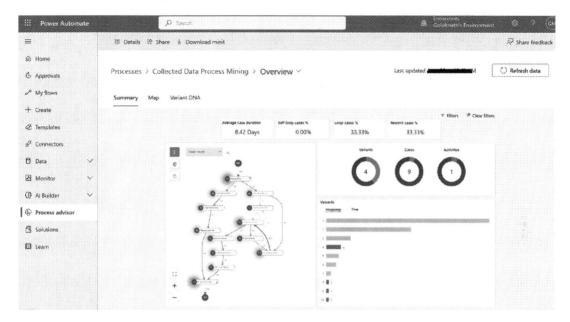

Figure 6-10. *A summary of your report appears*

Figure 6-11 shows the Map data of the report, which you can see when you click Map. If you click Variant DNA, you'll see the report shown in Figure 6-12.

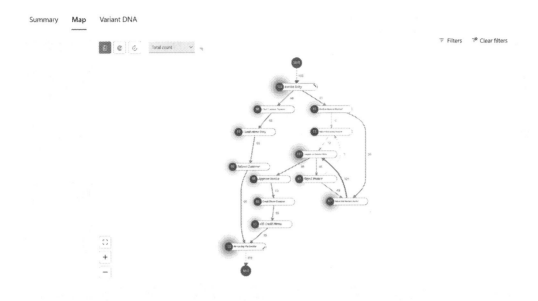

Figure 6-11. *Map data*

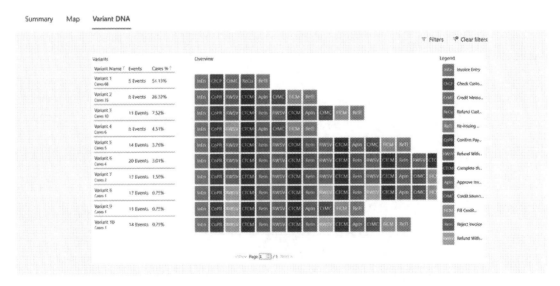

Figure 6-12. *The Variant DNA map*

You can also click on Summary to see a summary of the process, as shown in Figure 6-13.

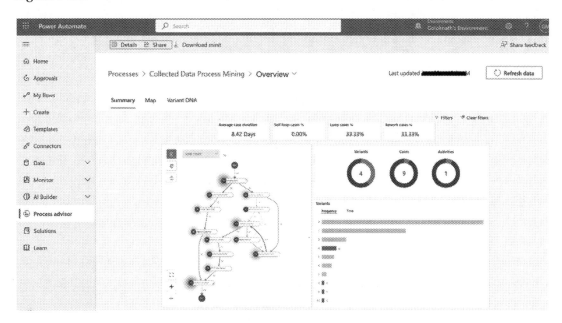

Figure 6-13. *Summary of the process*

You can click Details to see the details of the process, as shown in Figure 6-14.

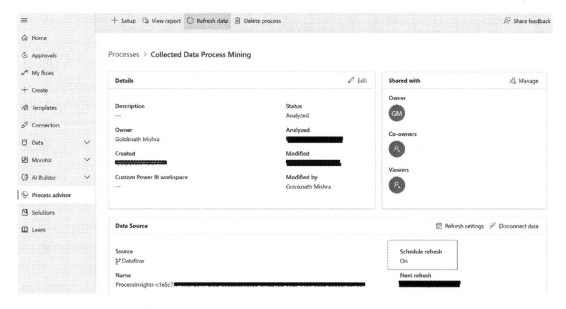

Figure 6-14. *Details of the process*

You can schedule the refresh by clicking Refresh Settings (see Figure 6-15). You can also click the Disconnect Data button to disconnect the data and click Setup to add the data again.

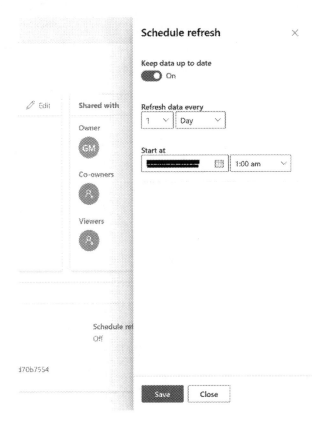

Figure 6-15. *Scheduling a refresh*

Figure 6-16 shows how to install the Minit desktop.

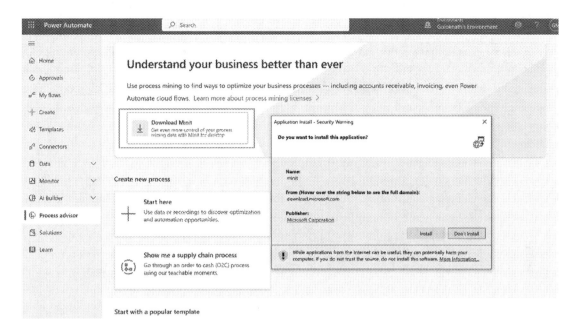

Figure 6-16. *Installing the Minit desktop*

Click Next Step to continue the installation, as shown in Figure 6-17.

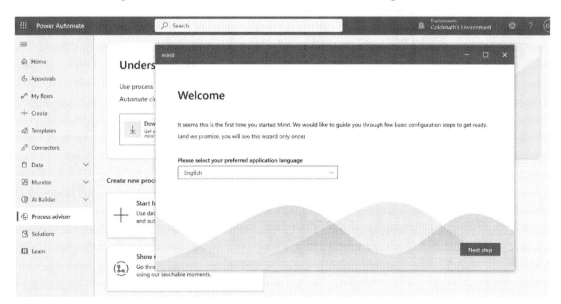

Figure 6-17. *Select a language when installing Minit*

Select a data storage location and then click Next Step, as shown in Figure 6-18.

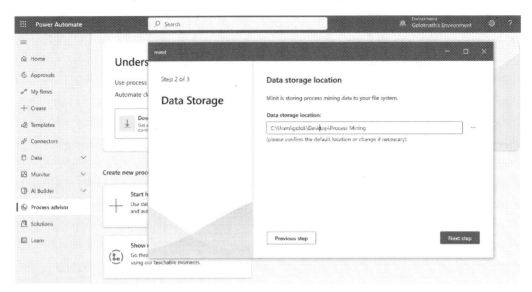

Figure 6-18. *Add or confirm the data storage location for Minit*

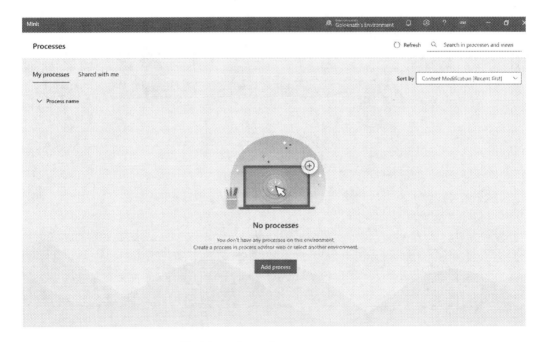

Figure 6-19. *Minit is installed but doesn't contain any processes*

After you install Minit and authenticate it with your credentials, the Minit desktop will look like Figure 6-19, because it doesn't contain any processes.

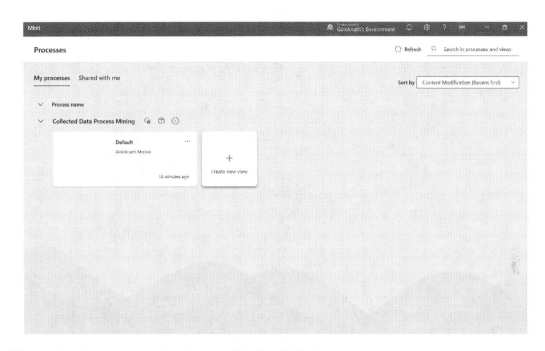

Figure 6-20. *A process has been added to Minit*

After you create a process and add it to Minit, your desktop will look similar to Figure 6-20.

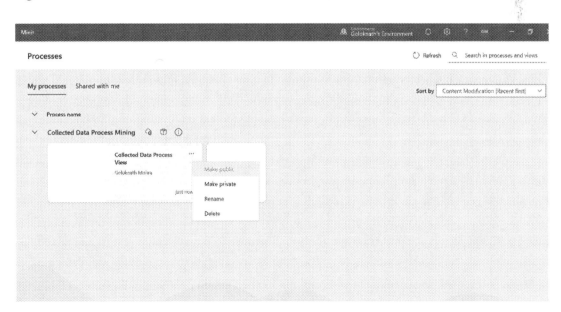

Figure 6-21. *You can rename your process, delete it, and make it private*

You can rename the process if you want, as shown in Figure 6-21.

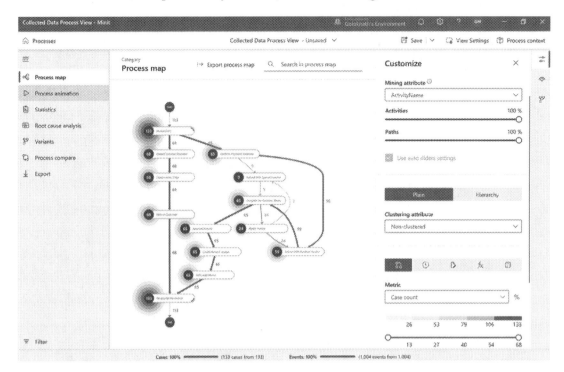

Figure 6-22. *The process map in Minit*

The Minit desktop helps you analyze the data in your process map. The options you have include Process Map, Process Animation, Statistics, Root Cause Analysis, Variants, Process Compare, and Export.

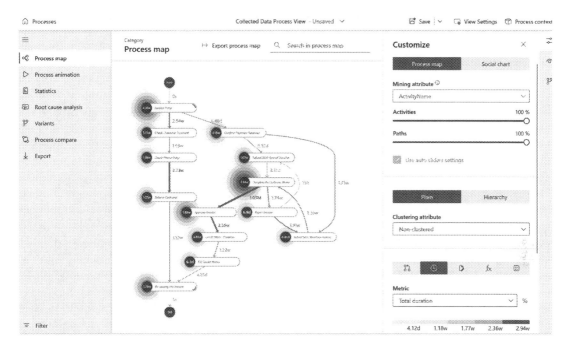

Figure 6-23. *Process map in action*

By customizing the parameter to Performance, you can change the process map, as shown in Figure 6-23.

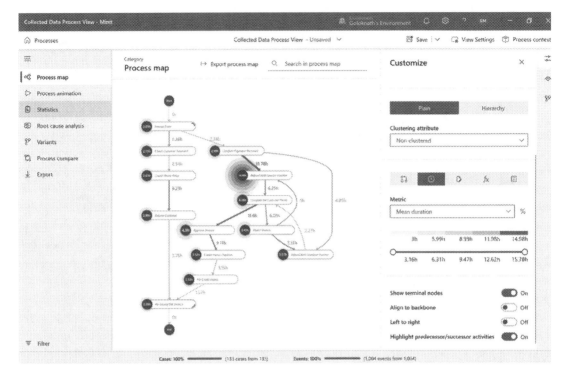

Figure 6-24. *Modifying the process map parameters*

When you change the duration from Metric to Mean, the map shows that the Refund with Special Voucher action takes more time. See Figure 6-24.

Task Mining

Task mining in the Process Advisor helps you capture detailed steps about the tasks performed on users' desktops. Task mining enables the following tasks:

- Prepare processes and recordings

- Analyze processes

- Visualize processes

- Identify automation recommendations

- Share processes

You can create a new process by clicking Start Here from the Process Advisor center page. Then select Recordings as the source and name the process, as shown in Figure 6-25.

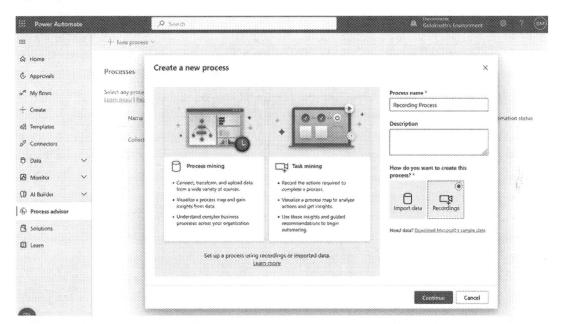

Figure 6-25. *Choose the Recordings button*

The system will display a dialog as the process is created. Click the Add a Recording button, as shown in Figure 6-26.

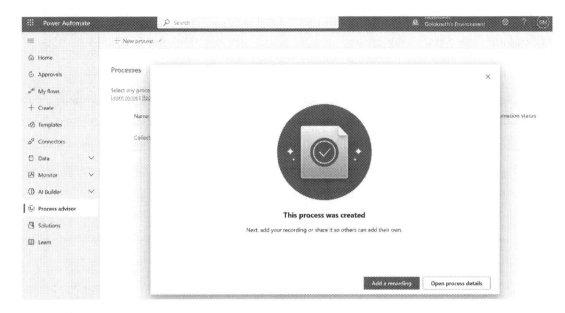

Figure 6-26. *Click the Add a Recording button*

The system will try to open the Power Automate Desktop, as shown in Figure 6-27.

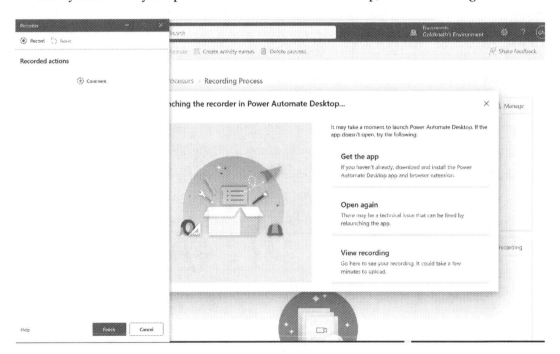

Figure 6-27. *Opening the Power Automate Desktop*

Once the recording is done, you can stop recording. The screen will look like Figure 6-28. Click View Recording.

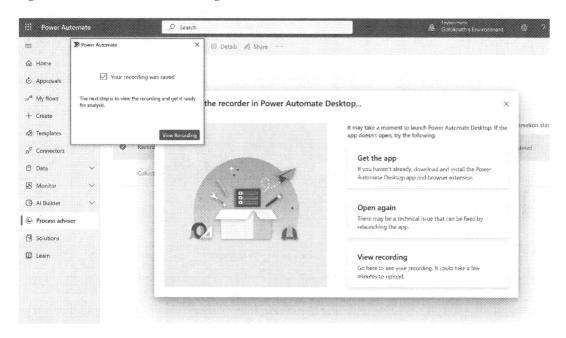

Figure 6-28.   *The recording has been saved*

When you click View Recording, you will see the screen in Figure 6-29. Click Save and Analyze to analyze the recording for task mining.

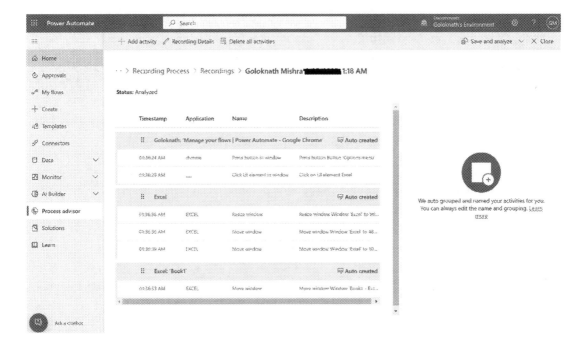

Figure 6-29. *Saving and analyzing the recording*

As shown in Figure 6-30, you can add recordings by using New Recording. You can analyze the recording by clicking the Analyze button.

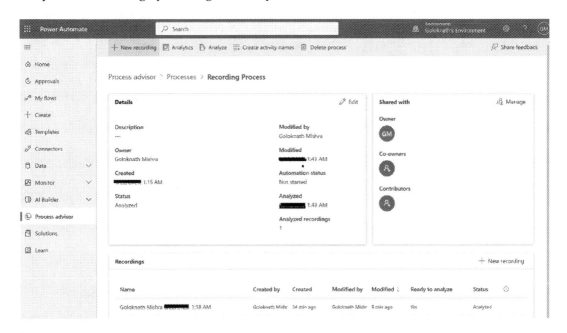

Figure 6-30. *You can add recordings by choosing New Recording*

After analysis, a report will be generated, as shown in Figure 6-31.

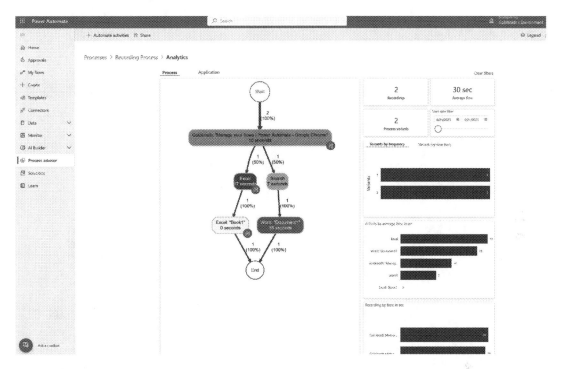

Figure 6-31.   *The process report is generated*

You can see the analytics report by clicking the Analytics button. The application report is shown in Figure 6-32.

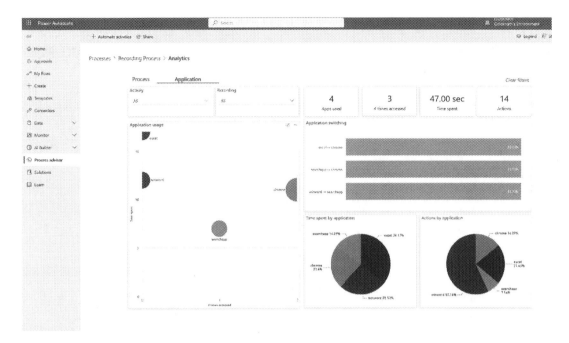

Figure 6-32. *The application report is generated*

If you click the Legend button, you'll see the legend information shown in
Figure 6-33.

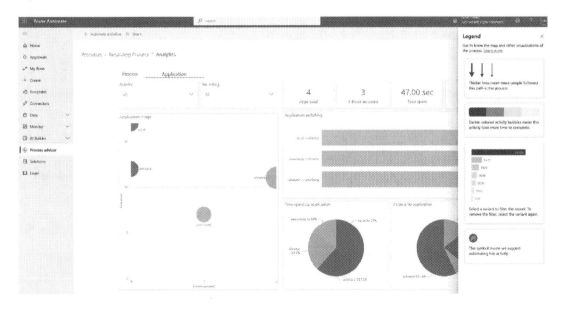

Figure 6-33. *The legend*

From the Automate Activities pane, you can start automating the processes that are taking too much time. See Figure 6-34.

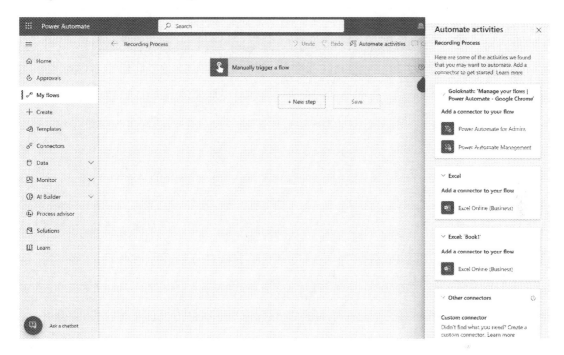

Figure 6-34. *You can automate slow and repetitive processes*

When you click the Automate Activities button, the system will suggest the Power Automate process it suggests you use for automation. See Figure 6-35.

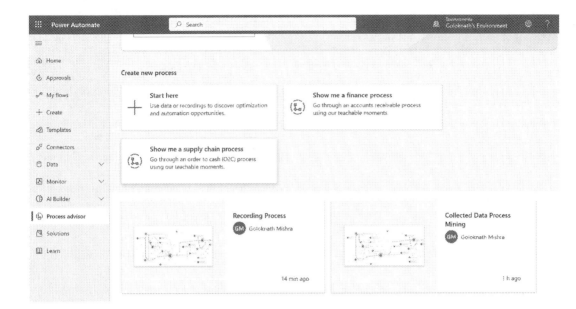

Figure 6-35. *Create a process for automation*

All the Process Advisor options—process mining and task mining—can be seen from the center pane of the Process Advisor.

Security and Administration

Process Advisor relies on the Power Platform environment's security and Microsoft Dataverse's security roles and privileges to grant access to its features in Power Automate.

The Application Process Advisor is an internal security role that Process Advisor uses. Don't assign this security role to users. Don't modify the set of privileges in the User or Application Process Advisor security roles.

Sharing processes and their recordings is essential to creating rich analysis and insights in Process Advisor. Users can add recordings to a process. They can then use Power Automate to record processes and import the processes into Process Advisor. Owners and contributors can see the data from the process and its recordings.

Only the export and import features of task mining (recordings) processes are currently supported. Process mining (data) processes can't be exported and imported by the Microsoft Power Platform solution.

Users can share the Process Advisors by using the Share option and providing the relevant privilege.

Summary

This chapter discussed the different Process Advisors. It covered what process mining is and how you use it. It also covered task mining, explained its significance, and described how you use it.

Answer a few questions based on your learnings:

1. How do you transfer processes from one environment to another?

2. What is a seeded license?

Keywords

Minit desktop

Power Automate Desktop

Process Advisor

Process mining

Task mining

CHAPTER 7

AI Builder

So far, you have learned what Power Automate is, as well as what Cloud Flows, Desktop Flows, and Business Process Flows are. You also learned when to implement RPA and how to optimize it. This chapter discusses Power Automate's AI capabilities.

This chapter explains what AI Builder is, and it covers the different types of AI models available, including the prebuilt and custom AI options. You also learn how to share, administer, and monitor these models.

What Is AI Builder

AI Builder allows you to easily add artificial intelligence (AI) capabilities to your applications. AI Builder is simple to use. It has a user-friendly interface and pre-built AI models, which can be customized to meet your specific business needs. Figure 7-1 shows the opening screen.

Tip   If you have experience with AI and Machine Learning, you can leverage features of Azure Machine Learning (`https://ml.azure.com/`) to build custom models from scratch.

© Goloknath Mishra 2023
G. Mishra, *Deep Dive into Power Automate*, https://doi.org/10.1007/978-1-4842-9732-2_7

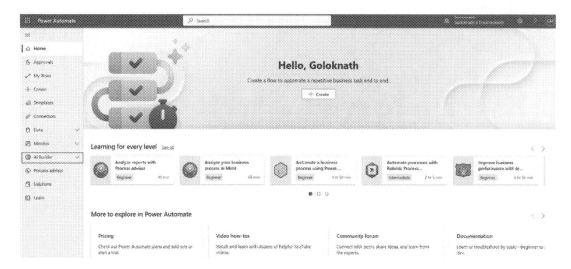

Figure 7-1. *The AI Builder opening window*

As highlighted in Figure 7-2, you can click AI Builder to expand the available sections:

- Explore

- Models

- Document Automation

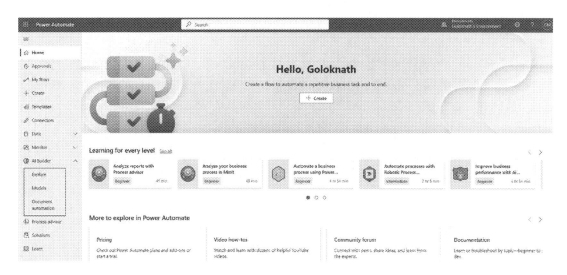

Figure 7-2. *The AI Builder menu options*

Accessing the Prebuilt and Custom Models

As shown in Figure 7-3, the Explore option contains a list of models that you can use to leverage AI capabilities.

- Models with use case scenarios that are common across different business types are called *prebuilt models*.

- Models with use case scenarios applicable to specific business scenarios are called *custom models*.

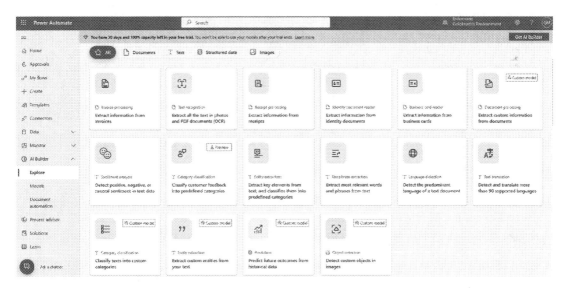

Figure 7-3. *AI models from the Explore option*

Using Prebuilt Models

These models are broadly classified into four types, based on operation.

- Document type models

- Text type models

- Structured data models

- Image models

Document Type Models

This type contains all the models that deal with documents, as listed in Table 7-1.

Table 7-1. *Document Type Models*

Prebuilt Models	
Invoice processing	Extract information from invoices
Text recognition	Extract all the text in photos and PDF documents (OCR)
Receipt processing	Extract information from receipts
Identity document reader	Extract information from identity documents
Business card reader	Extract information from business cards
Custom Models	
Document processing	Extract custom information from documents

Text Type Models

This type contains all the models that deal with text analysis, as shown in Table 7-2.

Table 7-2. *Text Type Models*

Prebuilt Models	
Sentiment analysis	Detect positive, negative, or neutral sentiment in text data
Category classification	Classify customer feedback into predefined categories
Entity extraction	Extract key elements from text and classify them into predefined categories
Key phrase extraction	Extract relevant words and phrases from text
Language detection	Detect the predominant language of a text document
Text translation	Detect and translate more than 90 supported languages
Azure Open AI Service	Create text, answer questions, summarize documents, and more with GPT
Custom Models	
Category classification	Classify text into custom categories
Entity extraction	Extract custom entities from your text

Structured Data

The Structured Data model deals with the structure of data, as shown in Table 7-3.

Table 7-3. *Structured Data Models*

Custom Models	
Prediction	Predict future outcomes from historical data

Image Models

This type contains models that deal with images, as listed in Table 7-4.

Table 7-4. *Image Type Models*

Prebuilt Models	
Text recognition	Extract all the text in photos and PDF documents (OCR)
Custom Models	
Object detection	Detect custom objects in images

Tip   The AI Builder Explore window also contains these options: Tutorials, Case Studies, How To Videos, Customer Stories, and What's New Coming Up in AI Builder.

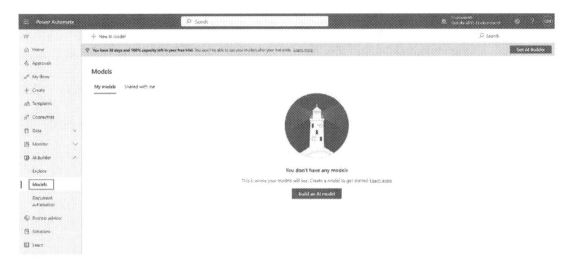

Figure 7-4. *AI models from the Models option*

As shown in Figure 7-4, the Models option contains list of the following

- Custom models created/modified by the user

- Custom model shared with users

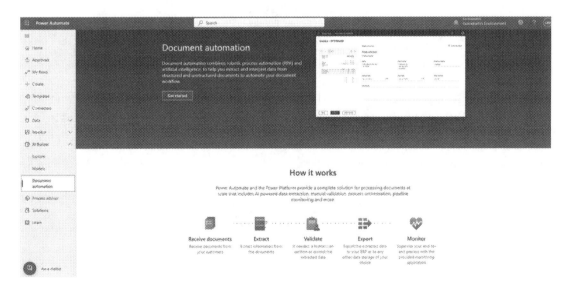

Figure 7-5. *Document Automation*

As shown in Figure 7-5, Document Automation uses the RPA capability to automate documents, whether they are structured or unstructured.

364

Building, Training, Managing, and Publishing Models

As illustrated in Figure 7-6, each model will pass through these four phases in order:

- Build

- Train

- Manage

- Publish

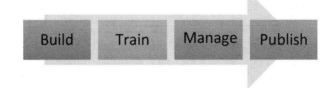

Figure 7-6. *Build, train, manage, and publish a model*

Building Models

To build a model using AI Builder, you must meet the following prerequisites:

- AI Builder requires Microsoft Dataverse storage to store and manage the business data

- AI Builder must be enabled for the environment

Training Models

Before using AI Builder models, you need to train them. The more you train a model with different samples, the better its accuracy will be. So, training is a vital activity in AI automation.

Training takes some time in AI Builder, depending on the level of difficulty. Once you train a model the first time, you should visit the Details page, where you can manage the model and see its performance score.

On the Details page, the training results appear in the last trained version section.

Managing Models

Optimizing an AI model is an iterative process and the results can vary depending on the configurations you set and the training data you provide. Updating these factors can affect the performance of your model.

After you train a model, its performance score will appear for each trained version. You can improve the model by adjusting the factors affecting the model.

After evaluating your model, you can determine whether it is perfectly fit, underfit, or overfit:

- **Underfit**: This occurs when your model performs below expectations. In this case, you need to train the model with more relevant information.

- **Overfit**: This occurs when your model provides accurate predictions for the training data, but not for any new data. In this case, you need to adjust the relevant parameters and retrain the model.

Figure 7-7. *Choose which version to train*

If your model has been published once already, you can choose between the published version and the last trained version when you want to edit it. Choose which one you want to use as the final version and publish it accordingly (see Figure 7-7).

Publishing Models

After your model has been trained successfully, you can publish to make it available. All users in your current environment will be able to use your published model when you publish it.

Different Model Usage

The Invoice Processing model extracts information from invoices, which can then be used with prebuilt or custom models, as shown in Figure 7-8.

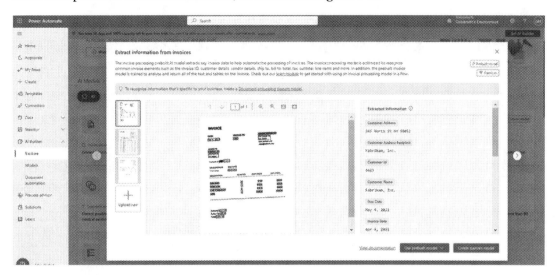

Figure 7-8. *The Invoice Processing model*

Let's start by choosing a prebuilt model here, which can be further used in a flow or in an app, as shown in Figure 7-9.

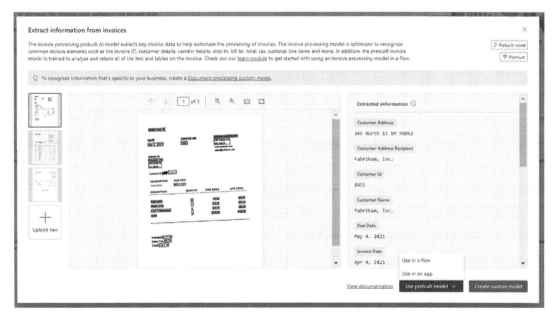

Figure 7-9. *Prebuilt models can be used in a flow or app*

Use the Prebuilt Model in an App

When you choose the Use in an App option, another browser tab will open showing the PowerApps Portal (`https://powerapps.microsoft.com/`). From there, you can create a Canvas app to use the prebuilt feature, as shown in Figure 7-10.

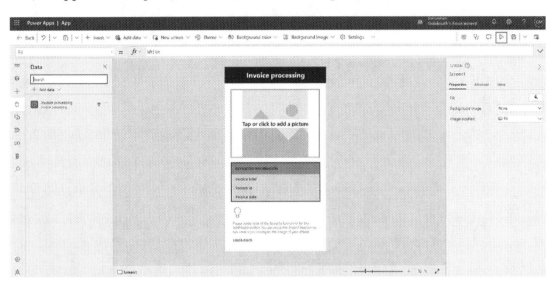

Figure 7-10. *Creating an invoice in an app*

When you click the Play button highlighted in Figure 7-10, the Canvas app plays, as shown in Figure 7-11.

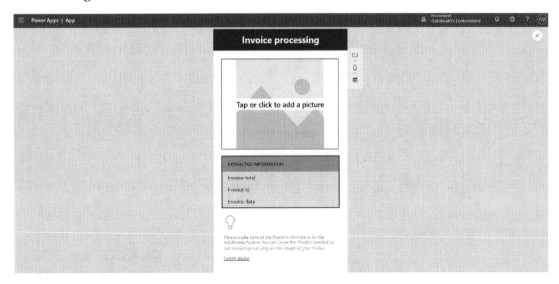

Figure 7-11. *The Canvas app, where you upload the image*

You upload the invoice to extract the pertinent information, as shown in Figure 7-12.

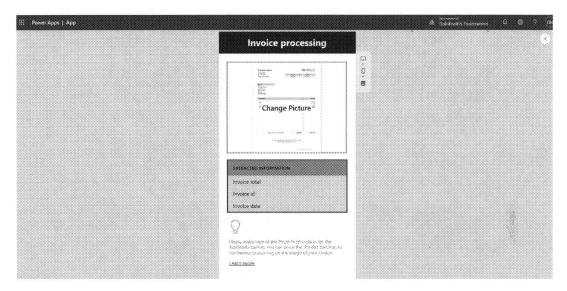

Figure 7-12. *The invoice has been uploaded*

The invoice sample used here is from the Internet and is shown in Figure 7-13.

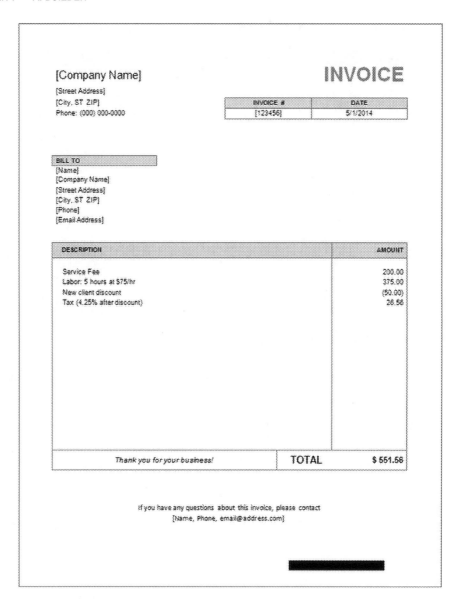

Figure 7-13. *The sample invoice used in this example*

After you upload the image to the Canvas app, the system will extract the relevant information, as shown in Figure 7-14.

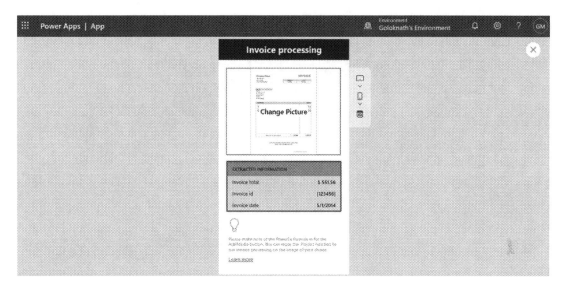

Figure 7-14. *Thee system extracts the relevant information*

Tip   If you don't have a PowerApps environment or account, the system will fail to open the PowerApps Portal and will display a 404 error instead.

Use a Prebuilt Model in a Flow

When you choose the Use in a Flow option, another browser tab will open. A prebuilt flow will extract information from the invoice and send the results by email, as shown in Figure 7-15.

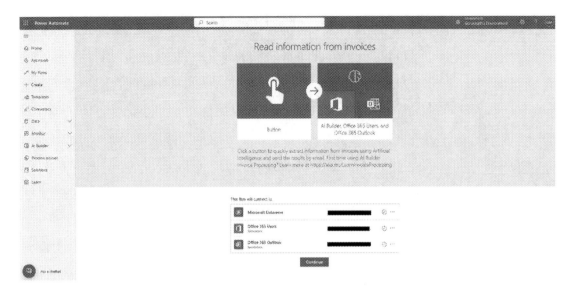

Figure 7-15. *The flow extracts information from the invoice*

When you click Continue, you will see the flow definition, which includes the steps shown in Figure 7-16.

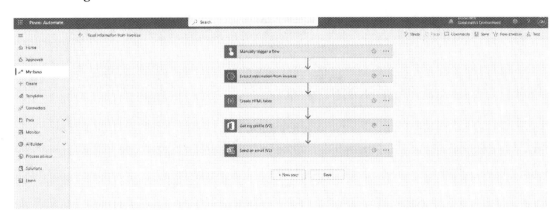

Figure 7-16. *Defining the flow*

If you expand the flow, you can see it's asking to upload the image to extract the invoice details. It is then creating an HTML table to send the email, as shown in Figure 7-17.

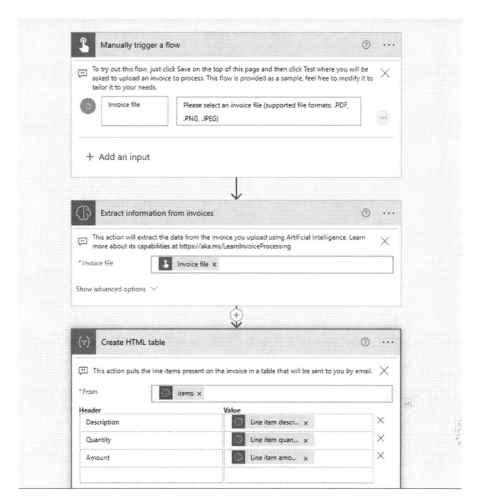

Figure 7-17. *The flow process*

If you run the flow (by clicking the Run button), you will notice that the flow will prompt for the invoice document that it needs to upload. See Figure 7-18.

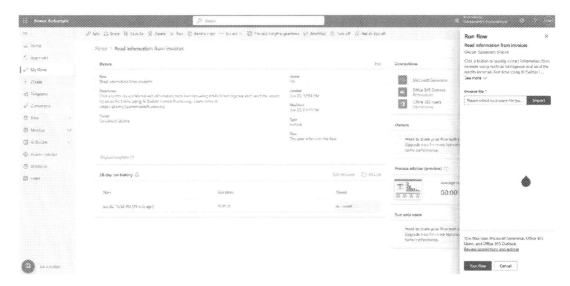

Figure 7-18. *Prompting you to upload the invoice file*

If you upload the image and click the Run Flow button, you'll see that the run flow starts successfully, as shown in Figure 7-19.

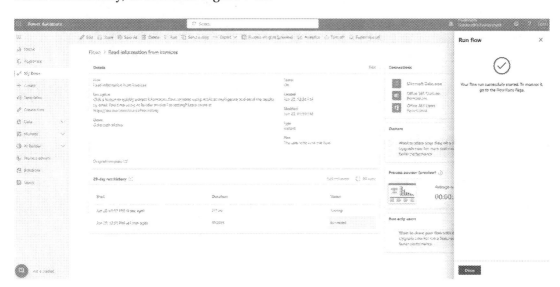

Figure 7-19. *The run flow is running*

After some time, the run flow status will show that it completed successfully, as shown in Figure 7-20.

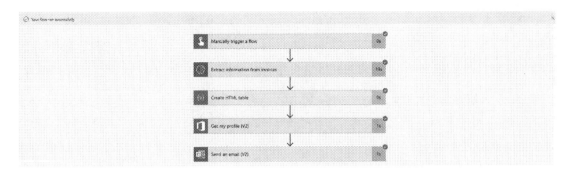

Figure 7-20. *The flow ran successfully*

You will receive an email with the invoice information, as configured as part of flow. See Figure 7-21.

Figure 7-21. *The email with the invoice information*

Supported Languages and Files

The following languages are supported: Dutch (Netherlands), English (Australia), English (Canada), English (India), English (United Kingdom), English (United States), French (France), German (Germany), Italian (Italy), Portuguese (Portugal), and Spanish (Spain).

To get the best results, provide one clear photo or scan per invoice. Other file requirements:

- The image format must be JPEG, PNG, or PDF.

- The file size must not exceed 20MB.

- The image dimensions must be between 50x50 pixels and 10,000x10,000 pixels.

- PDF dimensions must be at most 17x17 inches, which is the equivalent of the Legal or A3 paper sizes or smaller.

- For PDF documents, only the first 2,000 pages are processed.

Using Custom Models

Prebuilt models are designed to extract some common fields, but in real life you may want to extract information from additional fields that aren't part of any prebuilt model. In that case, you can use the custom model option (see Figure 7-22).

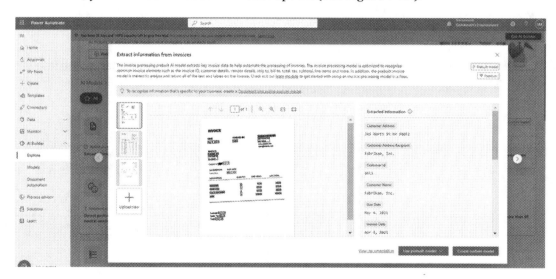

Figure 7-22. *Choose the Create Custom Model button*

If you want to use a custom model, you first need to add any fields that are not in the prebuilt model, as shown in Figure 7-23.

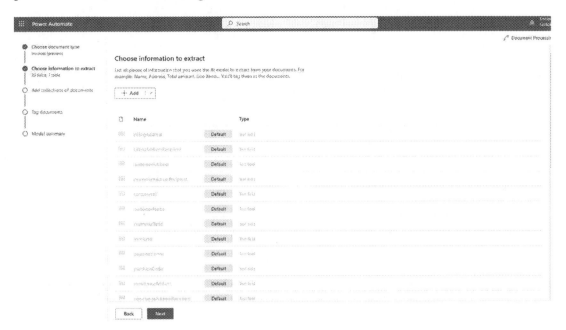

Figure 7-23. *Adding fields that aren't part of the prebuilt model*

This example uses the sample invoice shown in Figure 7-24, which includes the Salesperson and Payment Terms fields. These fields are not in the prebuilt model.

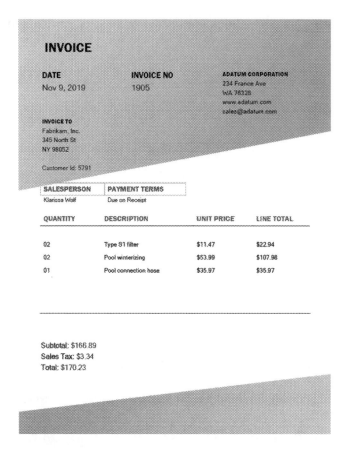

Figure 7-24. *Sample invoice with special fields*

Now you see how to add a text field from the list of available options to capture the salesperson and payment terms. Start by choosing Add. Figures 7-25 through 7-27 show this process.

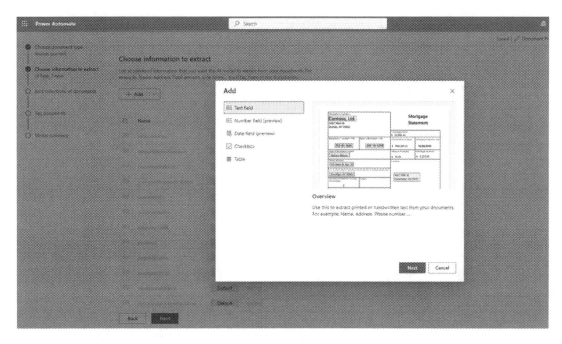

Figure 7-25. *Choose Add to add the text fields*

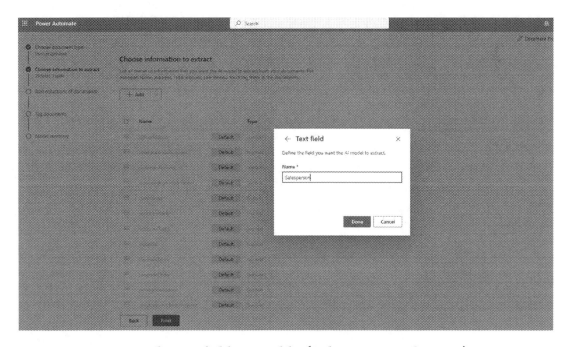

Figure 7-26. *Name the text field as you like (Salesperson in this case)*

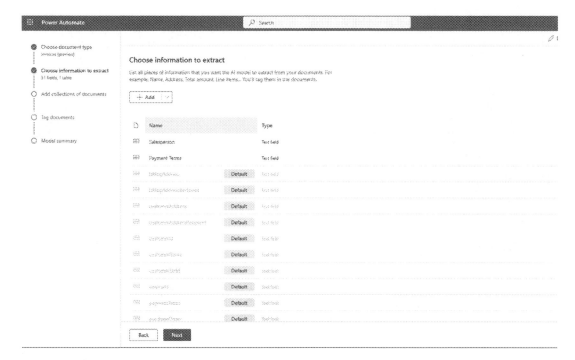

Figure 7-27. *The Salesperson field is now listed with the others*

Click Next to add a collection. You'll see the window in Figure 7-28.

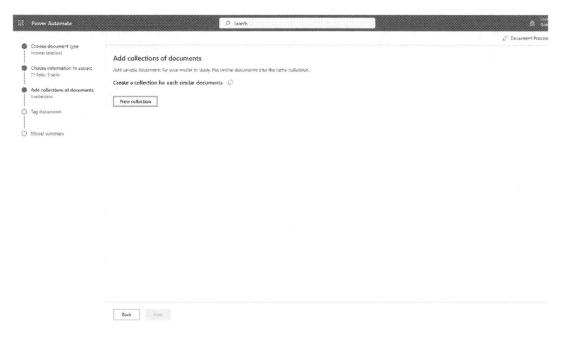

Figure 7-28. *Adding a collection*

This is the Training phase of the model. You have to train a minimum of five samples.

Click New Collection to create a collection of documents. These documents can be a single collection or multiple collections of similar documents. The source of these documents can be a local device, SharePoint, or Azure blob storage, as shown in Figure 7-29. Figure 7-30 shows the upload process.

Figure 7-29. *Choose the source of the documents for the collection*

Tip   A minimum of five documents need to be trained. They can be .JPG, .PNG, or .PDF documents, up to a size of 50MB or 500 pages.

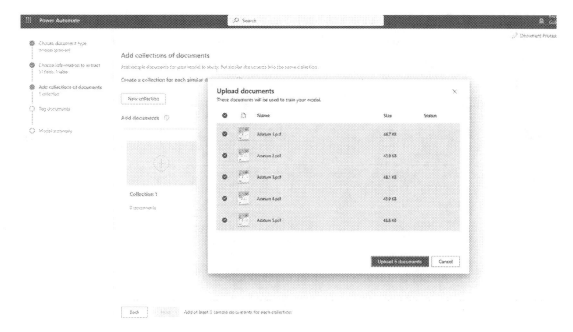

Figure 7-30. *Uploading the five documents*

Once you have selected the appropriate training documents, click Upload
Documents to move them to AI Builder. Figure 7-31 shows that the documents were
successfully uploaded.

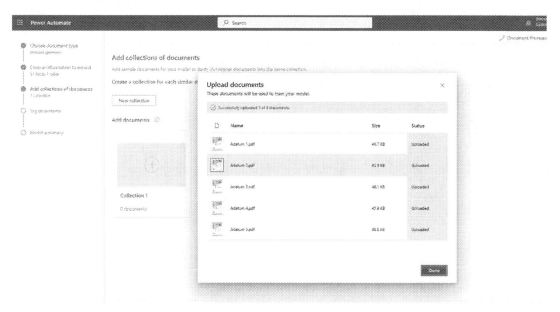

Figure 7-31. *The documents were successfully uploaded*

Once the documents are uploaded, click Done to see the documents in the collection. You can rename your model by clicking the top-right corner, as shown in Figure 7-32.

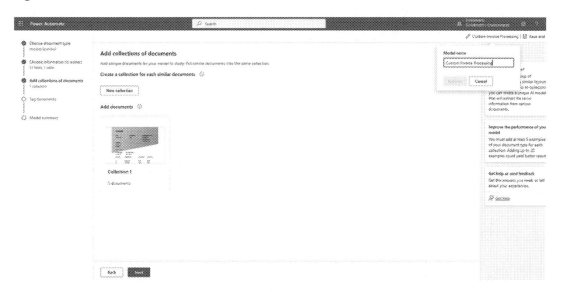

Figure 7-32. *You can rename your model by clicking the top-right corner*

Click Next to see the auto-tagged field based on the prebuilt training. You can validate if the tagging is correct or create a new tag (which the model is not able to identify).

In this case, the Salesperson and Payment Terms fields are new and haven't been trained yet, so the system cannot identify them. See Figure 7-33.

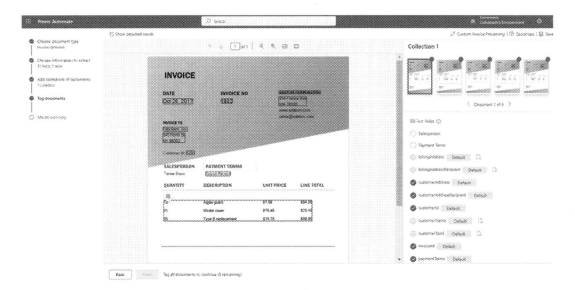

Figure 7-33. *The Salesperson and Payment Terms haven't been trained yet*

Train all five training documents individually by selecting the fields. You'll then see
the tick mark on each document, as shown in Figure 7-34.

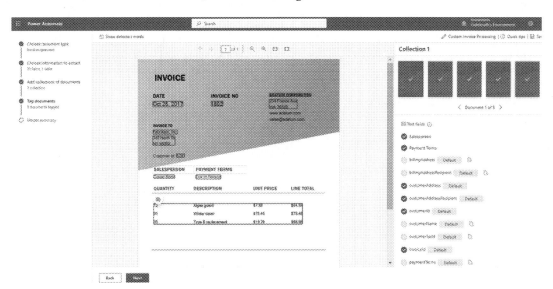

Figure 7-34. *Validating the new fields*

Click Next to see a list of fields to tag for extraction. Then click Train to start training the document. See Figure 7-35.

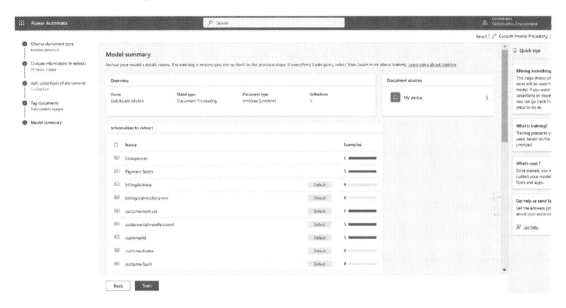

Figure 7-35. *Training the document*

Figure 7-36 shows the screen that appears during training. Once training is complete, you can click Go to Details Page to see the trained outcome.

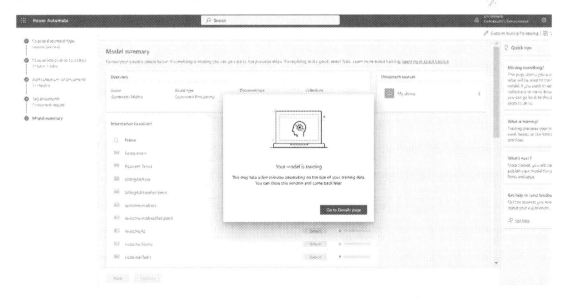

Figure 7-36. *Training is in process*

After training the model, you'll see an accuracy score, as shown in Figure 7-37. A score of 99% means it's good to publish.

Figure 7-37. *Accuracy score of the training*

Once the model has been published, you can view it in the My Models area, as shown in Figure 7-38.

Figure 7-38. *The My Models area shows your published models*

When you open the published model, you will see Use Model option, as shown in Figure 7-39.

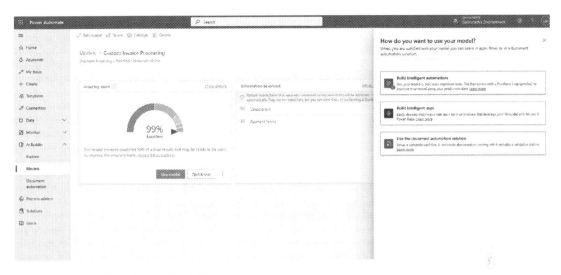

Figure 7-39. *The Use Model button*

If you choose the Build Intelligent Apps option on the right, you'll see the outcome of the model, which extracts the Salesperson and Payment Terms fields, along with other information. See Figure 7-40.

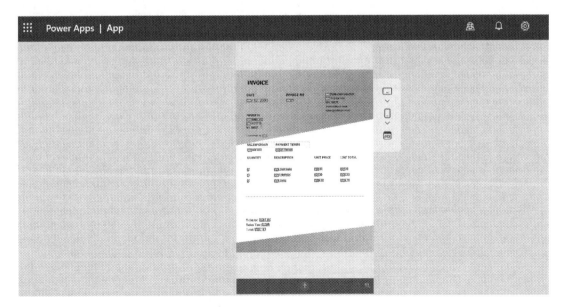

Figure 7-40. *The new fields have been extracted*

To use this custom model in Power Automate, you need to use the Predict action, as shown in Figure 7-41.

Figure 7-41. *Choose the Predict action*

Then you need to select the model in the Predict action. This model is called Custom Invoice Processing. Select that model, as shown in Figure 7-42, to create your desired flow action.

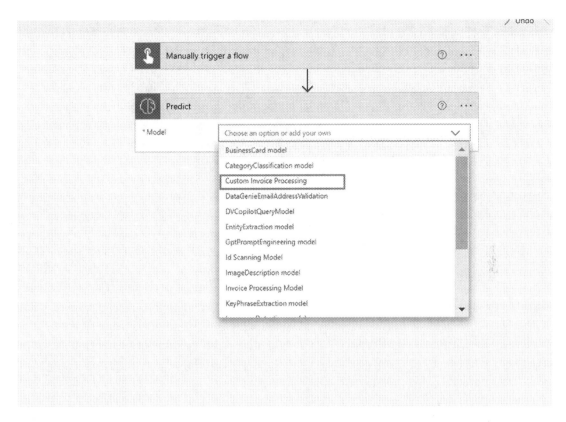

Figure 7-42. *Choose the Custom Invoice Processing model*

Text Recognition Model

This model is used to extract text from images and PDF documents using the built-in OCR (Optical Character Recognition) feature. When you click Text Recognition Model, you will see Figure 7-43.

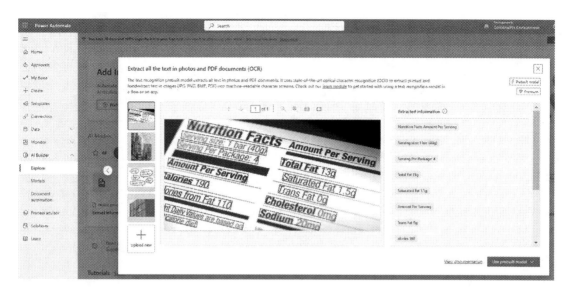

Figure 7-43. *The Text Recognition model*

In this case, choose Use Prebuilt Model ➤ Use in a Flow. A new tab will open showing a flow that extracts text from images and PDF documents. It does this using AI Builder's Text Recognition feature. See Figure 7-44.

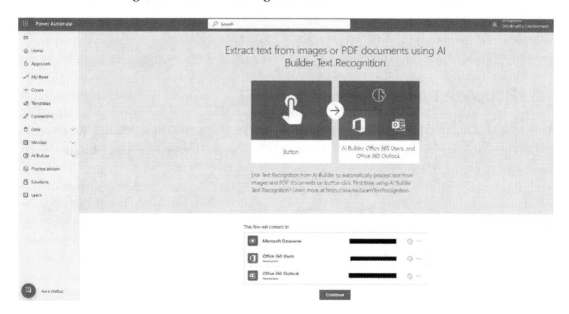

Figure 7-44. *AI Builder's Text Recognition feature*

Once the authentication is complete for Dataverse and Office 365, click Continue to see the flow steps in Figure 7-45.

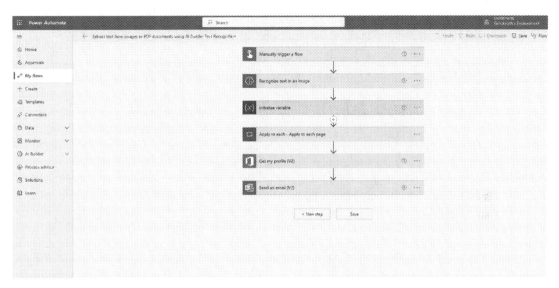

Figure 7-45. *The flow steps*

Figure 7-46 demonstrates the extraction process.

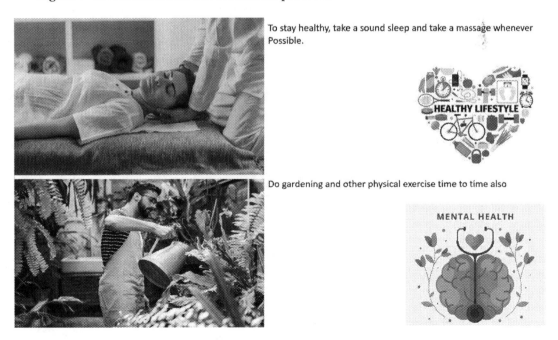

Figure 7-46. *The extraction process*

Save the flow and click Run the Flow. You will be prompted to upload the file, as shown in Figure 7-47.

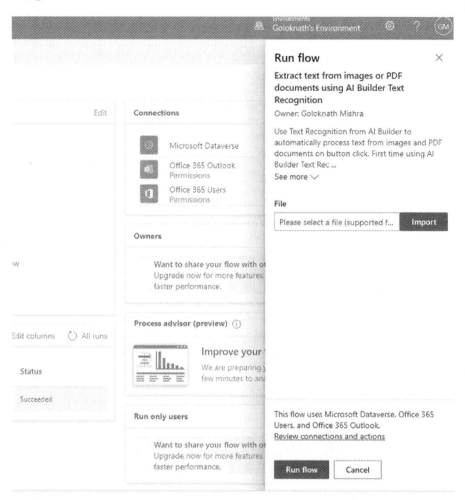

Figure 7-47. *Upload your file*

After uploading the file, click Run Flow. Once the run flow is complete, you will receive an email with the extracted text, as shown in Figure 7-48.

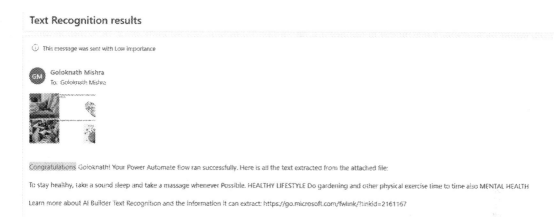

Figure 7-48. *The email with the extracted text*

You can also extract information from handwritten documents, as shown in Figure 7-49.

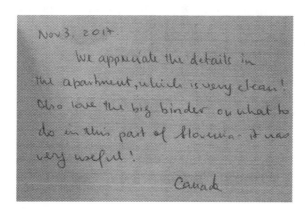

Figure 7-49. *OCR can extract information from handwritten documents*

Run the flow again. After uploading the file, click Run Flow. Once the run is completed, you will receive an email with the extracted text, as shown in Figure 7-50.

Text Recognition results

ⓘ This message was sent with Low Importance

GM Goloknath Mishra
To: Goloknath Mishra

Congratulations Goloknath! Your Power Automate flow ran successfully. Here is all the text extracted from the attached file:

Nov 3, 2017 We appreciate the details in the apartment, which is very clean! Also love the big binder on what to do in this part of florencia- it was very useful ! Canada

Figure 7-50. *The text from the note was extracted into the email*

Supported Languages and Formats

The languages that are supported for handwritten text are English, Chinese (Simplified), French, German, Italian, Japanese, Korean, Portuguese, and Spanish. Other requirements are as follows:

- Supported formats are JPG, PNG, BMP, and PDF

- File size is 20MB maximum

- For PDF documents, only the first 2,000 pages are processed

Document Processing Custom Model

This is a custom model that extracts custom information from documents, whether they are structured or unstructured. To use it, click Document Processing Model, which will display a dialog with a sample, as shown in Figure 7-51.

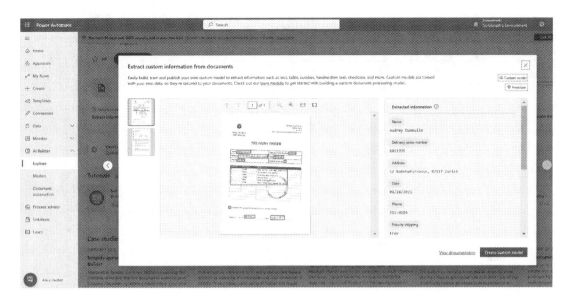

Figure 7-51. *The Custom Model window*

Click Create Custom Model to see the screen in Figure 7-52. Select the type of document you want to process.

Figure 7-52. *Choose the type of document to process*

Select Unstructured Documents, as shown in Figure 7-53.

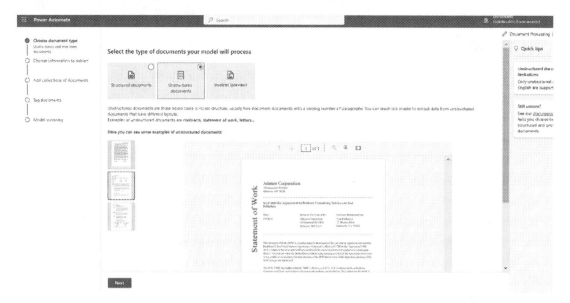

Figure 7-53. *Choose the Unstructured Documents option*

Say you have a residential lease document, which has lots of information you want to extract, such as the landlord's information, the tenant's name, and so on. See Figure 7-54.

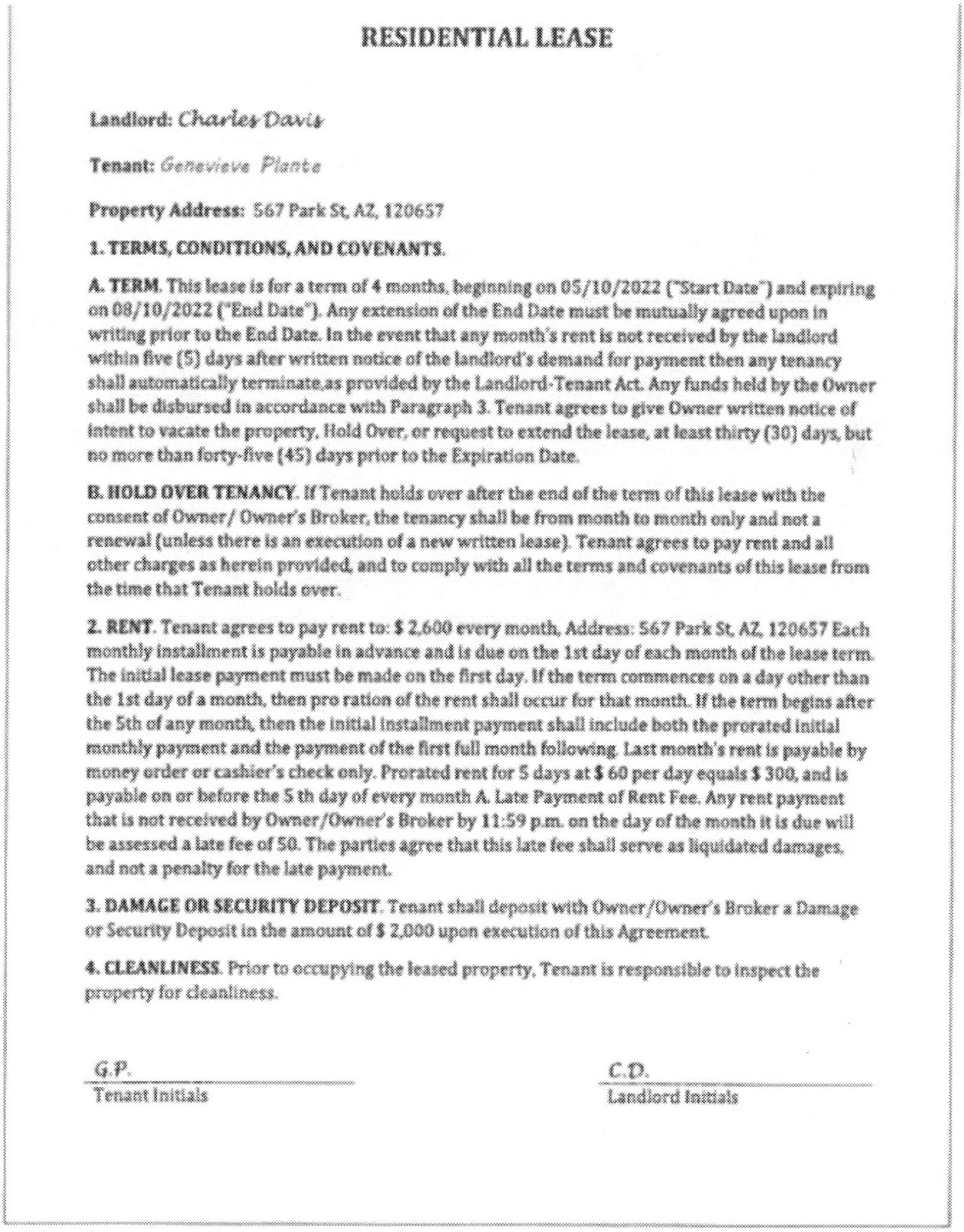

RESIDENTIAL LEASE

Landlord: *Charles Davis*

Tenant: *Genevieve Plante*

Property Address: 567 Park St, AZ, 120657

1. TERMS, CONDITIONS, AND COVENANTS.

A. TERM. This lease is for a term of 4 months, beginning on 05/10/2022 ("Start Date") and expiring on 08/10/2022 ("End Date"). Any extension of the End Date must be mutually agreed upon in writing prior to the End Date. In the event that any month's rent is not received by the landlord within five (5) days after written notice of the landlord's demand for payment then any tenancy shall automatically terminate,as provided by the Landlord-Tenant Act. Any funds held by the Owner shall be disbursed in accordance with Paragraph 3. Tenant agrees to give Owner written notice of intent to vacate the property, Hold Over, or request to extend the lease, at least thirty (30) days, but no more than forty-five (45) days prior to the Expiration Date.

B. HOLD OVER TENANCY. If Tenant holds over after the end of the term of this lease with the consent of Owner/ Owner's Broker, the tenancy shall be from month to month only and not a renewal (unless there is an execution of a new written lease). Tenant agrees to pay rent and all other charges as herein provided, and to comply with all the terms and covenants of this lease from the time that Tenant holds over.

2. RENT. Tenant agrees to pay rent to: $ 2,600 every month, Address: 567 Park St, AZ, 120657 Each monthly installment is payable in advance and is due on the 1st day of each month of the lease term. The initial lease payment must be made on the first day. If the term commences on a day other than the 1st day of a month, then pro ration of the rent shall occur for that month. If the term begins after the 5th of any month, then the initial installment payment shall include both the prorated initial monthly payment and the payment of the first full month following. Last month's rent is payable by money order or cashier's check only. Prorated rent for 5 days at $ 60 per day equals $ 300, and is payable on or before the 5 th day of every month A. Late Payment of Rent Fee. Any rent payment that is not received by Owner/Owner's Broker by 11:59 p.m. on the day of the month it is due will be assessed a late fee of 50. The parties agree that this late fee shall serve as liquidated damages, and not a penalty for the late payment.

3. DAMAGE OR SECURITY DEPOSIT. Tenant shall deposit with Owner/Owner's Broker a Damage or Security Deposit in the amount of $ 2,000 upon execution of this Agreement.

4. CLEANLINESS. Prior to occupying the leased property, Tenant is responsible to inspect the property for cleanliness.

G.P.
Tenant Initials

C.D.
Landlord Initials

Figure 7-54. *A residential lease document*

Click Next to add the fields you want to extract, exactly the same way you did for the invoice. This example adds the Landlord, Tenant, Rental Start Date, and Rental End Date fields, as shown in Figure 7-55.

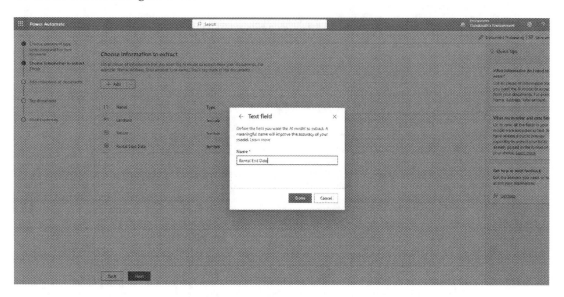

Figure 7-55. *Adding the fields to extract*

Then create a new collection and add the sample documents to that collection, as shown in Figure 7-56.

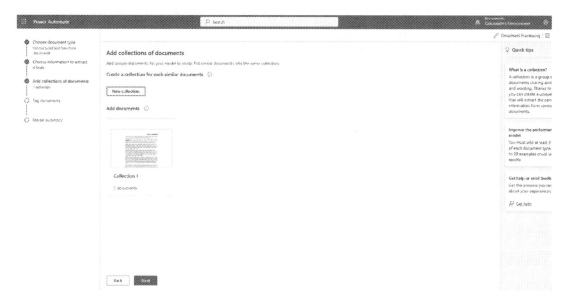

Figure 7-56. *Create a new collection*

Then click Next and tag the fields for training. See Figure 7-57.

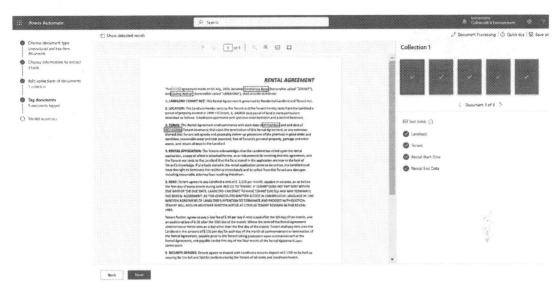

Figure 7-57. *Tagging the fields for training*

Once all the tagging is complete, the model summary will appear, as shown in Figure 7-58.

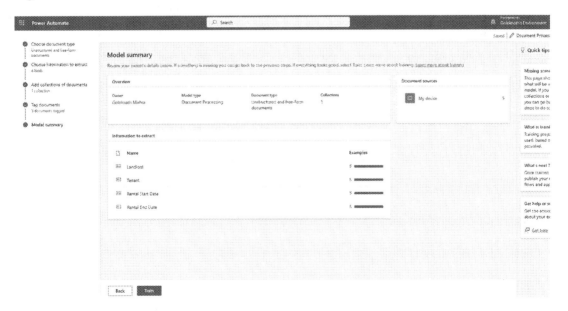

Figure 7-58. *The model summary*

Click the Train button to train the model. Figure 7-59 shows that the model is being trained.

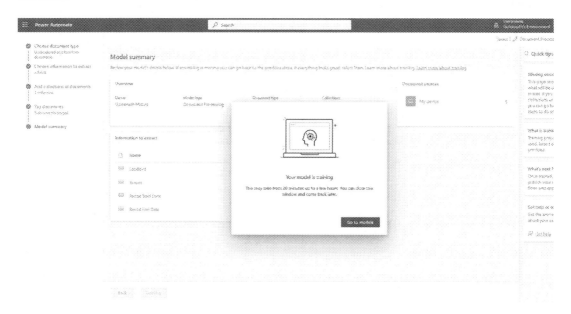

Figure 7-59. *The model is in the process of being trained*

You can click Go To Models to verify that the model is being trained, as shown in Figure 7-60.

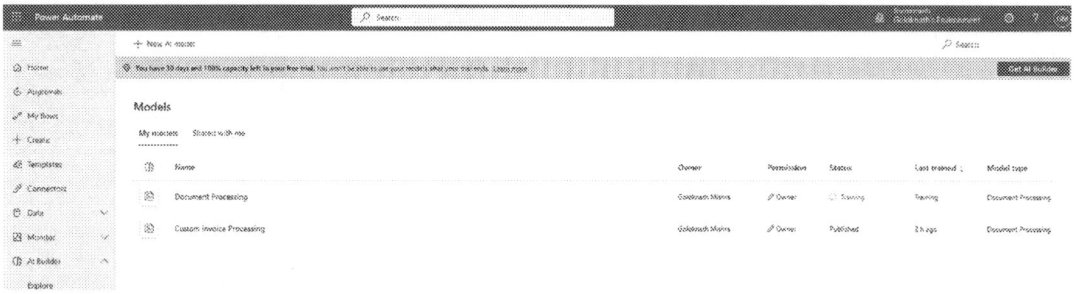

Figure 7-60. *Click Go To Models to see the status of all your models*

Once the model training process is complete, you can see the details in Figure 7-61. Click Publish to publish the model so all your users can use it.

Figure 7-61. *Click Publish to publish the model*

Once the model has been published, you will see two options: Use Model and Quick Test. See Figure 7-62.

Figure 7-62. *You now have two options: Use Model and Quick Test*

If you click Quick Test, you will see the window in Figure 7-63, where you can upload a document to test the model.

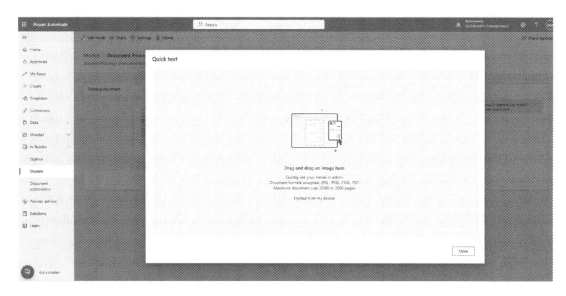

Figure 7-63. *Running a quick test*

After the test document is uploaded, the model will analyze the model and provide an outcome, as shown Figure 7-64.

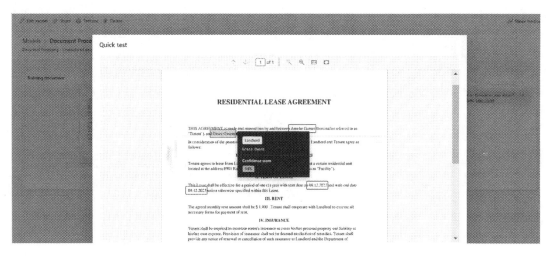

Figure 7-64. *The results of the quick test*

Sentiment Analysis Prebuilt Model

The Sentiment Analysis model is used to detect sentiment in text, whether it be positive, negative, or neutral. See Figure 7-65.

Figure 7-65. *The Sentiment Analysis model*

Choose Prebuilt Model ➤ Use in an App, as shown in Figure 7-66.

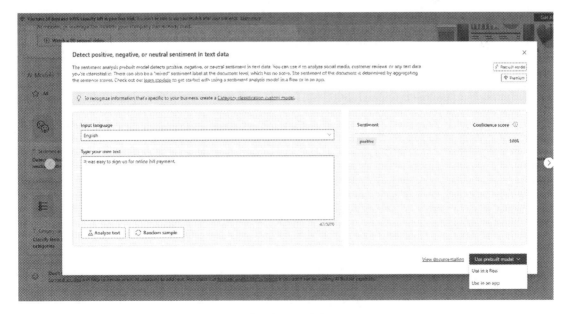

Figure 7-66. *Choose to use this prebuilt model in an app*

The system will open a Canvas app, in which you can analyze the sentiment by changing the text, as shown in Figure 7-67.

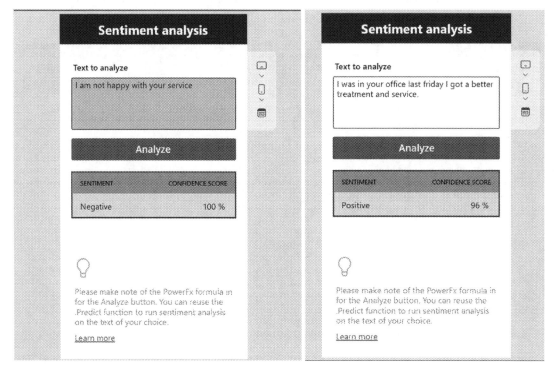

Figure 7-67. *The sentiment analysis app*

Text Translation Prebuilt Model

This model helps you translate text to 90 different supported languages. For this model, choose Use Prebuilt Model ➤ Use in an App. See Figure 7-68.

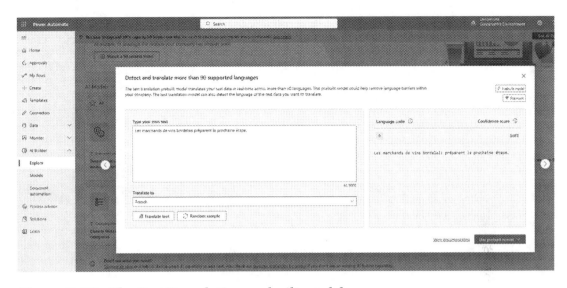

Figure 7-68. *The Text Translation prebuilt model*

You will see a new Canvas app, as shown in Figure 7-69. It helps translate the text to different languages.

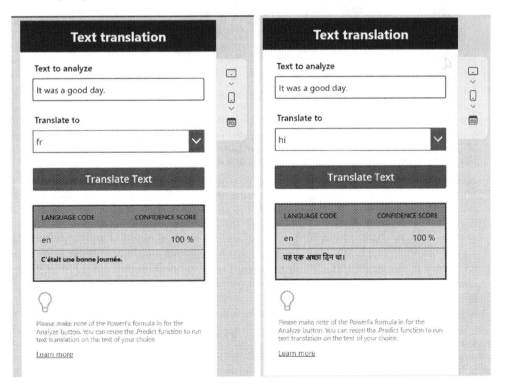

Figure 7-69. *The text translation Canvas app*

Tip   The text in this model can't exceed 10,000 characters.

Object Detection Custom Model

This is a custom model and can be used to detect objects in images. Choose Object Detection Model to see the dialog shown in Figure 7-70.

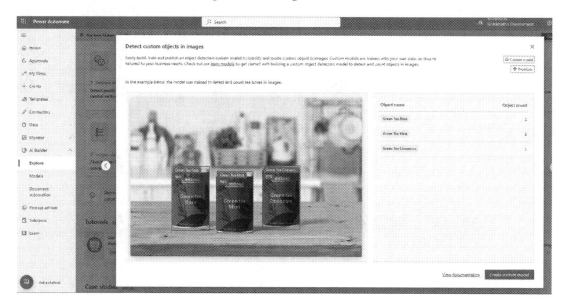

Figure 7-70. *The Object Detection model*

Click Create Custom Model. You will see the option to select an object. In this example, select Common Objects, as shown in Figure 7-71.

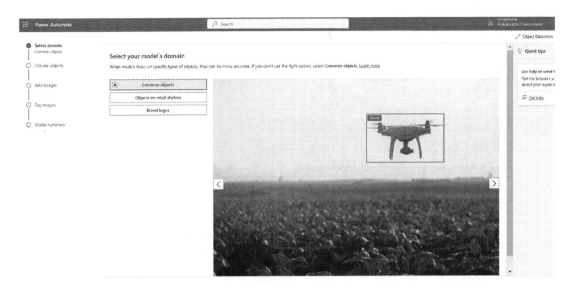

Figure 7-71. *Select Common Objects here*

Add new objects that you want the model to identify, as shown in Figure 7-72.

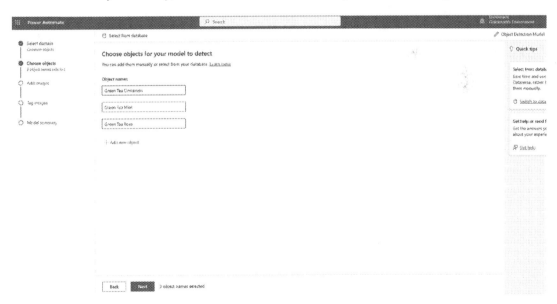

Figure 7-72. *Adding objects to detect*

Click Next to add the images. This model requires a minimum of 15 images of types .JPG, .PNG, or .BMP. They can be up to 6MB each. See Figure 7-73.

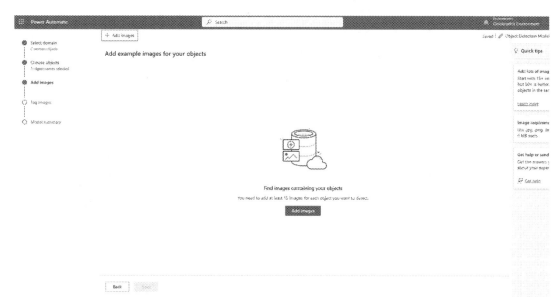

Figure 7-73. *Adding example images*

Once the images have been added, tag the images with the objects. When tagging is complete, you can see the images with tick marks, as shown in Figure 7-74.

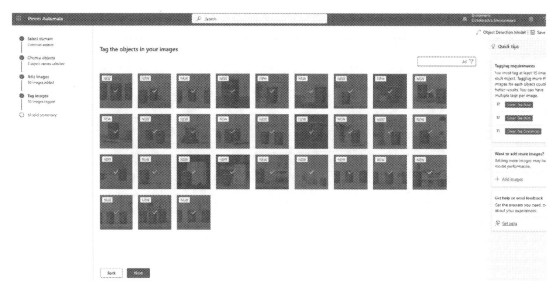

Figure 7-74. *Tagging the images*

Click Next to see the model summary, as shown in Figure 7-75.

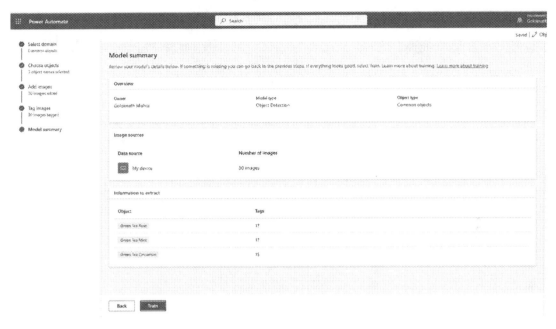

Figure 7-75. *The model summary*

Click Train to start training the model. The model training window will appear, as shown in Figure 7-76.

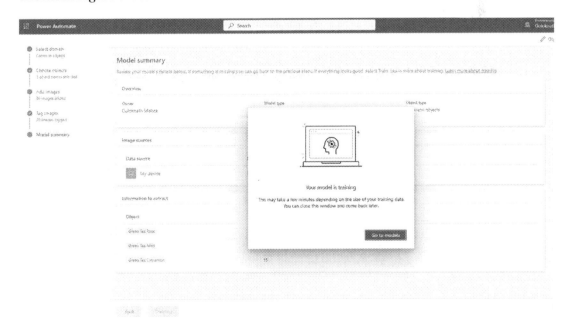

Figure 7-76. *Your model is being trained*

When the training process is done, you can view the performance score, along with options to Publish and Quick Test the model. See Figure 7-77.

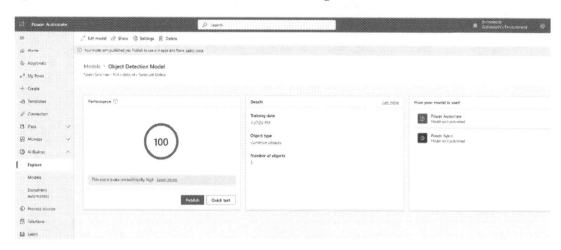

Figure 7-77. *The performance score of the training process*

Click Publish to allow users to access your model. You can access the Use Model and Quick Test options as well, as shown in Figure 7-78.

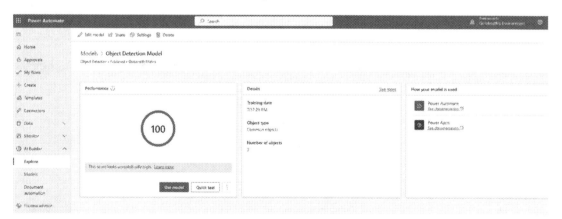

Figure 7-78. *Choose Use Model or Quick Test from this window*

Click Quick Test to check the model's usability. It will show a dialog asking you to upload an image with the object. The model's outcome is absolutely correct, as you can see in Figure 7-79.

Figure 7-79. *The model predicted correctly*

The Document Automation Toolkit

The Document Automation toolkit leverages features of AI Builder, Power Automate, Power Apps, and Microsoft Dataverse to allow you to set up rich and robust document processing solutions.

It provides a functional end-to-end solution that is ready to install and supports common processing patterns. This includes

- Receiving documents from a service mailbox.

- Automatically extracting data from these documents.

- Exporting the results to a target system like accounting, HR, or CRM.

The detailed process is shown in Figure 7-80.

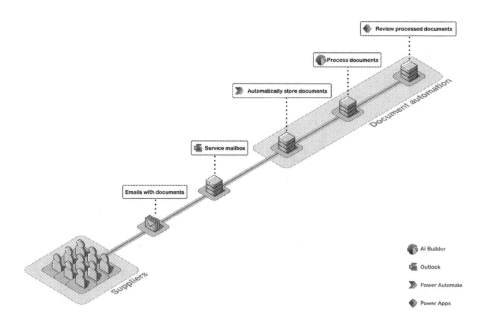

Figure 7-80. *The Document Automation process*

To start using Document Automation, navigate to Document Automation in Power
Automate within AI Builder. Then select Custom Documents and Invoices, as shown in
Figure 7-81.

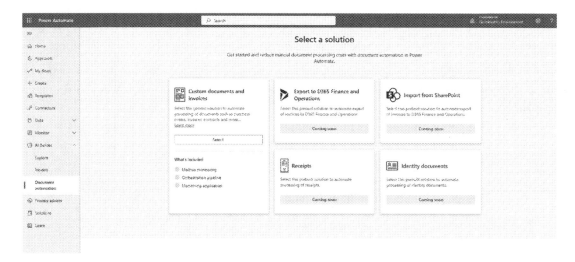

Figure 7-81. *Select Custom Documents and Invoices*

You will see the dialog in Figure 7-82, with the option to install a custom solution.

Figure 7-82. *Installing a custom solution*

Click to install the solution. Once the solution is installed, the mailbox and Dataverse apps need to be configured, as shown in Figure 7-83.

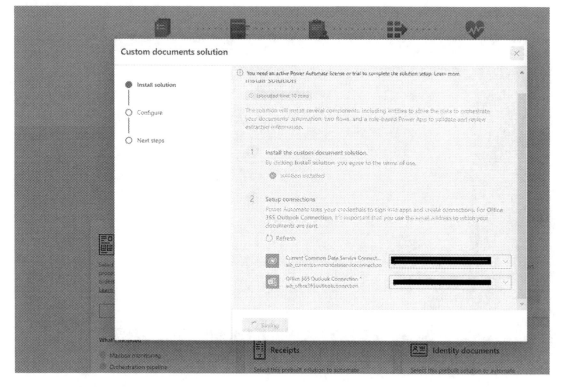

Figure 7-83. *Setting up the connections*

Configure the pertinent roles and permissions, as shown in Figure 7-84. Click Next when you're ready.

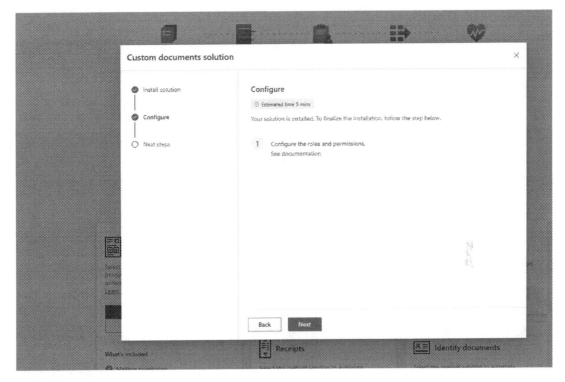

Figure 7-84. *Configure the roles and permissions*

Open the Microsoft Power Platform Admin Center (`https://aka.ms/ppac`) and select your environment. Then select Settings at the top.

Environments > Goloknath's Environment > **Settings**

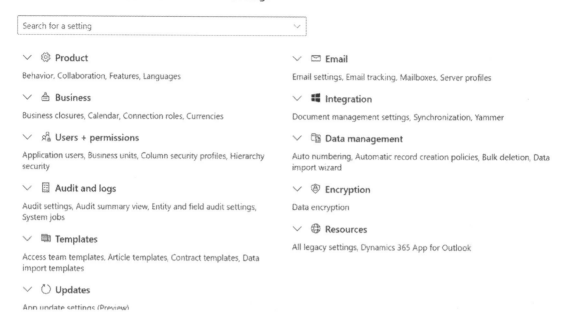

Figure 7-85. *The Microsoft Power Platform Admin Center*

Expand User + permissions and select Users. Then choose Manage Security Roles. Add the System Customizer role to Process Owners or add the Document Automation Reviewer role to Manual Reviewers. See Figure 7-86.

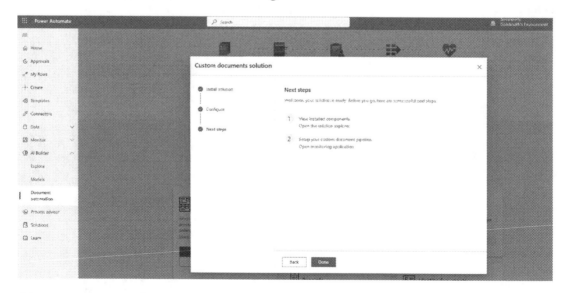

Figure 7-86. *Finishing the setup process*

In the Document Automation solution, click View Installed Components and then set up your custom document pipeline, as shown in Figure 7-87.

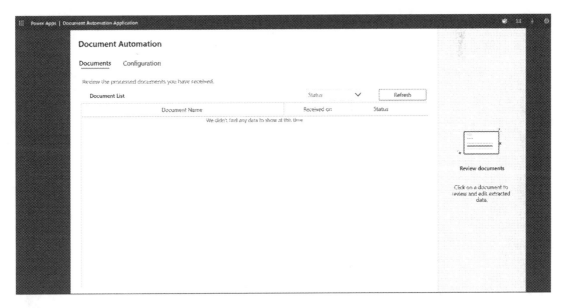

Figure 7-87. *Setting up your custom document pipeline*

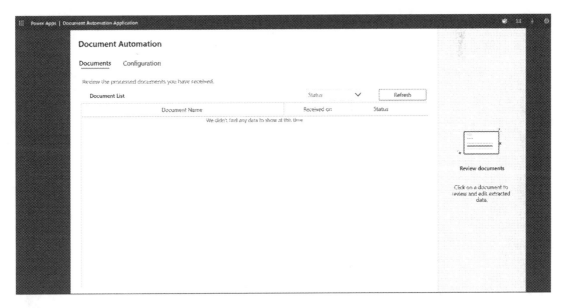

Figure 7-88. *Reviewing the documents*

Click the Configuration tab in the Document Automation Canvas app and select the model to associate with Document Automation. Then click Next, as shown in Figure 7-89.

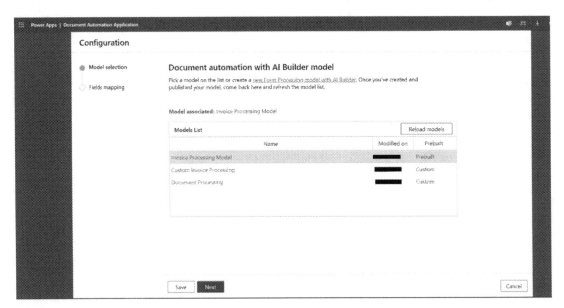

Figure 7-89. *Select the model you want to associate with Document Automation*

Do the field and tables mapping, as per the model, then save the configuration. See Figure 7-90.

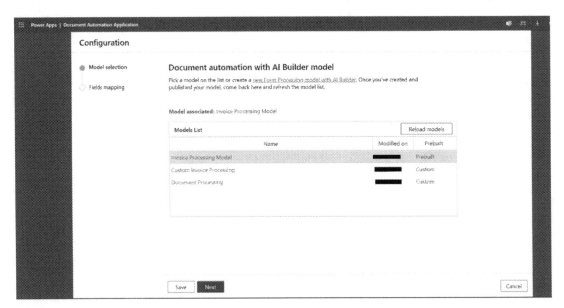

Figure 7-90. *Mapping the fields and tables*

The configuration is done for the Document Automation. Now trigger an email with the document to the mapped mailbox, as shown in Figure 7-91.

document automation example

GM Goloknath Mishra
    To: Goloknath Mishra

📎 6. 8901 Railroad St, MD, 781... ⌄
   76 KB

Please find the attached document

↩ Reply   ↪ Forward

Figure 7-91. *The email has been triggered*

The document will be extracted and will appear in the Documents tab of the Document Automation Canvas app, as shown in Figure 7-92.

Figure 7-92. *The document appears in the Documents tab*

Click the document to validate it, as shown in Figure 7-93.

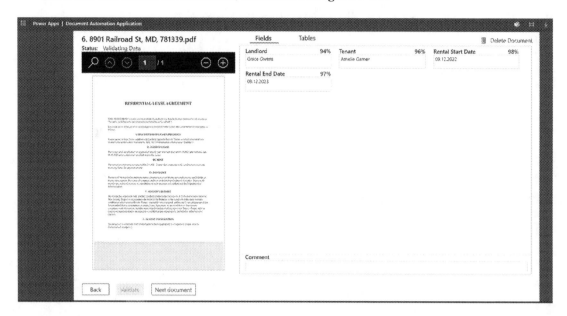

Figure 7-93. *Click Validate to check the document*

Sharing, Administering, and Monitoring Models

The states of a model are (in order) Draft, Training (Transient), Trained, Publishing (Transient), and Published. Other states of models include Unpublishing (Transient), Training Error, Importing (Transient), and Import Error. Figure 7-94 illustrates this lifecycle.

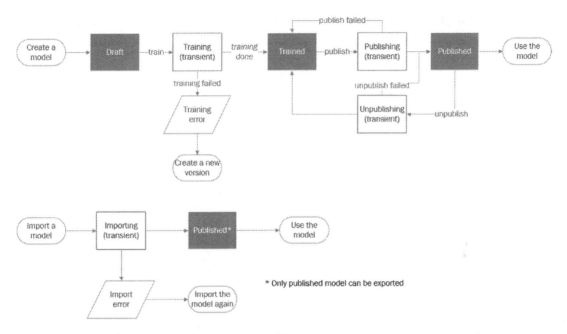

Figure 7-94. *Lifecycle states of a model (Ref: Microsoft documentation)*

Using the Power Platform Admin Center, you can track the AI Builder credit and its usage by navigating to Resources ➤ Capacity ➤ Summary, as shown in Figure 7-95.

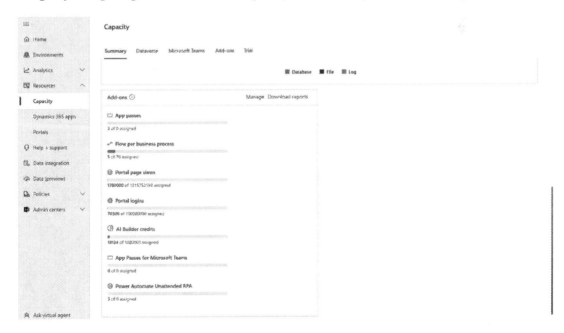

Figure 7-95. *Tracking the AI Builder usage*

Once a model has been created, you can edit it using the Edit Model option, as shown in Figure 7-96.

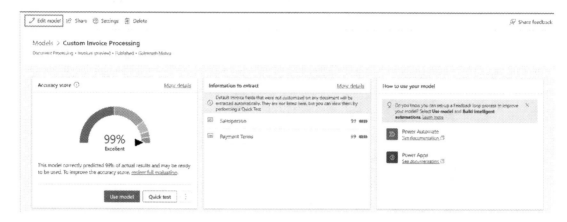

Figure 7-96. *Use Edit Model to change the model*

You can unpublish a model using the three dots, as highlighted in Figure 7-97.

Figure 7-97. *Unpublish a model using this button*

You can click the More Details link shown in Figure 7-98 to see a model overview.

Figure 7-98. *The More Details link*

You can filter fields by scores from the Model Evaluation window, as shown in Figure 7-99.

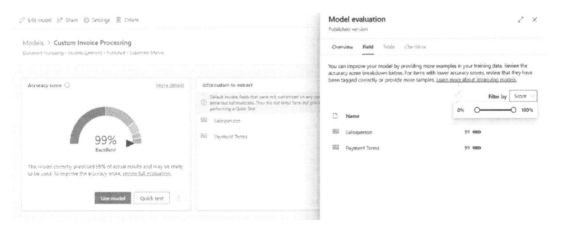

Figure 7-99. *The Model Evaluation window*

Choose Settings, as shown in Figure 7-100, to rename your model.

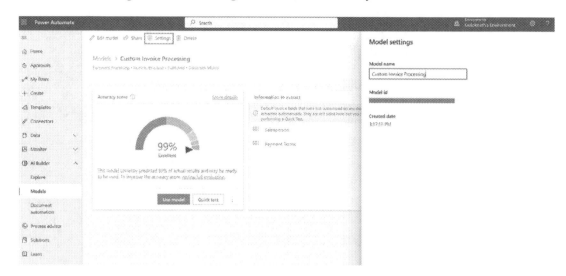

Figure 7-100. *The Model Settings window*

You can click the Share option to share the model with different users. You can sort or filter by name/email ID to find the user you want to share the model with. See Figure 7-101.

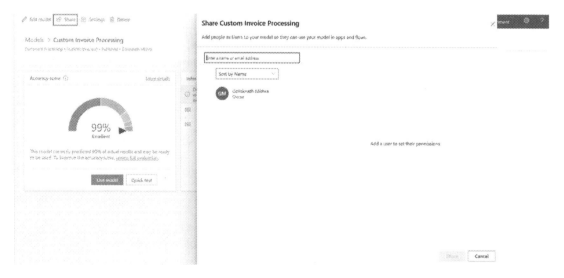

Figure 7-101. *Choose Share to share your model with other users*

You can also distribute an AI model as a *solution component*. After you create a model in AI Builder, you make it available to other environments by packaging it into a solution and then exporting it as a ZIP file. After the solution is imported in the target environment, the packaged AI model will be available for use.

Tip   When adding an AI model to a solution, only the model executable is included. The training data isn't included with the model.

AI Builder activity can be monitored by navigating to Monitor ➤ AI Builder Activity. See Figure 7-102. You can also click See More to see all the activities along or the activities of the last seven days.

Figure 7-102. *Monitoring AI Builder activity*

Call Limits

Table 7-5 lists the limits to calls made per environment across document processing models, including the receipt processing and invoice processing prebuilt models.

Table 7-5. *Limits to Calls Made Per Environment*

Action	Limit	Renewal Period
Calls (Per Environment)	360	60 seconds

Table 7-6 lists the limits to calls made per environment across the language detection, sentiment analysis, and key phrase extraction prebuilt models.

Table 7-6. *Limits to Calls Made Per Environment, Part 2*

Action	Limit	Renewal Period
Calls (Per Environment)	400	60 seconds

Table 7-7 lists the limits to calls made per environment for the text recognition model.

Table 7-7. *Limits to Calls Made Per Environment, Part 3*

Action	Limit	Renewal Period
Calls (Per Environment)	480	60 seconds

Table 7-8 lists the limits to calls made per environment for the ID reader and business card reader models.

Table 7-8. *Limits to Calls Made Per Environment, Part 4*

Action	Limit	Renewal Period
Calls (Per Environment)	24	60 seconds

Summary

This chapter explained what AI Builder is and how to use it. It also covered the steps for creating a custom model, the different types of prebuilt and custom models, and their use cases. It also explained how to monitor and administer models.

Answer a few questions based on your learnings:

1. How do you use a prediction model?

2. How do you use a category classification model?

3. How do you use an entity extraction model?

4. How do you use a business card and identity document reader model?

Keywords

AI Builder

Business card reader

Category classification

Custom model

Document automation

Document processing

Entity extraction

Entity extraction

Identity document reader

Invoice processing

Key phrase extraction

Language detection

Object detection

OCR

Prebuilt model

Prediction

Receipt processing

Sentiment analysis

Text recognition

Text translation

CHAPTER 8

Licensing Considerations

In earlier chapters, you learned what Power Automate is and does, including the kinds of flows in Power Automate, broadly classified as cloud flows, desktop flows, and business process flows.

This chapter discusses the different licensing models you can purchase, including the standalone plan, the seeded plan, the developer plan, and the add-on plans. If you don't know which licensing model to use, you might accidently incur additional expenses for licenses that are already available as part of your existing purchased plan.

This chapter dives deeply into the licensing models available in Power Automate.

Power Automate Licenses

Power Automate licenses are classified as follows:

- Standalone plan
    - Per user plan
    - Per user with attended RPA
    - Per flow plan
    - Pay-as-you-go plan
- Seeded plan
    - Power Automate + Microsoft 365
    - Power Automate + Dynamics 365
- Developer plan

© Goloknath Mishra 2023
G. Mishra, *Deep Dive into Power Automate*, https://doi.org/10.1007/978-1-4842-9732-2_8

The Standalone Licensing Plan

A standalone license is an individual license that you need to purchase separately. It's not tied to any other plan or model. The standalone license is explained in Table 8-1.

Table 8-1. *Standalone Plan Options with Descriptions*

Plan	Description
Per user plan	User can run an unlimited number of flows (within service limits) with the full capabilities of Power Automate.
	This includes standard connectors, premium connectors, business process flows, custom connectors, and on-premises gateways, based on their unique needs for a monthly fixed cost for each user.
Per user plan with attended RPA	User can run an unlimited number of flows (within service limits) with the full capabilities of Power Automate.
	This includes standard connectors, premium connectors, business process flows, custom connectors, and on-premises gateways, based on their unique needs for a monthly fixed cost for each user.
	As well as
	The ability to automate legacy apps on a desktop via robotic process automation (RPA) in attended mode.
	And
	AI Builder supporting scenarios like forms processing, object detection, prediction, text classification, and recognition.
Per flow plan	With this plan, organizations can implement flows with reserved capacity that serve a team, a department, or an entire organization without having to license each user separately.
	This plan starts with a fixed monthly cost for five active flows.
	There's a monthly fee for each additional active flow (beyond the five flows that are included in the base fee).

(continued)

Table 8-1. (*continued*)

Plan	Description
Pay-as-you-go plan	With this plan, organizations can get started building flows without any license commitment or upfront costs and use their Azure subscription to pay only when their flows run.
	A flow can be cloud flow, an attended desktop flow, an unattended desktop flow, or a Microsoft-hosted machine group. Pricing is as follows:
	• Premium flows that run in the cloud or attended cost $0.60 per run
	• Premium flows that run unattended cost $3.00 per run
	• Premium flows that run with hosted machine group cost $3.00 per run
	No charges will be incurred if you're testing your flow in the designer or resubmitting failed runs.
	If you use the Child Flow feature for cloud flows or attended flows, there will only be a single charge for the parent flow run. No charges are incurred for child flow runs.
	For unattended flows, both parent and child flow runs are charged.

For automated or scheduled flows, the license entitlements of the flow owner apply. For instant and Power Apps-triggered flows, the license entitlements of the user running the flow apply.

The Seeded Licensing Plan

If an organization has any of the following licenses, it is eligible to use Power Automate as a seeded plan:

- Microsoft 365 (Office 365)
- Dynamics 365 Enterprise
- Dynamics 365 Professional
- Dynamics 365 Team member
- Power Apps (Canvas and model-driven apps) per app plan
- Power Apps per user plan
- Windows license

431

When you use seeded plans, your flows must run within the context of the application in which the seeded plan is available. If the flow is isolated and has nothing to do with the application, a standalone Power Automate license must be purchased. Figure 8-1 displays the different license plans and their limits.

| ✓ Included | ⊘ Not included | ⚓ Supported in the context of app |

License	Power platform limits/day	Standard connectors	Premium connectors, Business Process flows, Custom connectors, On-premise gateway/ connectors	RPA Attended	AI builder credits	Dataverse Database capacity (accrued per USL/Flow)	Dataverse File capacity (accrued per USL/Flow)
Power Automate per flow plan - $500 for 5 flows/month	Actual limit -250K/flow Transition period limit - 500K/flow	✓	✓	⊘	⊘	50MB	200MB
Power Automate per user plan - $15/user/month	Actual limit- 40K Transition period limit -100K	✓	✓	⊘	⊘	50MB	200MB
Power Automate Per User with Attended RPA plans - $40/user/month	Actual limit- 40K Transition period limit -100K	✓	✓	1 bot	5000	50MB	200MB
Office 365 plan	Actual limit - 6K Transition period limit -10K	✓	⊘	⊘	⊘	⊘	⊘
Power Apps Per User plans	Actual limit- 40K Transition period limit -100K	✓	⚓	⊘	⊘	250MB	2GB
Power Apps Per App plan	Actual limit- 6K Transition period limit -10K	✓	⚓	⊘	⊘	50MB	400MB
Dynamics Team member	Actual limit- 5K Transition period limit -100K	✓	⚓	⊘	⊘	⊘	⊘
Dynamics 365 Professional [1]	Actual limit- 40K Transition period limit -100K	✓	⚓	⊘	⊘	⊘	⊘
Dynamics 365 Enterprise applications [2]	Actual limit- 40K Transition period limit -100K	✓	⚓	⊘	⊘	⊘	⊘
Windows licenses		⊘	⊘	Limited RPA via PAD only	⊘	⊘	⊘

Figure 8-1. *Licensing plans and their inclusions*

Premium connectors aren't included in the Microsoft 365 license, but they are included in all standalone plans. Flows with a per flow license can make 250,000 requests in 24 hours, but they can't make more than 100,000 requests within five minutes. See Figure 8-2.

License	Power platform limits/day
Power Automate per flow plan - $500 for 5 flows/month	Actual limit -250K/flow Transition period limit - 500K/flow
Power Automate per user plan - $15/user/month	Actual limit- 40K Transition period limit -100K
Power Automate Per User with Attended RPA plans - $40/user/month	Actual limit- 40K Transition period limit -100K
Office 365 plan	Actual limit - 6K Transition period limit -10K
Power Apps Per User plans	Actual limit- 40K Transition period limit -100K
Power Apps Per App plan	Actual limit- 6K Transition period limit -10K
Dynamics Team member	Actual limit- 5K Transition period limit -100K
Dynamics 365 Professional [1]	Actual limit- 40K Transition period limit -100K
Dynamics 365 Enterprise applications [2]	Actual limit- 40K Transition period limit -100K

Figure 8-2. License limits

The Developer Licensing Plan

The Developer plan is a free plan used to learn the technology. It can't be used in a production environment or for any commercial purposes. Anyone interested in learning Power Automate can use this plan. You can sign up for the Developer plan from this link:

```
https://powerapps.microsoft.com/en-us/developerplan/
```

Power Automate Add-ons

A few functionalities in Power Automate require additional add-on licenses. These capabilities are not available in any of the standard plans. They are discussed next.

AI Builder

You can infuse AI into your flows with custom or prebuilt models using AI Builder. To calculate the AI Builder requirements and costs, you can use the following calculator:

`https://powerautomate.microsoft.com/en-sg/ai-builder-calculator/`

Each AI Builder add-on unit is a pack of 1 million service credits pooled at the tenant level. AI Builder also available as an add-on for Power Automate, Power Apps, and the Dynamics 365 paid subscription.

Unattended RPA

You can automate legacy apps on your desktop or virtual machines using robotic process automation (RPA) in unattended mode. It features the following attributes:

- Desktop flows in unattended mode

- 5,000 AI builder service credits per month

Hosted RPA

You can run robotic process automation (RPA) as a service with hosted machine options. This includes:

- Microsoft hosted machine

- Desktop flows in unattended mode

- 5,000 AI builder service credits per month

More details about pricing and capabilities can be found in the Microsoft Power Platform Licensing Guide at `https://go.microsoft.com/fwlink/?linkid=2085130`.

Summary

This chapter covered the different licensing options available with Power Automate. It explained the difference between standalone licenses and seeded licenses. It also included add-on license information.

Answer these few questions based on your learnings:

1. What is a pay-as-you-go license?

2. What is a seeded license?

Keywords

Attended RPA

Developer license

Pay-as-you-go

Power Automate per user

RPA

Seeded license

Standalone license

Unattended RPA

CHAPTER 9

Mini Project

Now that you have all relevant tools and knowledge to use Power Automate, in this chapter, you develop a mini project. It illustrates Power Automate's end-to-end functionality and utilization.

This mini project is called *Booking Management System.* It completes the vendor booking process through an automated program that captures information from a Microsoft form. This project includes the following steps:

- Creating a demo environment

- Creating a model-driven app, called the Booking Management System

- Modifying the Contact table in the model-driven app

- Submitting data automatically from the Microsoft form into the Booking Management System

- Creating a volunteer approval flow

- Exporting a solution from one environment and importing it into another

© Goloknath Mishra 2023
G. Mishra, *Deep Dive into Power Automate*, https://doi.org/10.1007/978-1-4842-9732-2_9

Creating a New Environment

Create a new environment using `https://aka.ms/ppac` and following these steps:

1. After logging in to the admin center, navigate to Environments ➤
   New, as shown in Figure 9-1.

Figure 9-1. *Choose to create a new environment*

2. The New Environment dialog will open. Fill in the required
    information, as shown in Figure 9-2. Call this environment **Demo**.

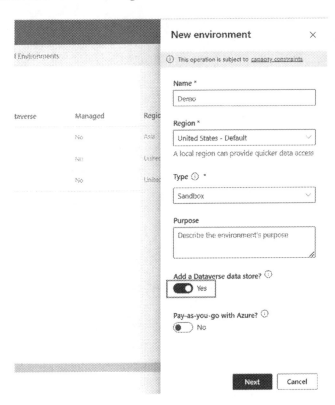

Figure 9-2. *Fill in the required information*

3. Click Next. You then need to fill in the relevant information, as shown in Figure 9-3.

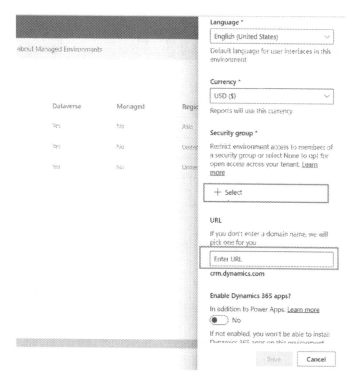

Figure 9-3. *Continue to define the new environment*

4. Click Save. Your new environment will be in the Preparing state, as you can see in Figure 9-4.

Figure 9-4. *The new environment is in the Preparing state*

5. Once the environment has been created successfully, you'll see
   Ready as the state, as shown in Figure 9-5.

Figure 9-5. *The environment is now ready*

6. If you click the environment name, you can see the details shown
   in Figure 9-6.

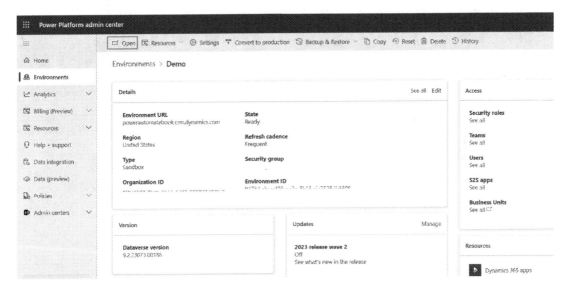

Figure 9-6. *The Demo environment's details page*

Creating a Model-Driven App

1. Click Open to navigate to the URL. This will display the
    PowerApps environment with the default apps. Click Create New
    App, as shown in Figure 9-7.

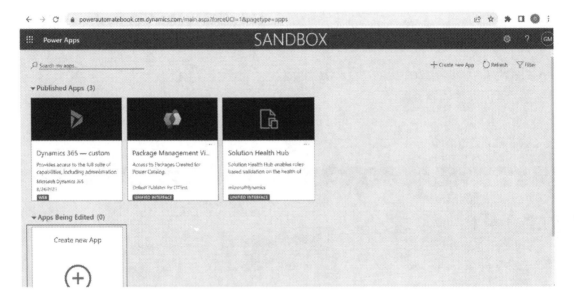

Figure 9-7. *Choose Create New App*

2. A new model-driven app window will appear. Enter a name and description, as shown in Figure 9-8.

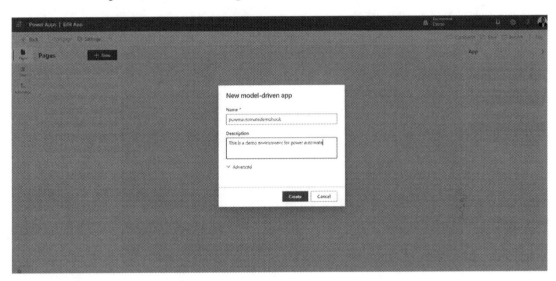

Figure 9-8. *Enter a name and description*

3. Click Create to create the app in the environment. Once the app has been created, you can change the name and the icon, as highlighted in Figure 9-9. Click Save to save the app.

Figure 9-9. *You can change the app's name and icon*

4. Click the Select Icon button. A dialog will appear so you can
    select the icon. If you want to create a new icon, click +New Web
    Resource. See Figure 9-10.

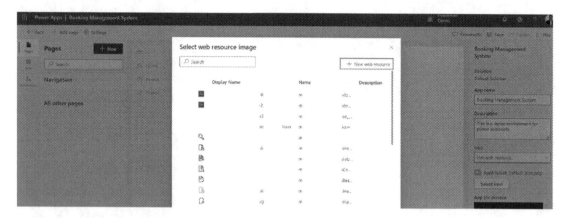

Figure 9-10. *Choose the new icon*

5. Log in to https://make.powerapps.com/ and navigate to
    Solutions. Select Environment Demo, as shown in Figure 9-11.
    Click +New Solution to create the solution.

Figure 9-11. *Creating a new solution*

6. A New Solution dialog box will open, where you provide the name and publisher. If you want to create a new publisher, you can do that here as well, as shown in Figure 9-12. Click Create when you're ready.

Figure 9-12. *Defining the new solution*

7. A new blank solution will be created. Click + New to create a new component or choose Add Existing to add existing component, as shown in Figure 9-13.

Figure 9-13. *You can create a new component or add an existing one*

Now, you'll add the model-driven app called Booking Management System to this solution for further edits, as shown in Figure 9-14.

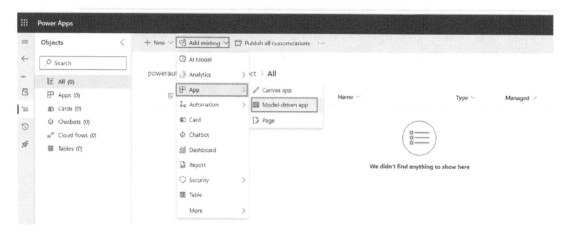

Figure 9-14.   *Adding a model-driven app*

1.   Select the app and click Add, as shown in Figure 9-15.

Figure 9-15.   *Find the app and click Add*

2. The model-driven app will be added to the new solution, as shown in Figure 9-16.

Figure 9-16. *The Booking Management System app has been added*

3. Choose Booking Management System to see the options you can edit, as shown in Figure 9-17.

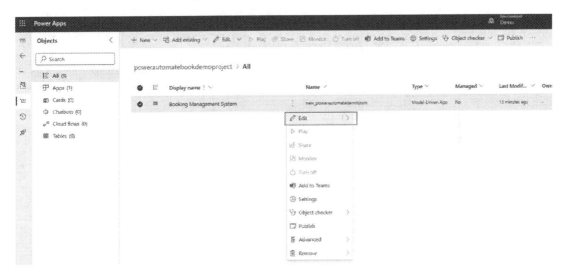

Figure 9-17. *Choose the app and then click to choose Edit*

4. The model-driven app will open, this time within the new solution instead of the default solution. See Figure 9-18.

Figure 9-18. *The app is now part of the new solution*

Modifying a Table

Follow these steps to modify a table:

1. Click Add Page to create a navigation for model-driven app. Then select Dataverse Table and click Next, as shown in Figure 9-19.

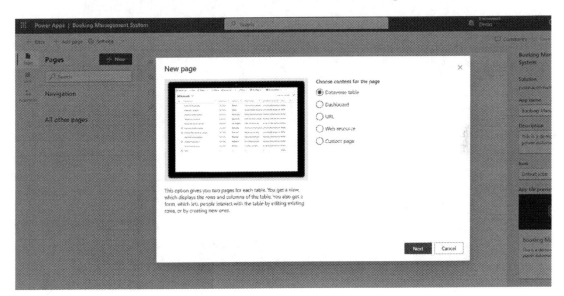

Figure 9-19. *Select Dataverse Table here*

2. You can select an existing table or create a new one. This example selects the Contact table, which is the default table in the Dataverse. See Figures 9-20 and 9-21.

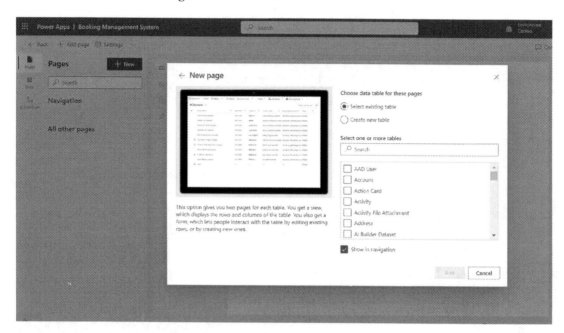

Figure 9-20.   *Choosing the Contact table*

Figure 9-21.   *Click Add to add the table*

3. Once you click Add, the model-driven app will appear as shown in Figure 9-22.

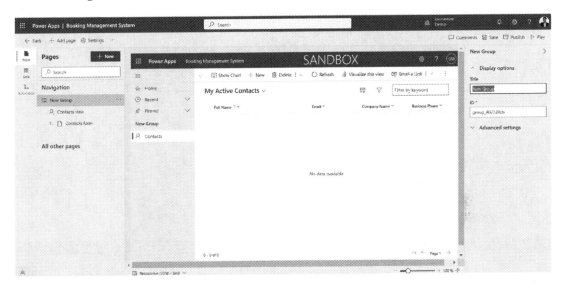

Figure 9-22. *The model-driven app appears*

4. Rename the group Customer Information and click Save, as shown in Figure 9-23.

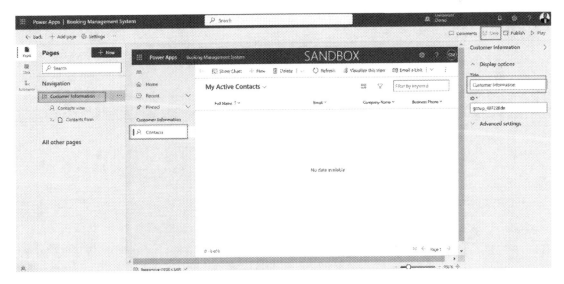

Figure 9-23. *Rename the group Customer Information*

5. In the solution, you can see three components, as shown in Figure 9-24—model-driven app, table, and site map.

Figure 9-24. *Note the three components*

6. Choose Tables and then Contact, as highlighted in Figure 9-25.

Figure 9-25. *Choose the Contact table*

7. Click Columns under Schema to create new columns. See Figure 9-26.

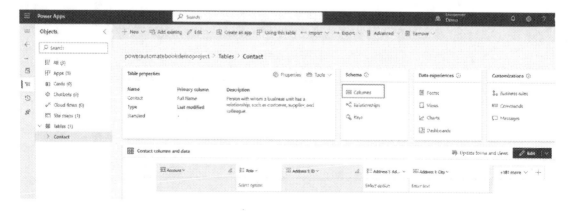

Figure 9-26. *Creating new columns*

8.   Click +New Column, as shown in Figure 9-27.

Figure 9-27. *Add a new column*

Submitting Data Automatically

In this section, you learn how to add an auto-numbering field for the contact ID so you can select/enter the required information (the Display Name, Datatype, Autonumber Type, and Format), as shown in Figure 9-28.

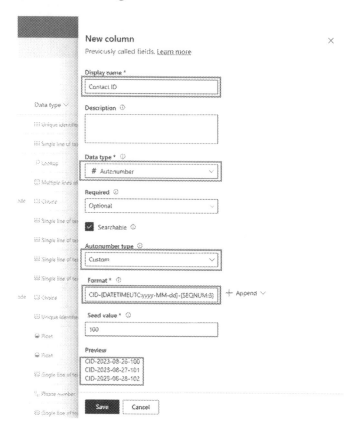

Figure 9-28. *Adding an auto-numbering field*

Now you'll add another field type so you can upload files, as shown in Figure 9-29.

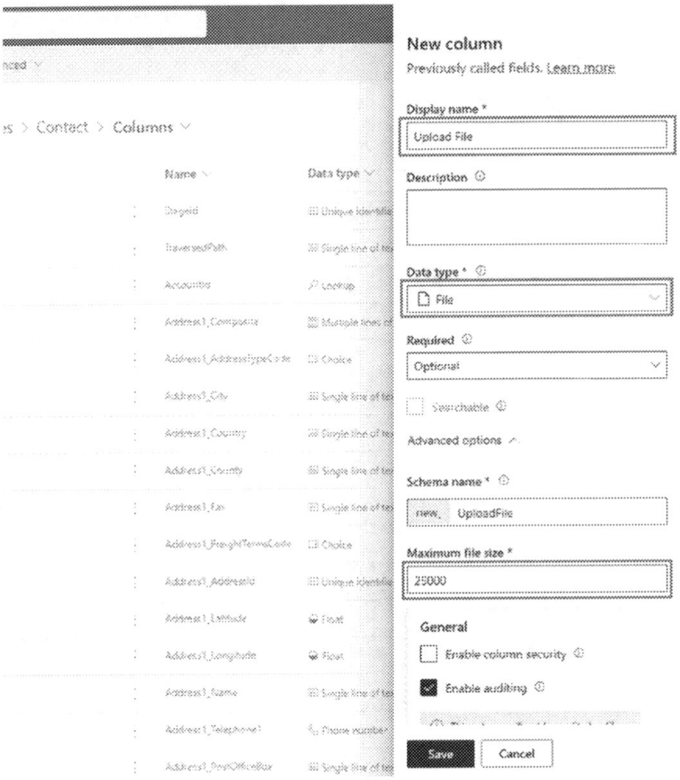

Figure 9-29. *Adding a field to upload files*

You can also add choice (Yes/No) fields, as shown in Figure 9-30.

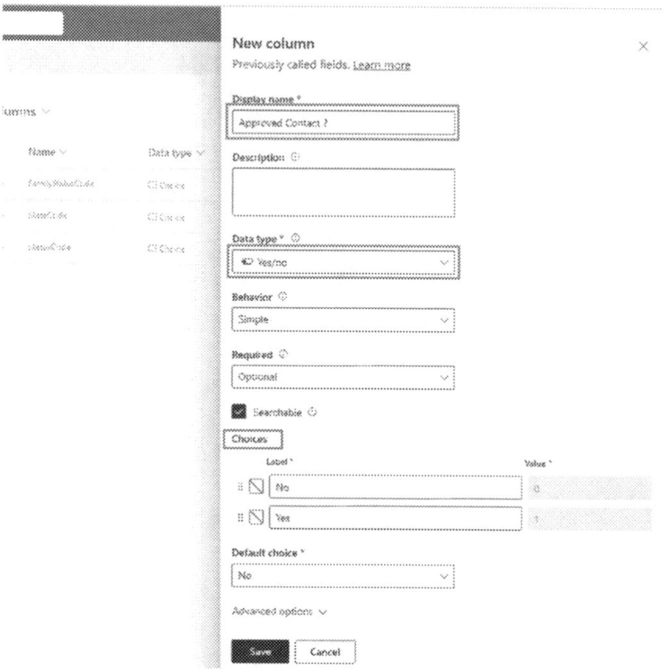

Figure 9-30. *Adding a yes/no choice field*

Now navigate to the form and choose Edit to change it, as shown in Figure 9-31.

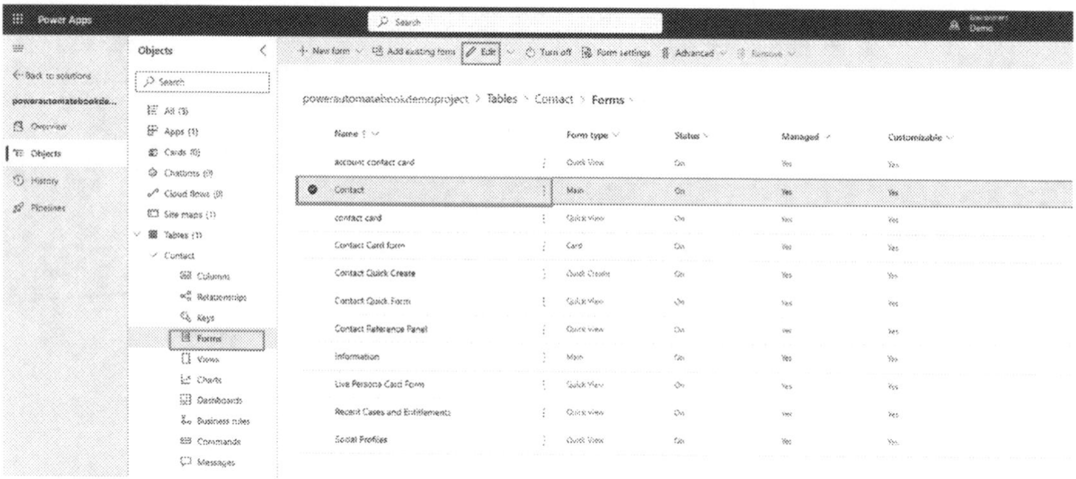

Figure 9-31. *Modifying a form*

The form's wireframe view will appear, where you can add, select, and rearrange fields. You can and search for and select a field to add to the form, as shown in Figure 9-32.

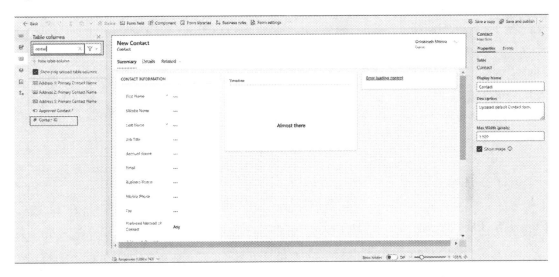

Figure 9-32. *Searching for fields to modify*

After you add all the fields by dragging them to the form, the form will resemble Figure 9-33. Click Save and Publish if you like how it looks.

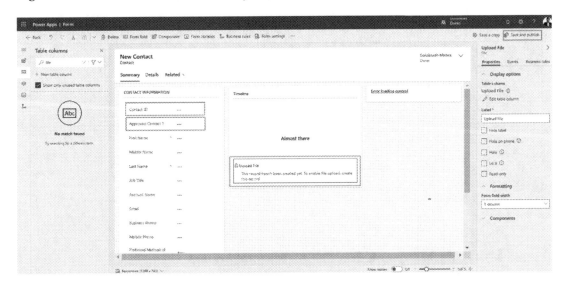

Figure 9-33. *The form with the new fields*

Go back to the solution and navigate to Apps. Click Play. See Figure 9-34.

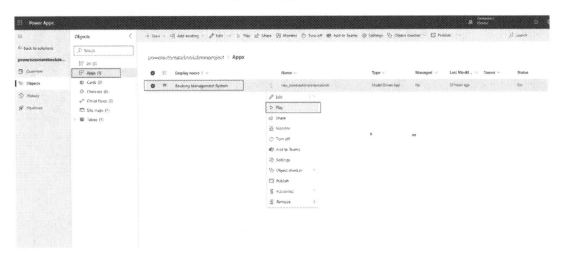

Figure 9-34. *Choose Play from the solution area*

The app will open with Contacts table showing, as shown in Figure 9-35. Click +New to create a new contact.

Figure 9-35. *The app opens with Contacts table showing*

When you click +New, you will see your modified form. Fill in the form with the required information and click Save to enable the Upload File feature, as shown in Figure 9-36.

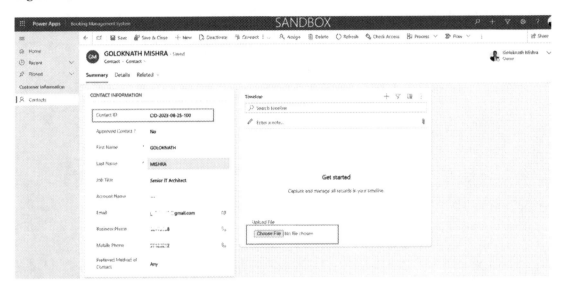

Figure 9-36. *Using the Upload File feature*

Creating a Volunteer Approval Flow

This section explains how to create a Microsoft form so that volunteers can be registered, as shown in Figure 9-37.

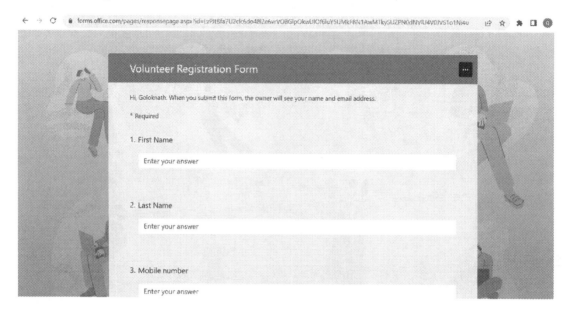

Figure 9-37. *Volunteer registration form*

You can use an integrated system where the form data will be passed to the system automatically. To achieve that feat, you'll add a Cloud Flow, as shown in Figure 9-38. Follow these steps to do so:

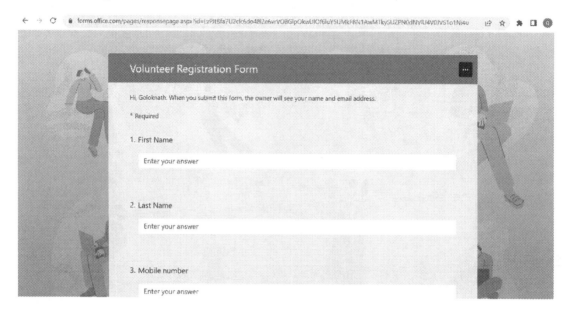

Figure 9-38. *Adding an automated Cloud Flow*

1. Name the flow and select the When a New Response Is Submitted trigger. Click Create. See Figures 9-39 and 9-40.

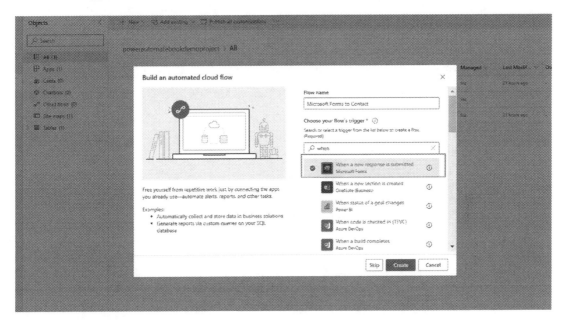

Figure 9-39. *Select the When a New Response Is Submitted trigger*

2. Select Form ID to pull the data to Dataverse, as shown in Figure 9-40.

Figure 9-40. *Select Form ID here*

3. Get the response details, as shown in Figure 9-41.

Figure 9-41. *Adding the response details*

4. Select Dataverse ➤ Add a New Row and map the fields to retrieve. Then click Save, as shown in Figure 9-42.

Figure 9-42. *Adding a new row and mapping the fields*

5. Submit a form with the relevant data. You'll now notice that the
    flow will run automatically and pull the information to the contact
    record. Figure 9-43 shows that the flow ran successfully.

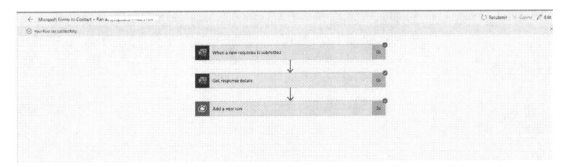

Figure 9-43. *The flow automatically pulls information to the contact record*

6. Notice that data is parsed from the forms to the model-driven app,
    as shown in Figure 9-44.

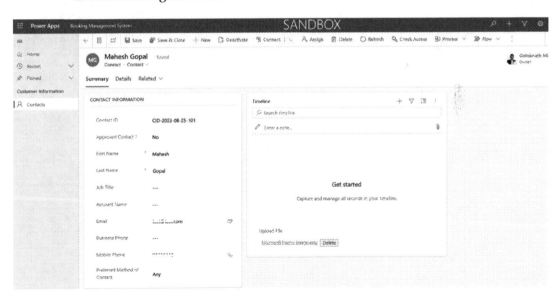

Figure 9-44. *Data is parsed from the forms to the model-driven app*

7. Now create another flow to approve the volunteer. When the
    Approved Contact? field is set to Yes, the volunteer is considered
    approved. See Figure 9-45.

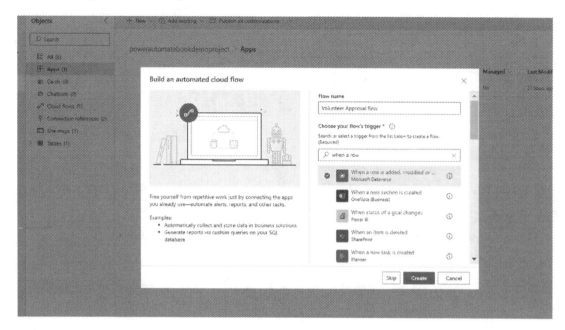

Figure 9-45. *Creating a volunteer approval flow*

8. Select the relevant parameters, as shown in Figure 9-46.

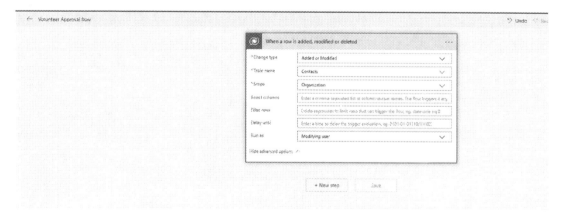

Figure 9-46. *Select the relevant parameters for the new flow*

9. Create an approval, as shown in Figure 9-47. If it is approved, update the flag to Yes. If it's not approved, the flag should be set to No. See Figure 9-47.

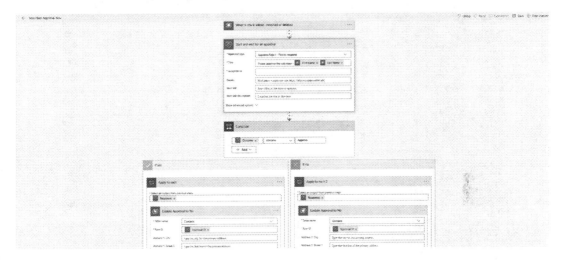

Figure 9-47. *Setting the flag for approval*

10.   Update a form to see the response. See Figures 9-48 and 9-49.

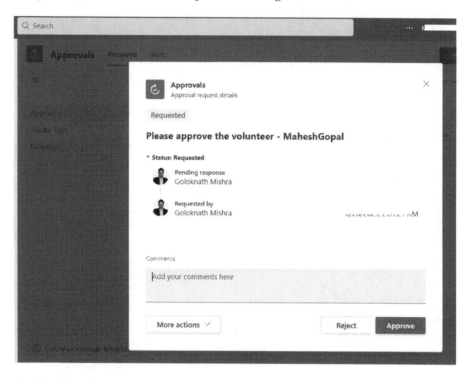

Figure 9-48.   *The form shows the proper response*

Figure 9-49.   *The approval process is working*

11.   Once it has been approved, the status will be updated to
       Approved, as shown in Figure 9-50.

Figure 9-50.   *The status has been updated to Approved*

12.   You can also check if the flow execution completed successfully,
       as shown in Figure 9-51.

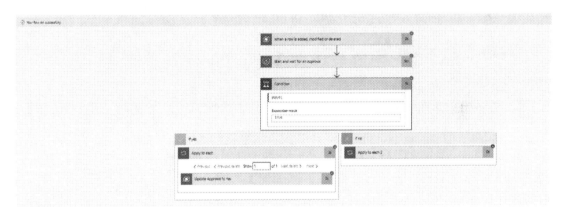

Figure 9-51.   *The flow execution completed successfully*

The Approval Status has also been updated, as shown in Figure 9-52.

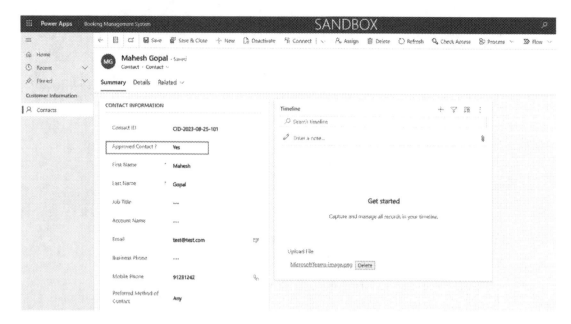

Figure 9-52. *The Approval Status has been updated*

For each item, the system created connection references, as you can see in Figure 9-53.

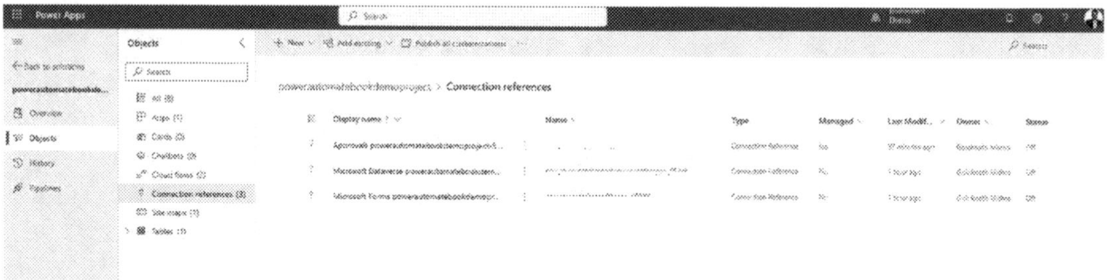

Figure 9-53. *All the items' connection references*

All of the solution components are shown in Figure 9-54.

Figure 9-54. *The solution's components*

Exporting a Solution to a Different Environment

You can migrate a solution to another system by exporting it. Follow these steps to do so:

1. Select the solution and then click Export Solution, as shown in
    Figure 9-55.

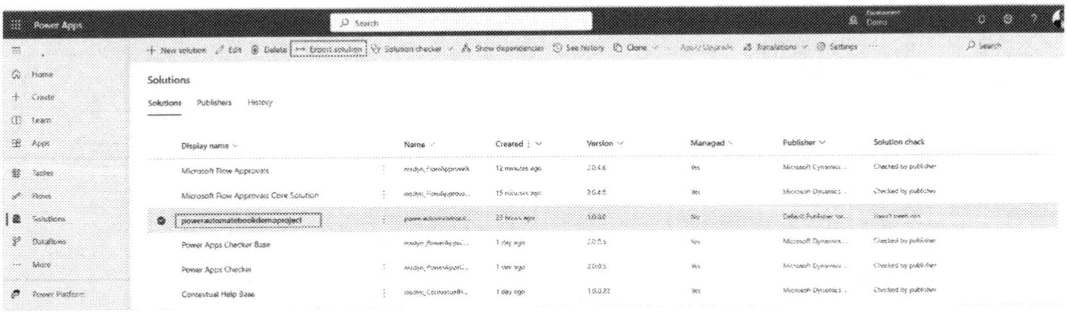

Figure 9-55. *Exporting a solution*

2. Click Publish and Next, as shown in Figure 9-56.

Figure 9-56. *Choose Publish and then Next*

3. Select the version and type of solution (managed or unmanaged), as shown in Figure 9-57.

Figure 9-57. *Include the version and the type of solution*

4. Once you click Export, a ZIP file of the solution is generated. You can import that file into a different environment.

Summary

This chapter covered end-to-end implementation of Power Automate in real time. You also learned how to migrate the solution from one environment to another as part of the project.

Index

A

Academic subjects, 150
Actions, 64, 69
AI Builder, 25, 27, 42
    business card reader, 426
    call limits, 425, 426
    capabilities, 359
    document automation toolkit
        configuration tab, 418
        connections, 413, 414
        detailed process, 411
        document pipeline, 417
        documents/invoices, 412
        documents tab, 419
        field/tables mapping, 418
        functional end-to-end
          solution, 411
        installation, 413
        mailbox, 419
        predictions, 366
        reviewing documents, 417
        roles/permissions, 415
        settings process, 415, 416
        setup process, 416
        validation, 420
    document processing, 362
    entity extraction, 362
    identity document reader, 362
    IPA, 9
    key phrase extraction, 362, 426
    language detection, 362, 426
    licensing model, 434
    menu options, 360
    opening screen, 359
    opening window, 360
    PAD features, 19
    portal pane, 41
    prebuilt models (*see* Prebuilt/
      custom models)
    receipt processing, 425
    sentiment analysis, 362
    sharing/administering/
      monitoring models
        details link, 423
        edit model, 422
        lifecycle states, 420, 421
        model evaluation window, 423
        monitoring, 425
        settings window, 424
        share option, 424
        solution component, 425
        tracking model, 421
        unpublish model, 422
Artificial intelligence (AI), 14
    builder, 359 (*see* AI Builder)
    IPA/RPA, 12
Associated apps, 120
    Process Mining, 122
    search, 121
    setting up, 120
Attended RPA, 3, 430
Authentication type, 162, 163

G. Mishra, *Deep Dive into Power Automate*, https://doi.org/10.1007/978-1-4842-9732-2

Printed in the United States
by Baker & Taylor Publisher Services